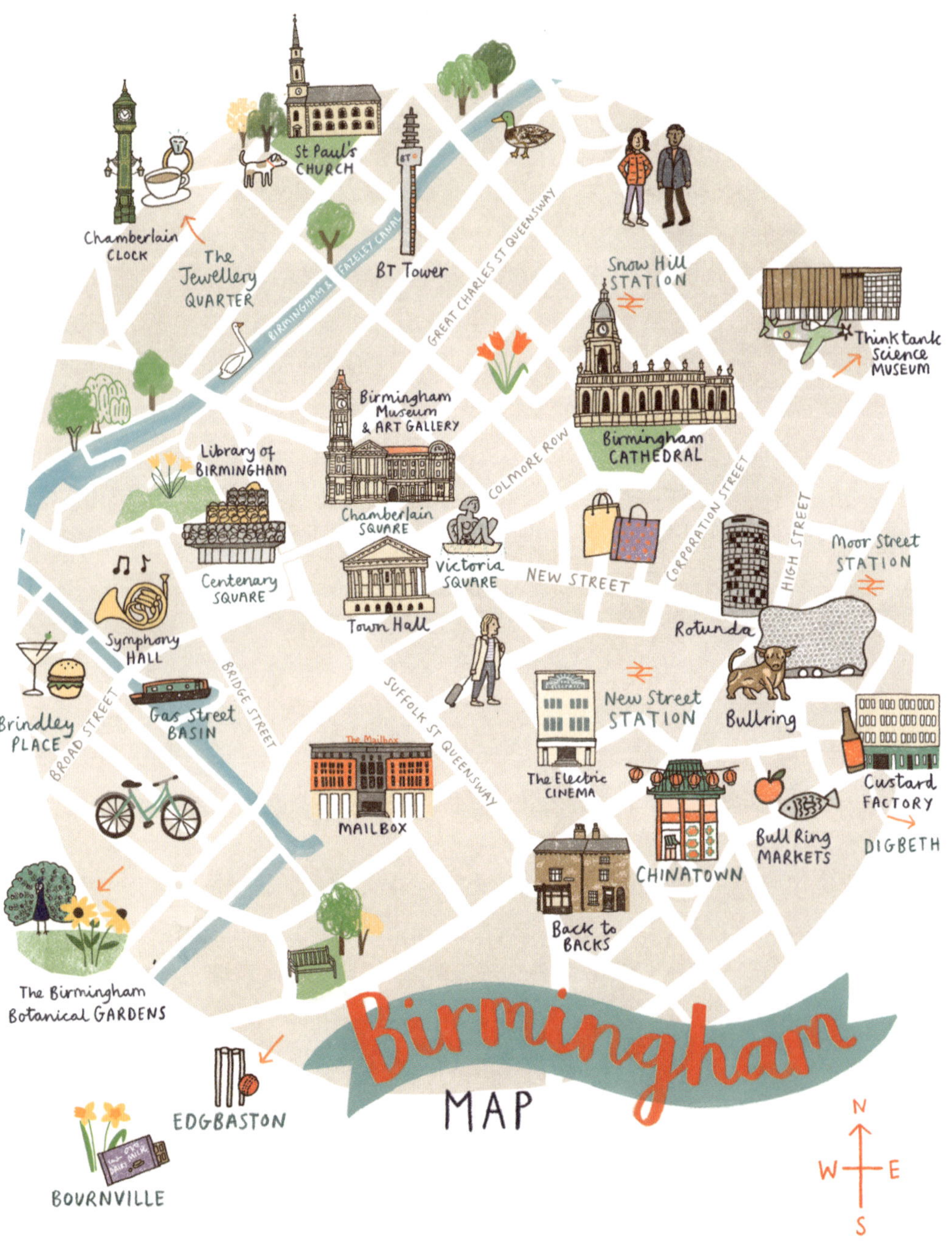

Chamberlain CLOCK
The Jewellery QUARTER
St Paul's CHURCH
BT Tower
BIRMINGHAM & FAZELEY CANAL
GREAT CHARLES ST QUEENSWAY
Snow Hill STATION
Think tank Science MUSEUM
Birmingham Museum & ART GALLERY
Library of BIRMINGHAM
Chamberlain SQUARE
COLMORE ROW
Birmingham CATHEDRAL
Centenary SQUARE
Victoria SQUARE
NEW STREET
CORPORATION STREET
HIGH STREET
Moor Street STATION
Symphony HALL
Town Hall
Rotunda
Brindley PLACE
BROAD STREET
Gas Street BASIN
BRIDGE STREET
SUFFOLK ST QUEENSWAY
New Street STATION
Bullring
Custard FACTORY
The Electric CINEMA
Bull Ring MARKETS
DIGBETH
MAILBOX
The Mailbox
CHINATOWN
Back to BACKS
The Birmingham Botanical GARDENS
Birmingham
MAP
EDGBASTON
BOURNVILLE
N
W E
S

*This book shows a unique view of Birmingham,
a city that still holds a substantial bit of my heart*

DAME JULIE WALTERS, ACTOR (HARRY POTTER,
MAMMA MIA!, PADDINGTON, EDUCATING RITA)

*This is like being given a pair of magic spectacles through
which you can see Birmingham's unusual, oft hidden, oft unappreciated
beauty, more clearly and more exhilarating than you ever did before.*

FRANK SKINNER, WRITER, COMEDIAN, TV AND RADIO PRESENTER,
CO-WRITER OF SEMINAL FOOTBALL ANTHEM *THREE LIONS*

*We are a city that's quietly understated yet brilliant! If you want to know
about it, stand and stare, you'll know why so many still want to live here.*

RUBY TURNER MBE, SINGER, SONGWRITER, ACTOR

*I am proud to be associated with a city that can produce
such stunning, artistic creations and in such numbers - remarkable.*

JASPER CARROTT OBE, COMEDIAN, ACTOR AND AUTHOR

*Amazing and thought-provoking images from 59 incredible artists,
proving that Birmingham really is at the centre of it all!*

JOSIE LAWRENCE, COMEDIAN AND ACTOR

*The Birmingham Art Book is a visual feast of historic and futuristic beauty,
created by local artists who live within the heart of this bustling, vibrant city.*

TOYAH WILLCOX, ACTOR, SINGER AND AUTHOR

*The artists who are inspired by the city of my birth light up its
architecture, its sensations, its spirit and its multiculturalism, in the most creative
and imaginative ways. It is our artists that make our city shine so brightly in the
universe. You have to love them. This book loves them.*

BENJAMIN ZEPHANIAH, WRITER AND POET

Published by UIT Cambridge Ltd

www.uit.co.uk

PO Box 145, Cambridge CB4 1GQ, England

Phone: +44 (0) 1223 302 041

First published in 2022, in England.

ISBN: 9781912934256 (hardback)

ISBN: 9781912934263 (ebook)

ep-1-1

THE BIRMINGHAM ART BOOK

The City Through the Eyes of its Artists

EDITED BY

EMMA BENNETT

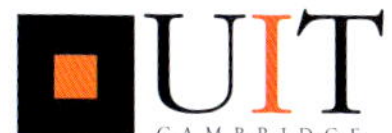

Acknowledgements

The Birmingham Art Book has been made possible with the enthusiasm and talent of the contributing artists and to them I am eternally grateful.

In the bustling city of Birmingham, an illustrious panel of local art and city experts helped select images for publication. I am indebted to them for their creative input. They are:

- Claire Birch, Producer, Cultural Programme, Birmingham 2022 Commonwealth Games

- Steve Evans, President, Royal Birmingham Society of Artists

- Richard Russell, Director, The Purple Gallery

- Jo Tunmer, Lead Panellist, *The City Through The Eyes of Its Artists*® series

- Helen Wheeler, Course Director, BA Illustration, Birmingham City University

I thank Sheila Stickley and Niall Mansfield at UIT for their continued support for *The City Through The Eyes of Its Artists*® series.

I grew up with the tantalizing aroma of chocolate in the air, from the nearby Cadbury factory in Bournville. Having now lived away from the city for thirty years, I see Birmingham afresh through the eyes of a visitor, whilst remembering fondly my childhood and teenage years growing up in the city suburbs. From my Brum years, thanks to Liz Thwaite (neé Liz Child) for the roller skating, pick 'n' mix and general growing up shenanigans. To Sam Clay, grey eggs? and don't believe her about that broken elbow!

Thank you to my family who still connect me with the city, particularly Mom, Dad, Ann, Andy, Adam and Aunty Jean. To Geoff Smith, Sonia Cater and all the grandparents, aunts and uncles formerly of this city, you are missed.

Thanks for on-going support from Craig, Molly and William Bennett. To Jo Tunmer thanks for keeping me focused on work trips and to Alison Schuldt and Julia Sadler for usual proofreading, thank you so much. To Pat Seymour (Aka Marial) who loves Birmingham so much, this book will guide your next visit.

Emma Bennett

CONTENTS

FOREWORD

Birmingham, as I'm sure you're aware, is the best city in the world. And the art here is the best in the world too. I am not biased. This is a fact. I will fight anyone who disagrees with this to the death.

The art here is often really funny. We don't take ourselves too seriously. We have a healthy mix of talent, ambition, cynicism, sarcasm, focus, jokes, skill, patience and plenty of time getting on the lash.

The people of this city avoid, above all else, any sense of pretentiousness. They are genuine people, no nonsense, just getting by. We're not fussed with awards and showing off. But we're proud, quietly, of what and who we are.

Enjoy our art. But don't go on about it too much. We'd hate that!

Joe Lycett
Comedian, television presenter and proud Brummie

PREFACE

Birmingham is a city based on a strong industrial and manufacturing past, but with a futuristic feel unlike many other UK cities. Cleverly combining the old with the new, Birmingham is bold and certainly not afraid to be different. Factories and buildings that once made custard or sorted the city's mail now have a new purpose in a modern world.

Sitting at the heart of the UK and with 35 miles of canals, once vital to Victorian Britain, Birmingham's waterways reach out like fingers connecting every part of the city. Sounds of the canals are never far away.

Birmingham is a genuine city, often underappreciated. Where else can you go to stroke a bull; ride on a barge; see modern and historic architecture in the same view; purchase a diamond; splash through a fountain; buy anything from a saucepan to an apple from an abundance of colourful market stalls; watch world class cricket; have a chat with someone from the furthest corner of the globe or stand up close to a shark, all in the same day?

Brum has so much to offer that you will want to come back again and again. A more welcoming city you will be hard pressed to find: 'Brummies' are, after all, widely known for their humour and friendly disposition. This welcome and the diversity within the city is why Birmingham was awarded the prestigious 2022 Commonwealth Games.

It is little wonder then, that this city provides endless inspiration to its artists. The Birmingham Art Book is the seventh in *The City Through The Eyes of Its Artists*[®] series (with Cambridge, Oxford, Edinburgh, Liverpool, Dublin and Bristol and Bath) and represents just some of the talented artists working in and around Birmingham.

With The Birmingham Art Book in your hand, take a stroll through this fantastic city and stand for a while in the footsteps of an artist.

Emma Bennett

Creator and Editor of *The City Through The Eyes of Its Artists*[®] series

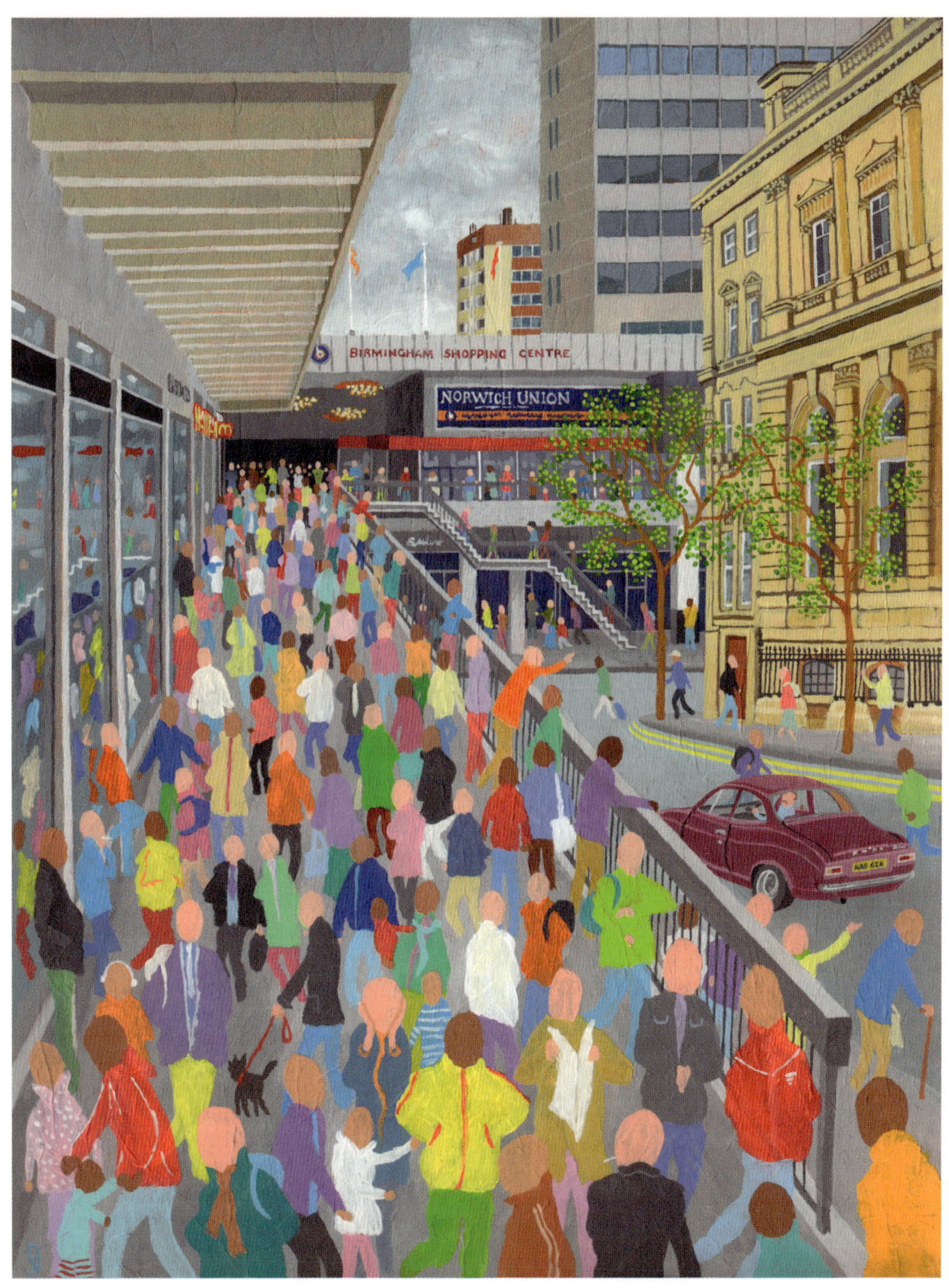

DAVID NEWTON, THE RAMP, STEPHENSON PLACE

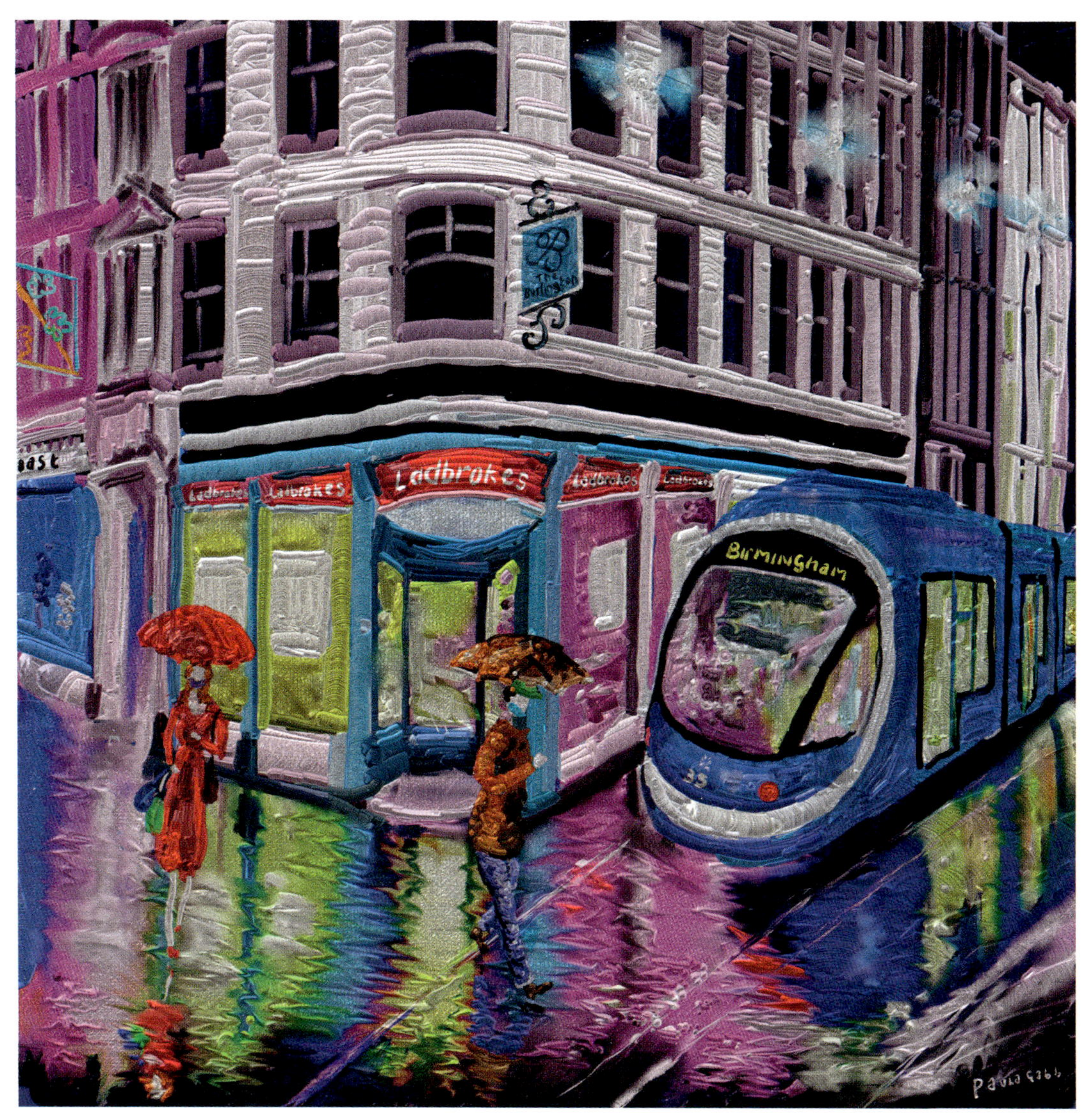

PAULA GABB, STEPHENSON STREET

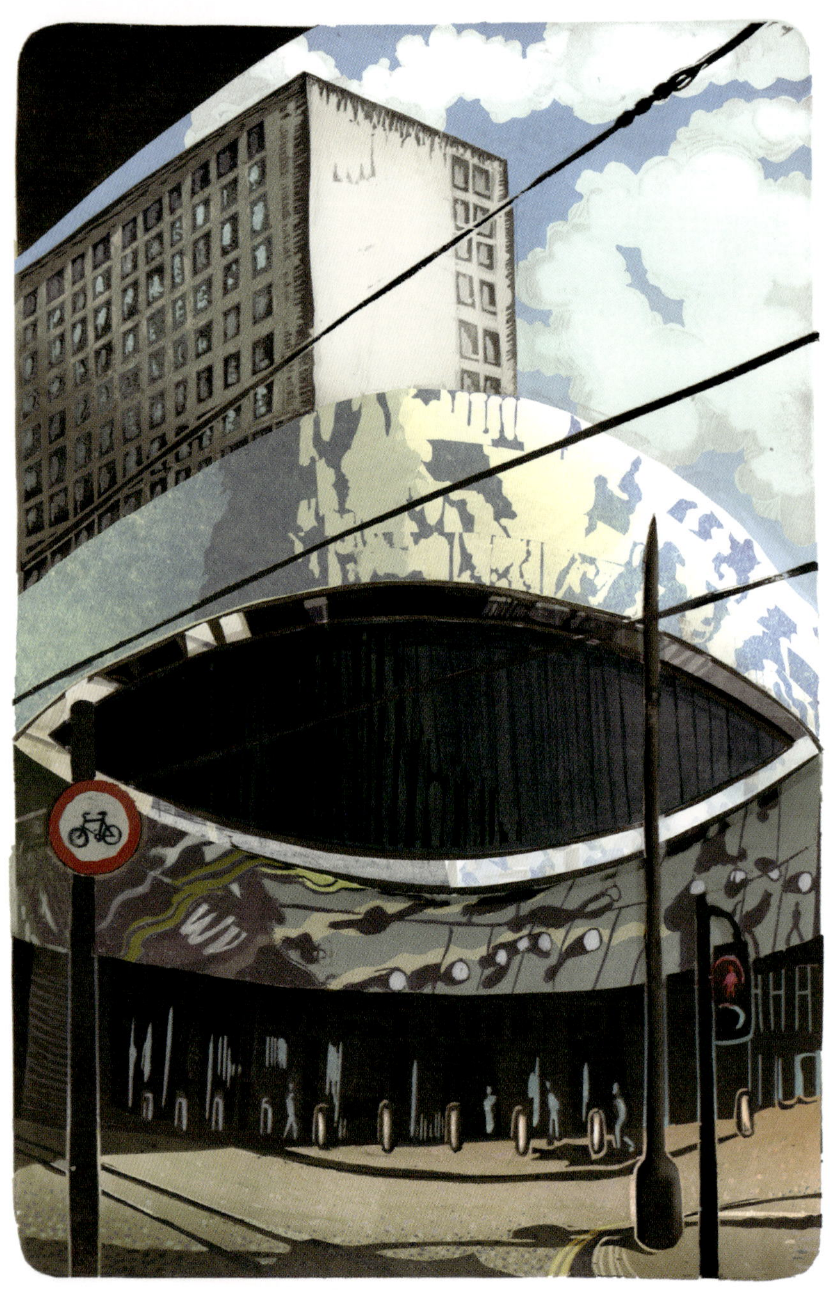

MIKE ALLISON, GRAND CENTRAL, BIRMINGHAM NEW STREET STATION entrance

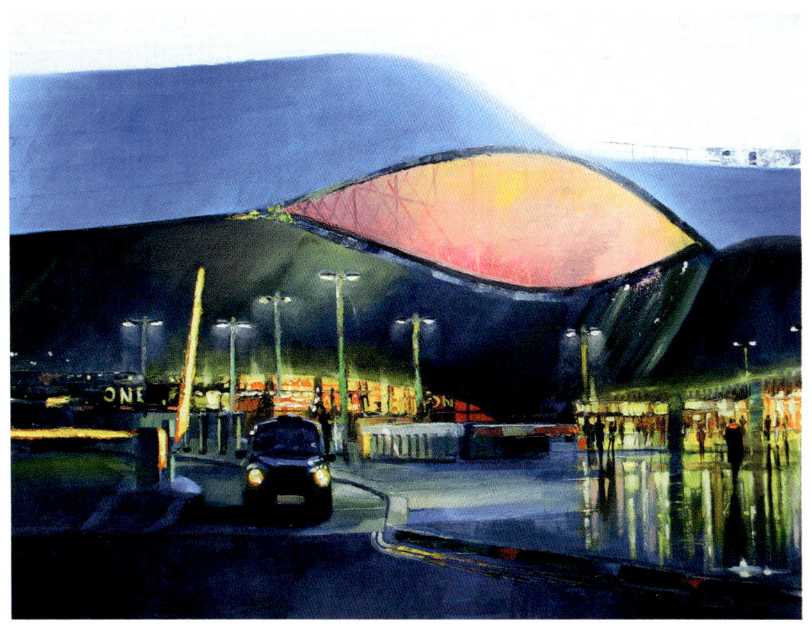

CARRICK SIDDELL, GRAND CENTRAL

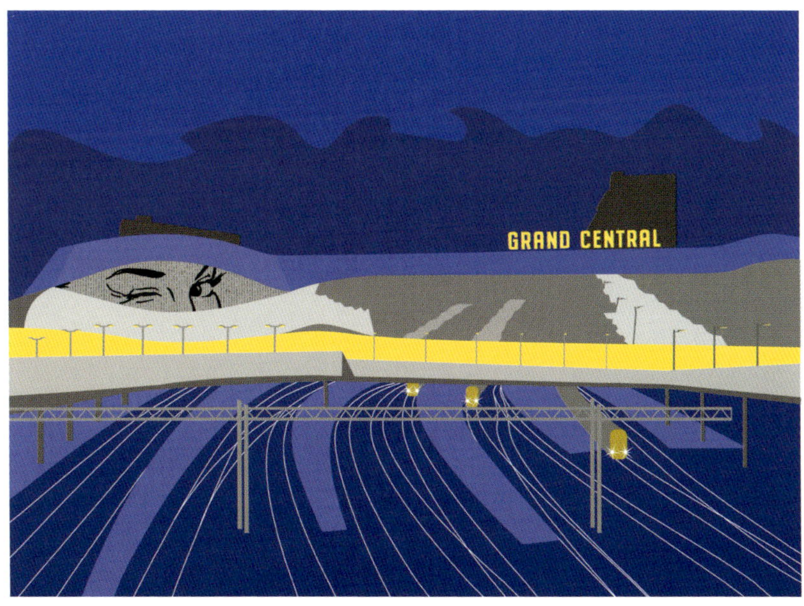

ANNA REUBEN, GRAND CENTRAL

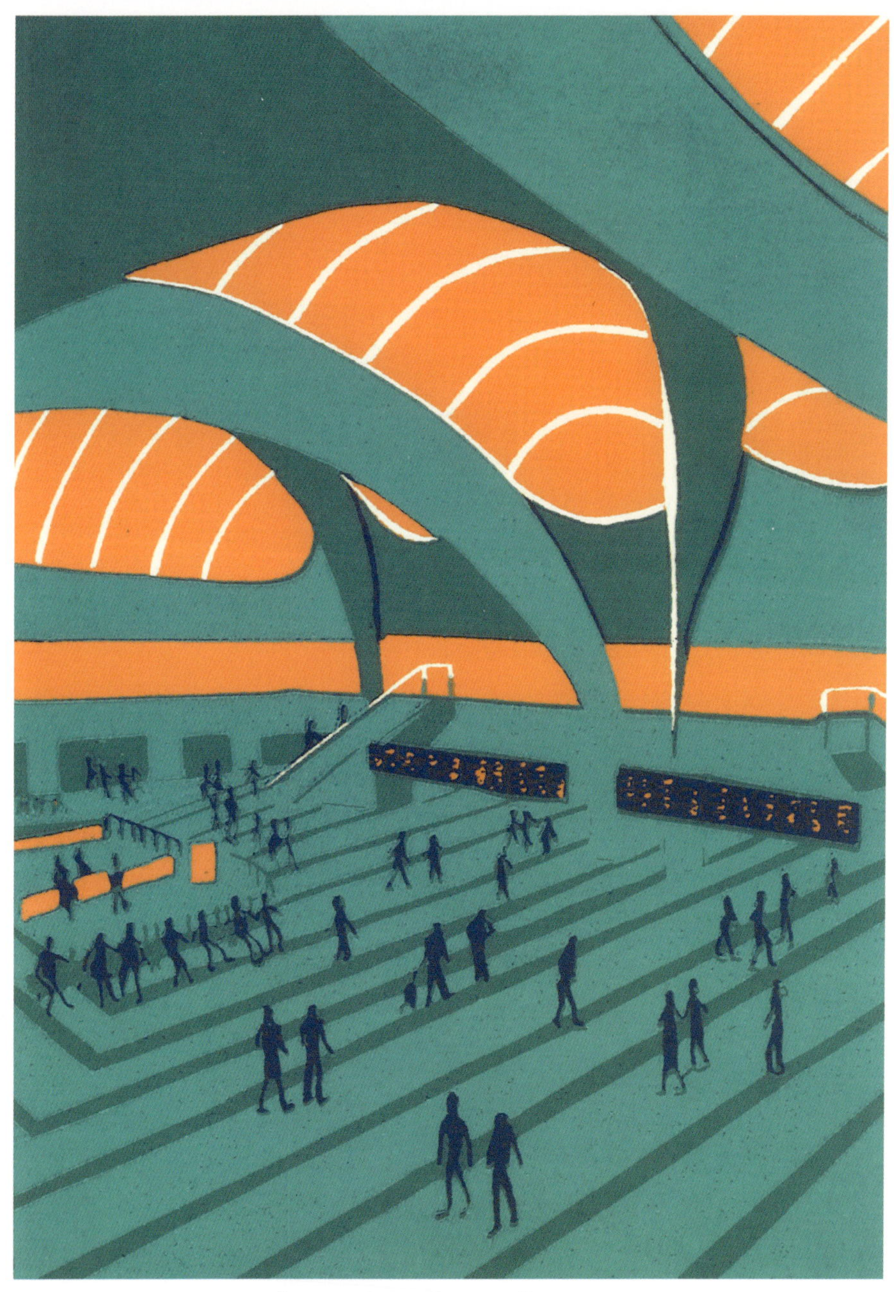

JENNIE ING, GRAND CENTRAL

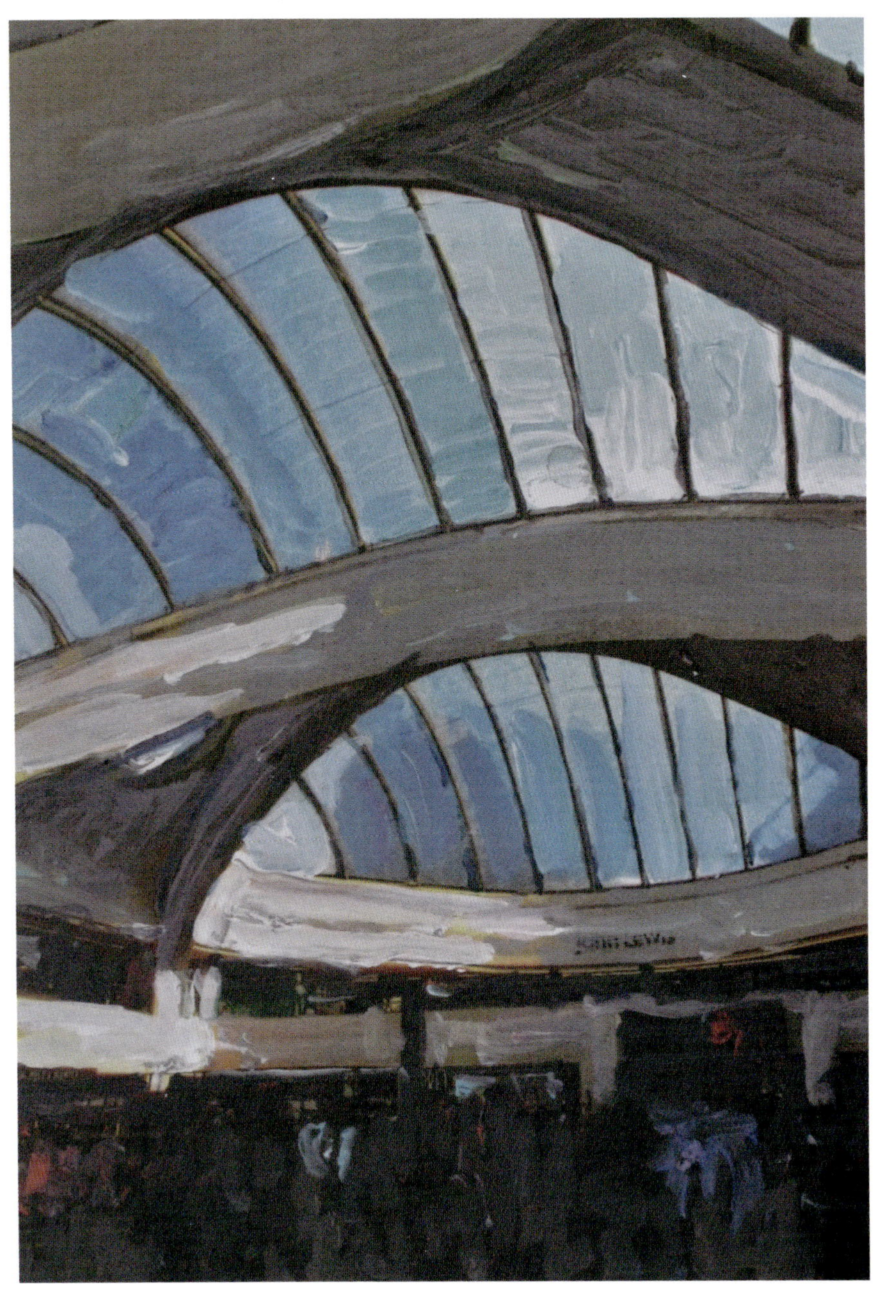

DANIEL STEDMAN, GRAND CENTRAL

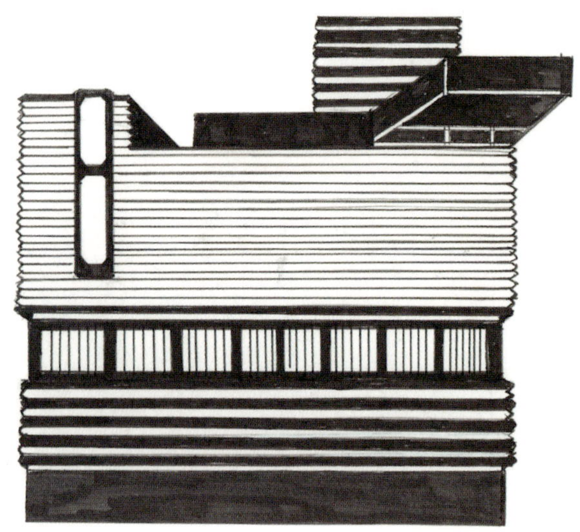

BETHANY DARTNELL, BIRMINGHAM NEW STREET SIGNAL BOX

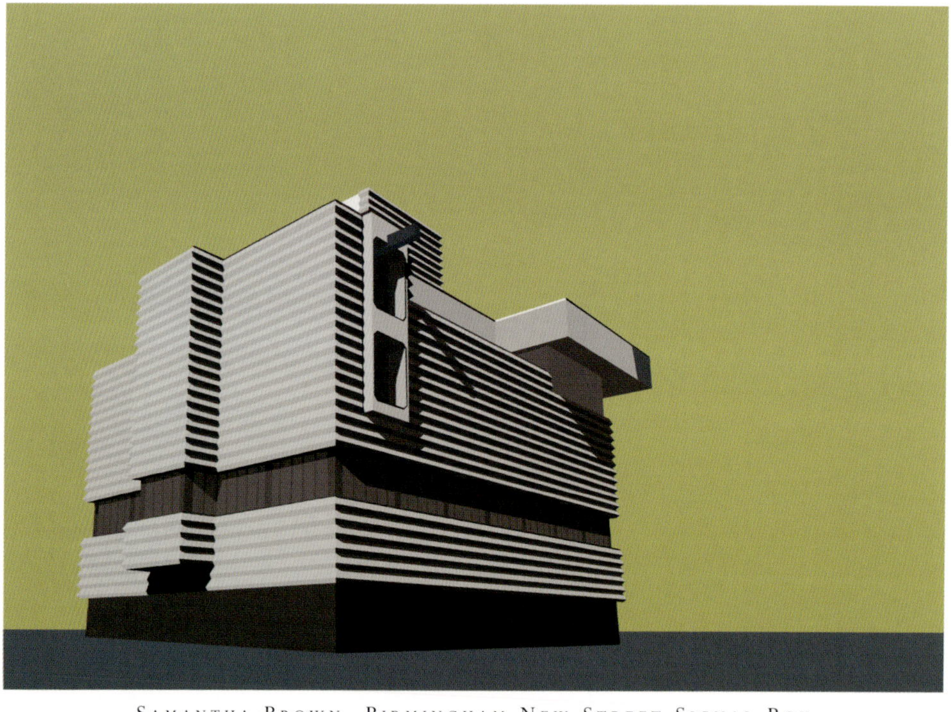

SAMANTHA BROWN, BIRMINGHAM NEW STREET SIGNAL BOX

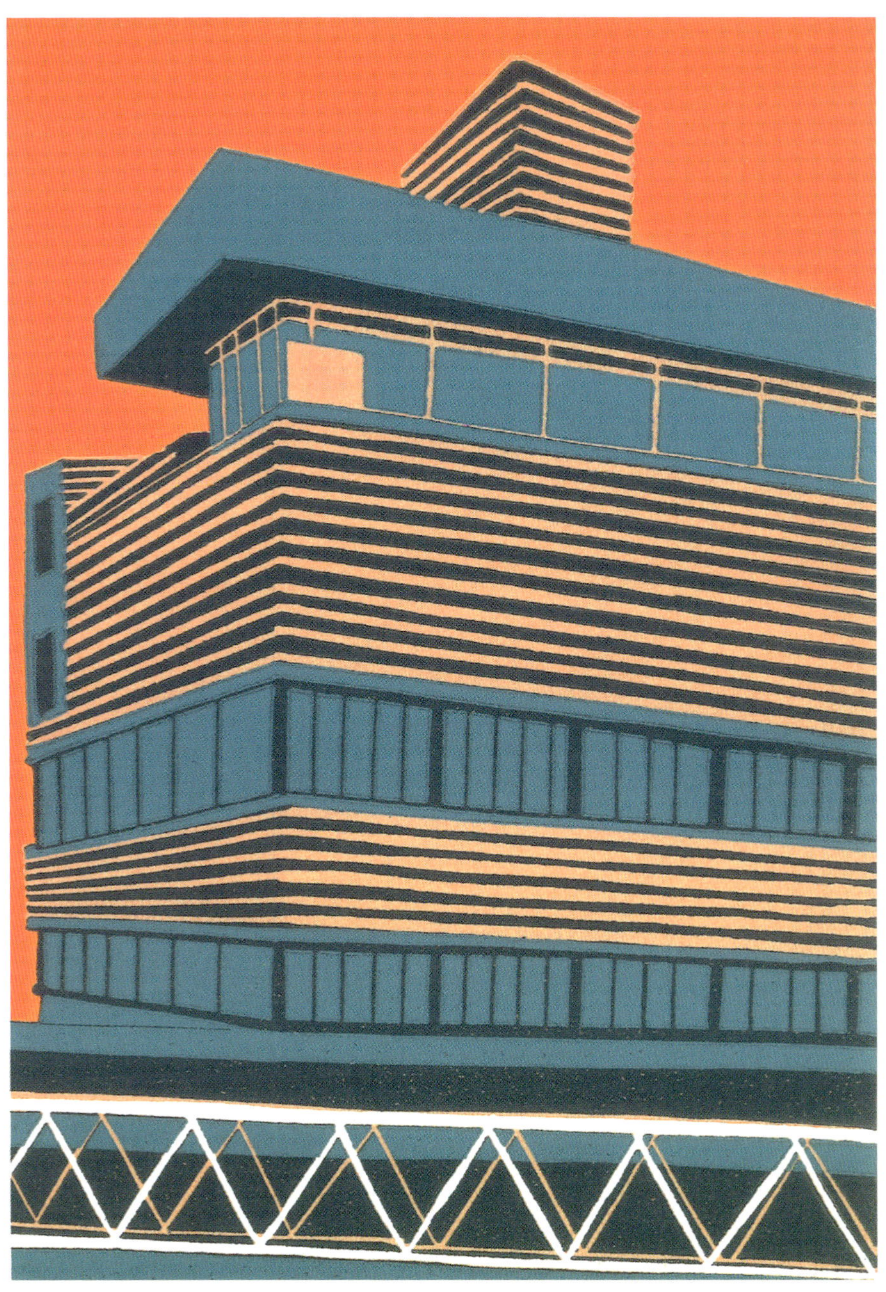

JENNIE ING, BIRMINGHAM NEW STREET SIGNAL BOX

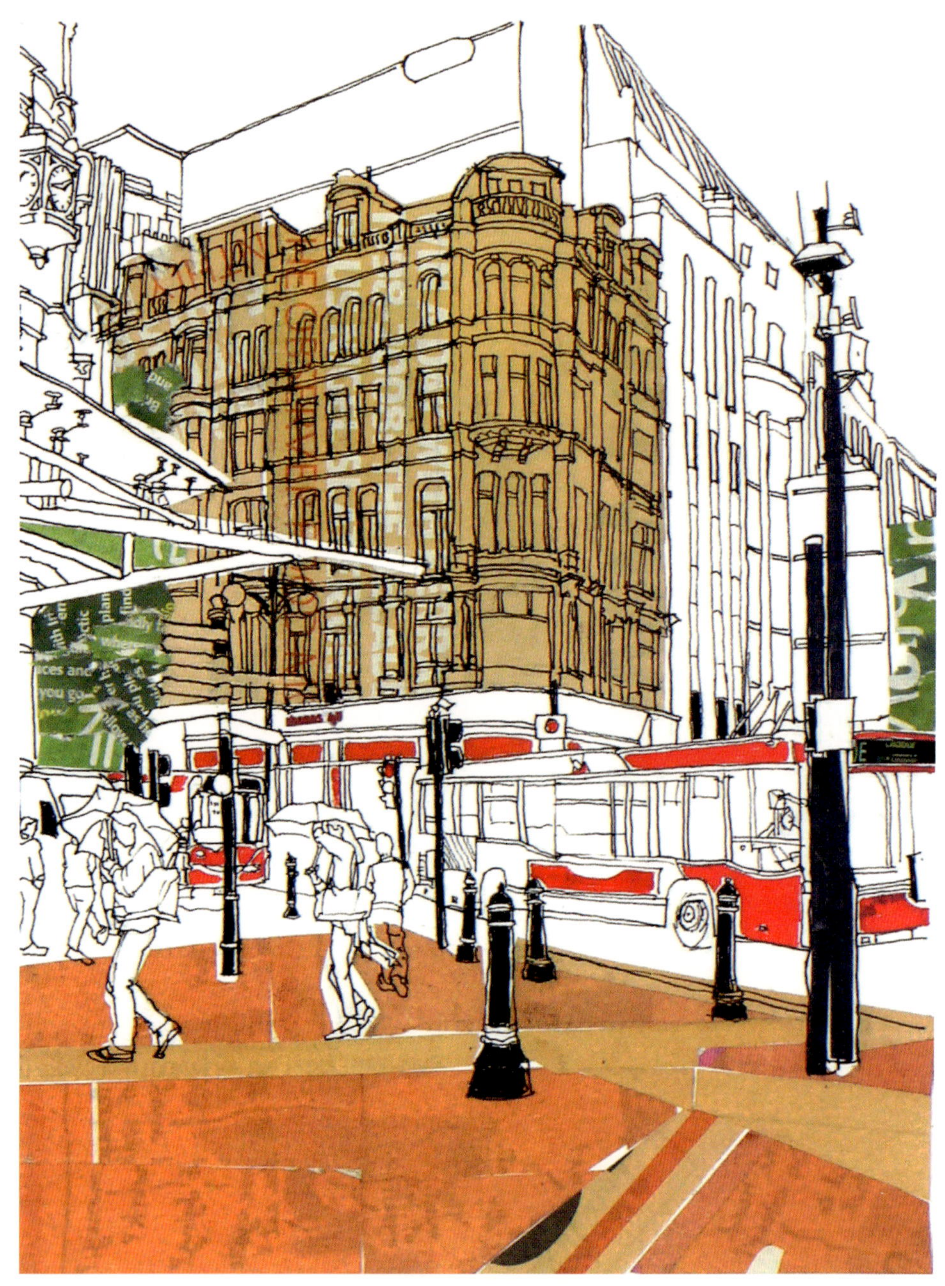

CAROLINE JOHNSON, NEW STREET

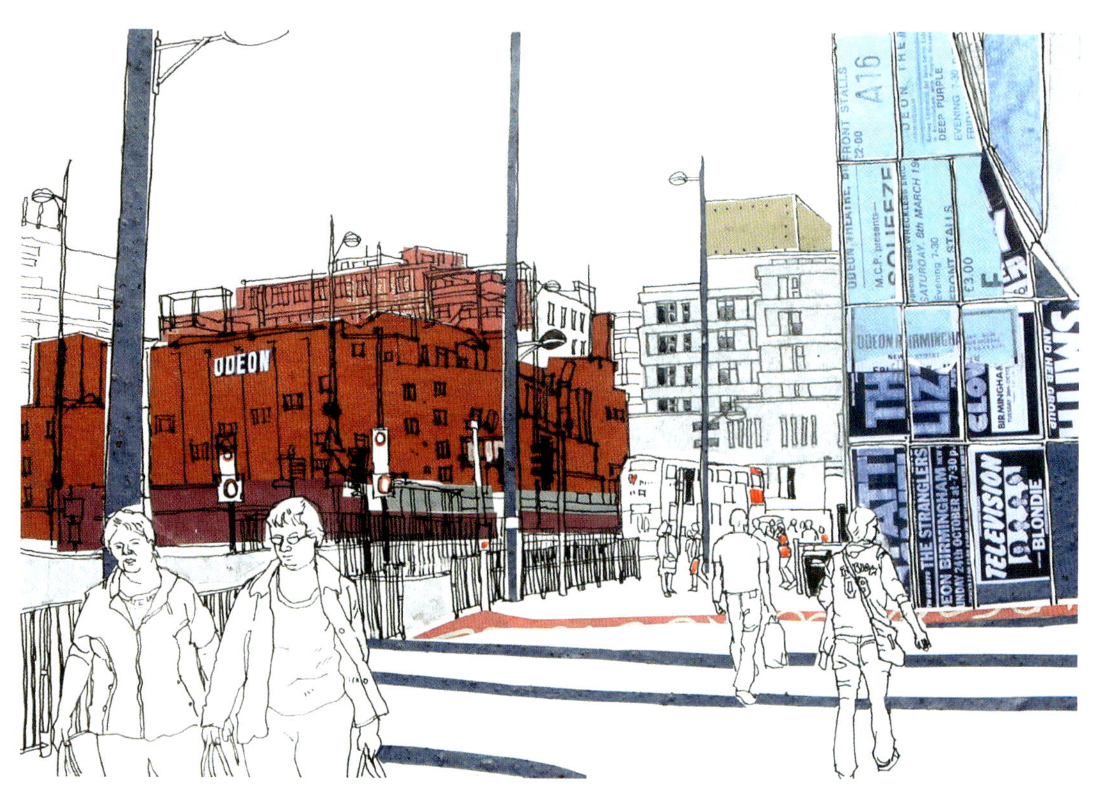

CAROLINE JOHNSON, THE ODEON

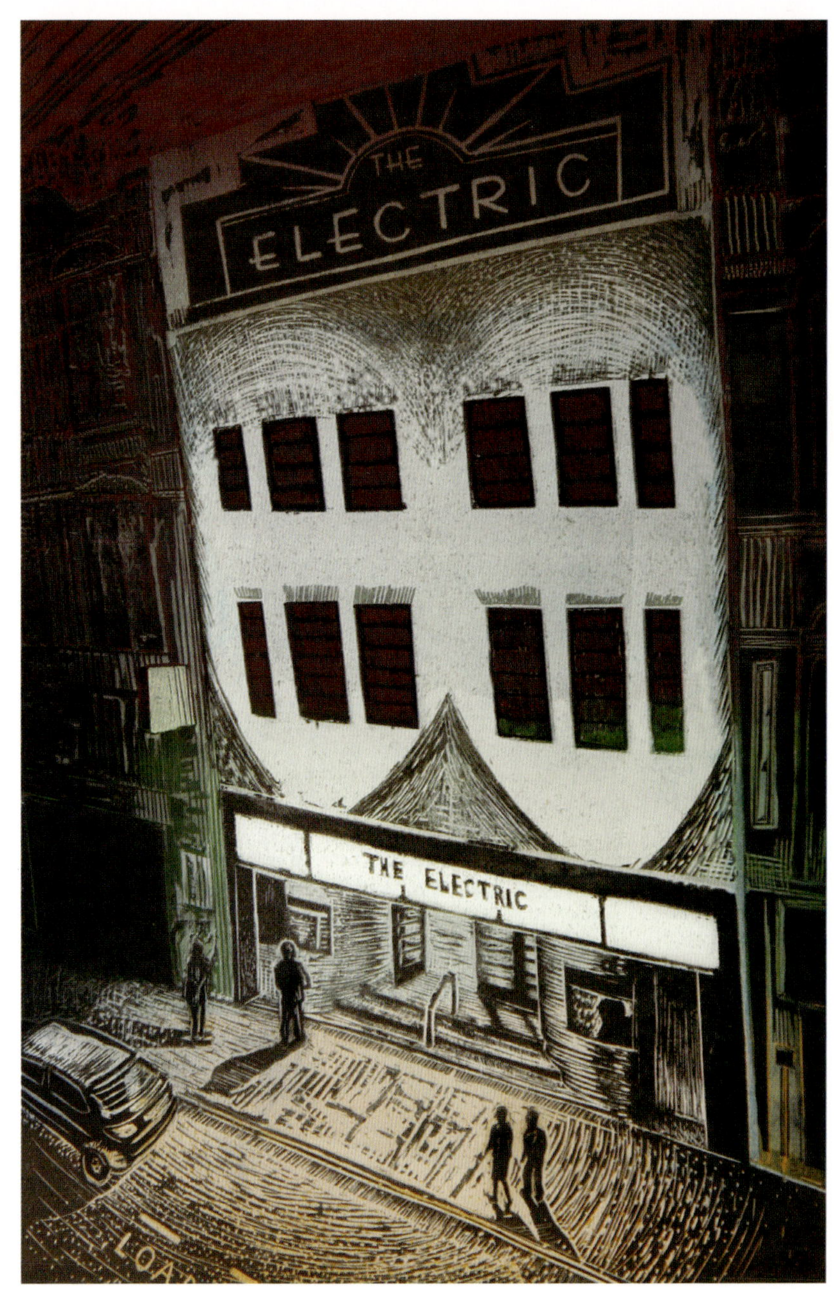

MIKE ALLISON, THE ELECTRIC CINEMA

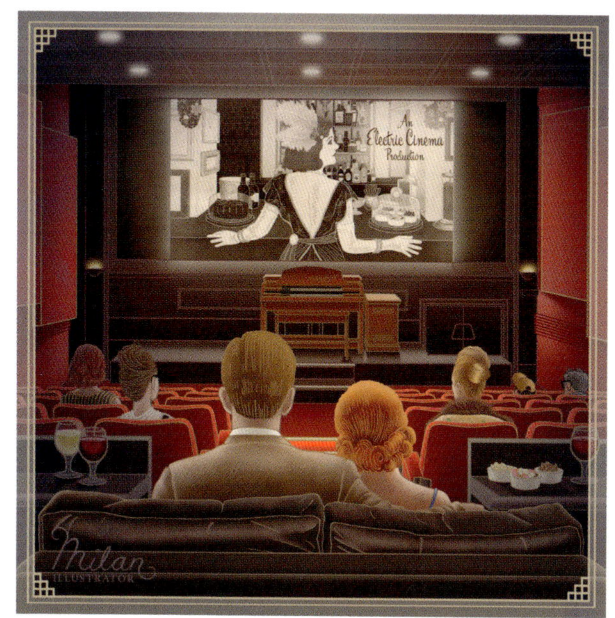

MILAN TOPALOVIĆ, THE ELECTRIC CINEMA

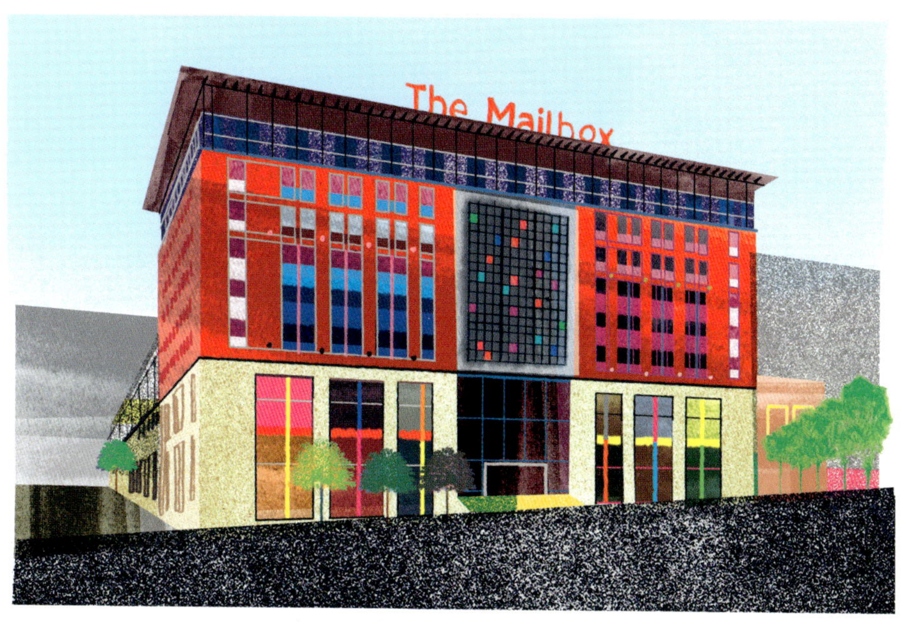

ILONA DREW, THE MAILBOX

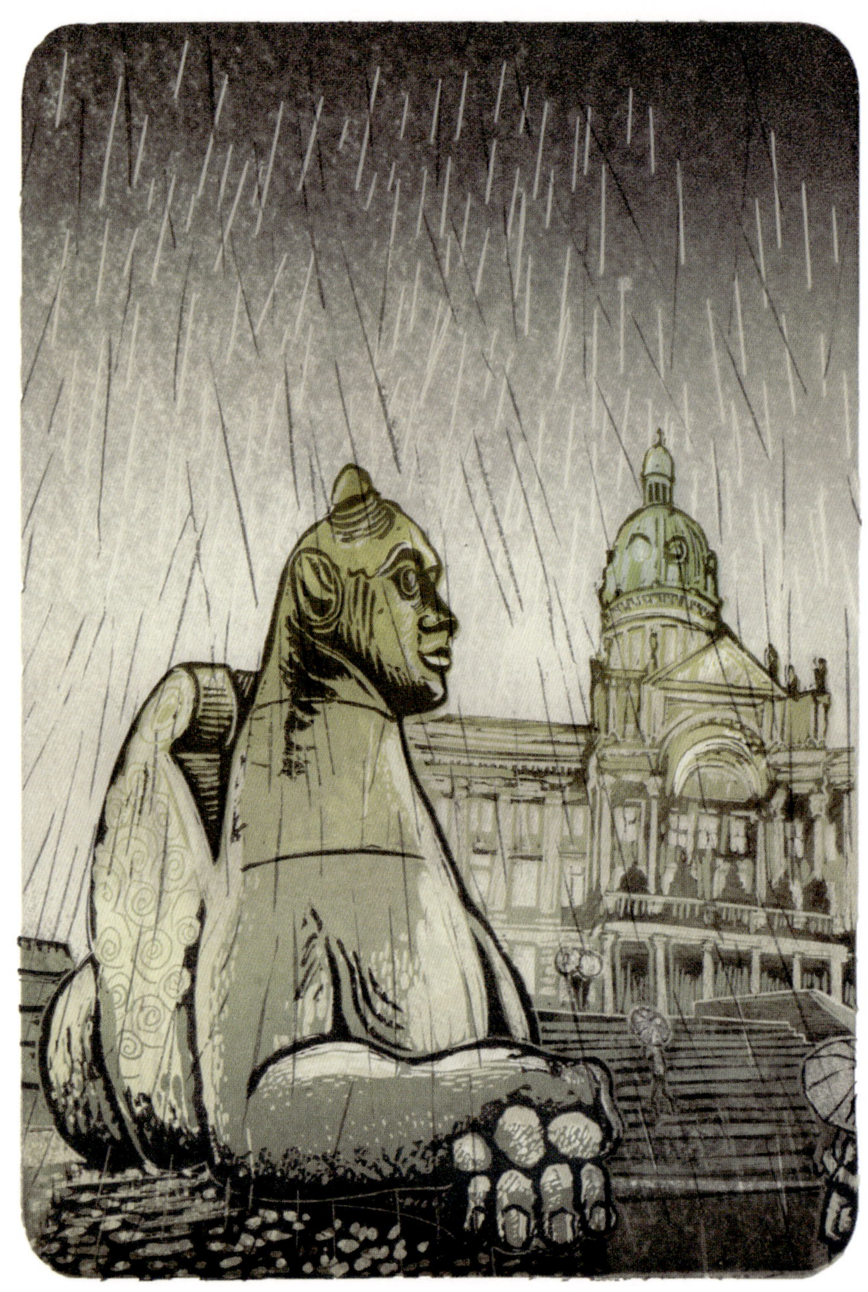

MIKE ALLISON, THE GUARDIAN, VICTORIA SQUARE

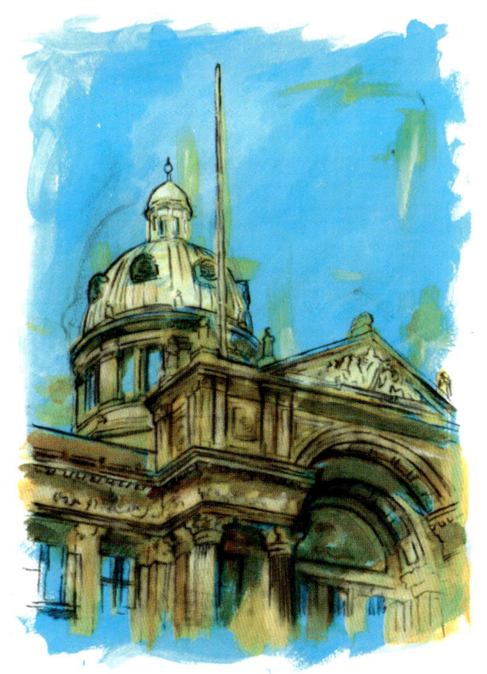

GEORGIA CHAPMAN, BIRMINGHAM CITY COUNCIL HOUSE

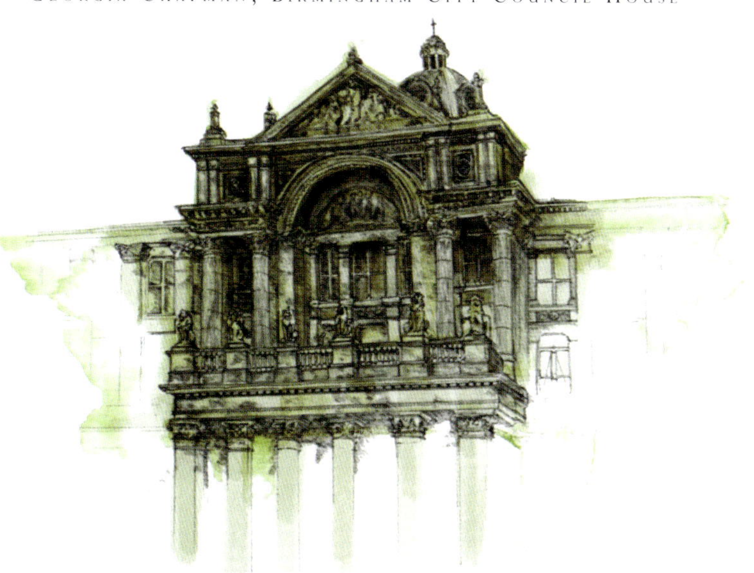

GRACE WARREN, BIRMINGHAM CITY COUNCIL HOUSE

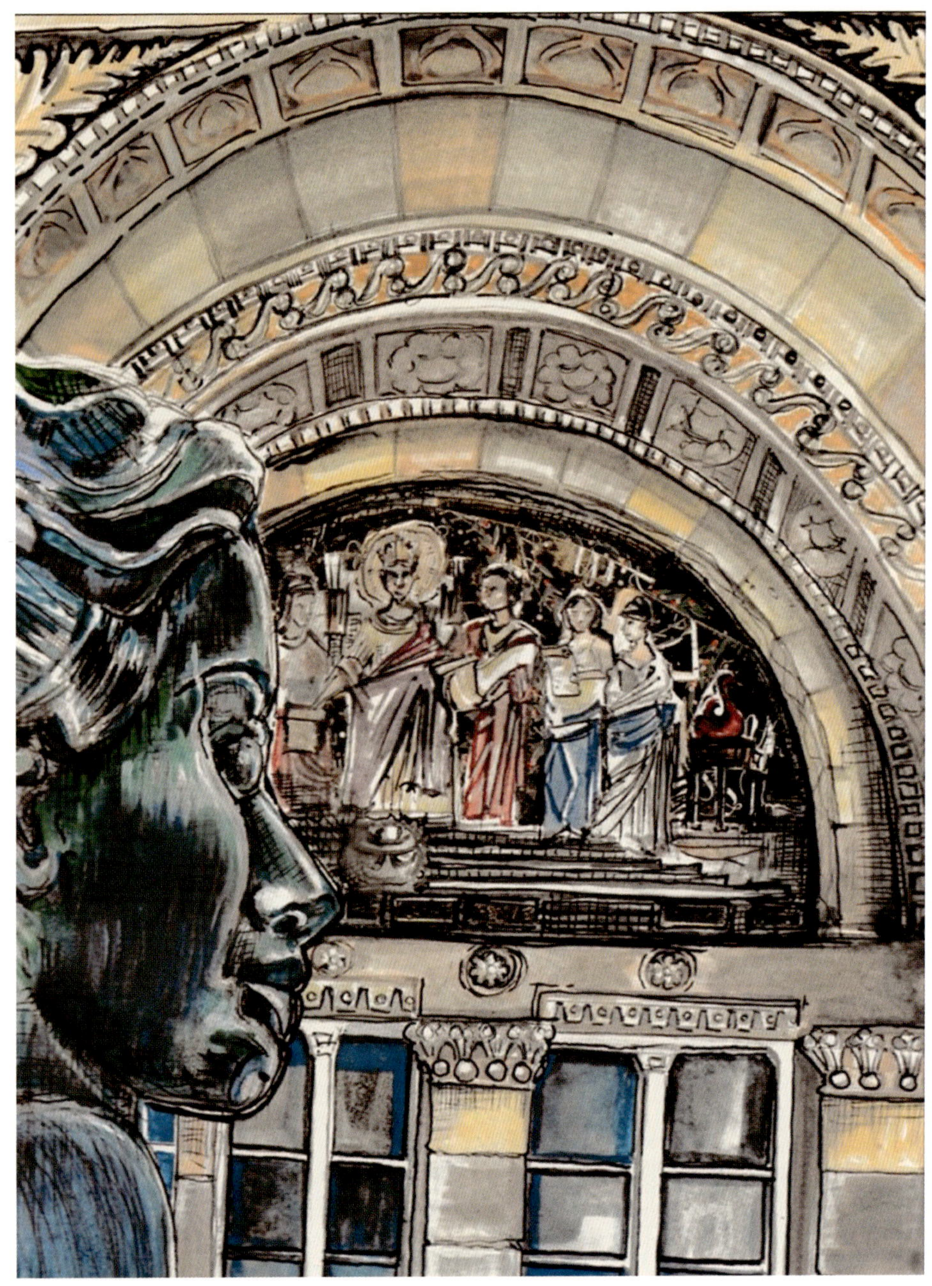

AMANDA GODDEN, THE FLOOZY IN THE JACUZZI

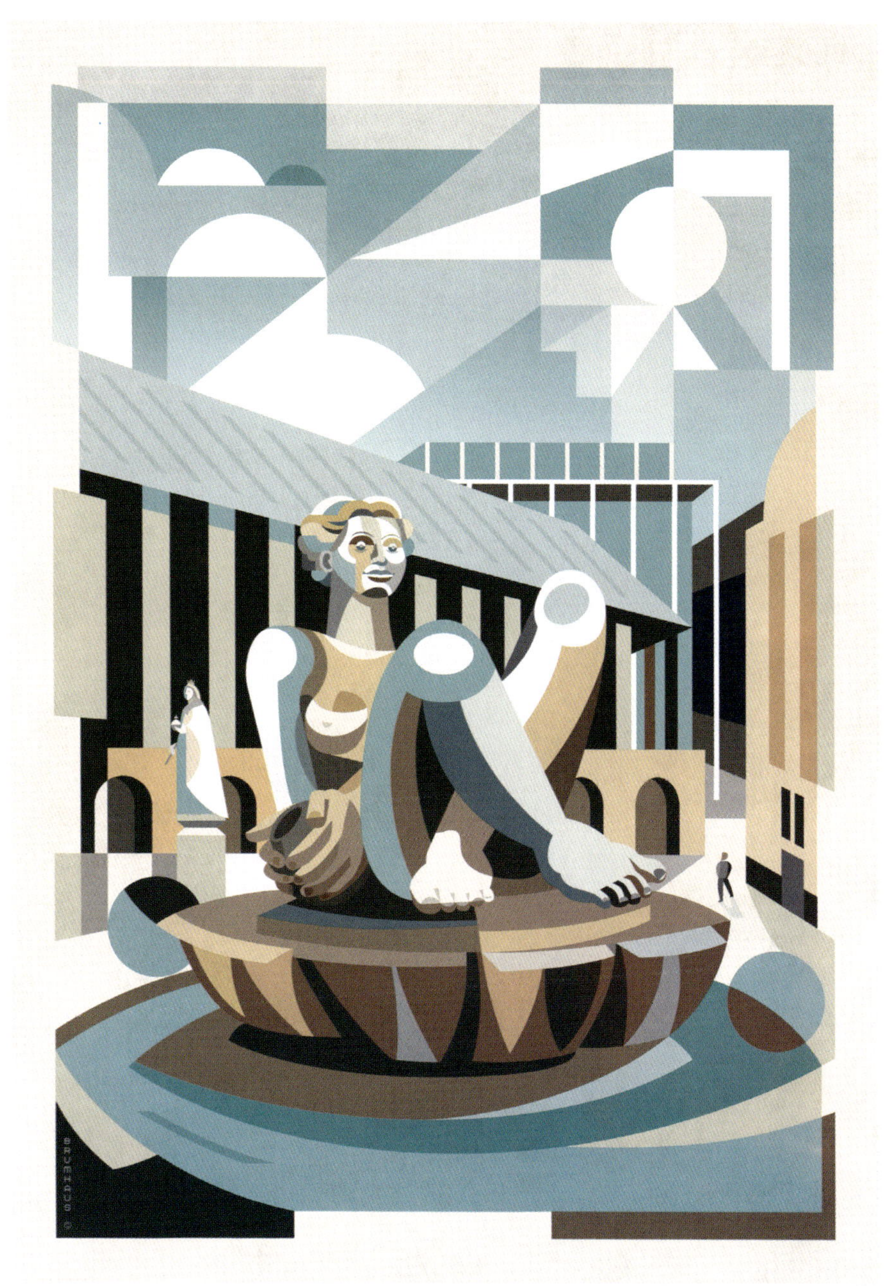

ALEXANDER EDWARDS (BRUMHAUS), THE FLOOZIE IN THE JACUZZI

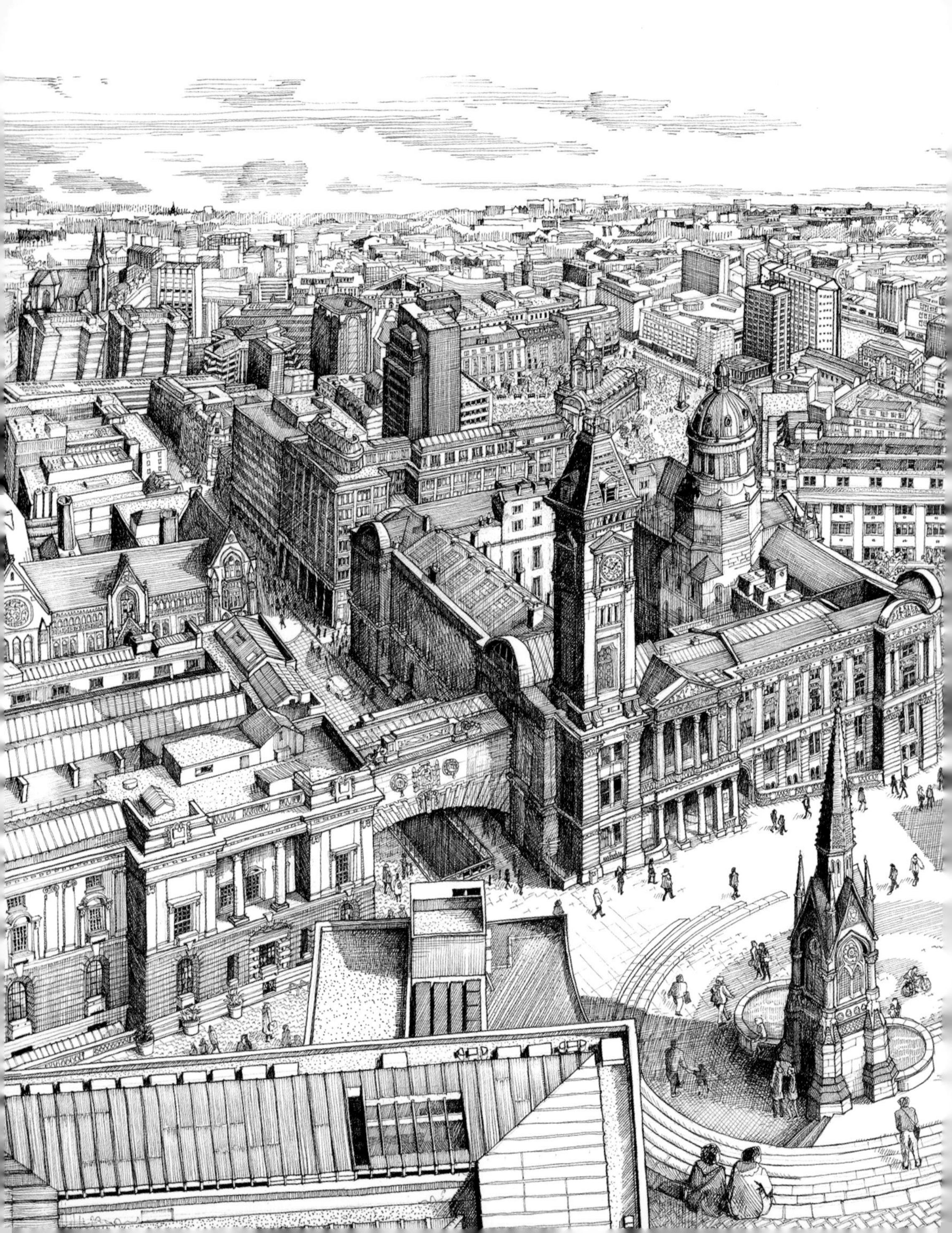

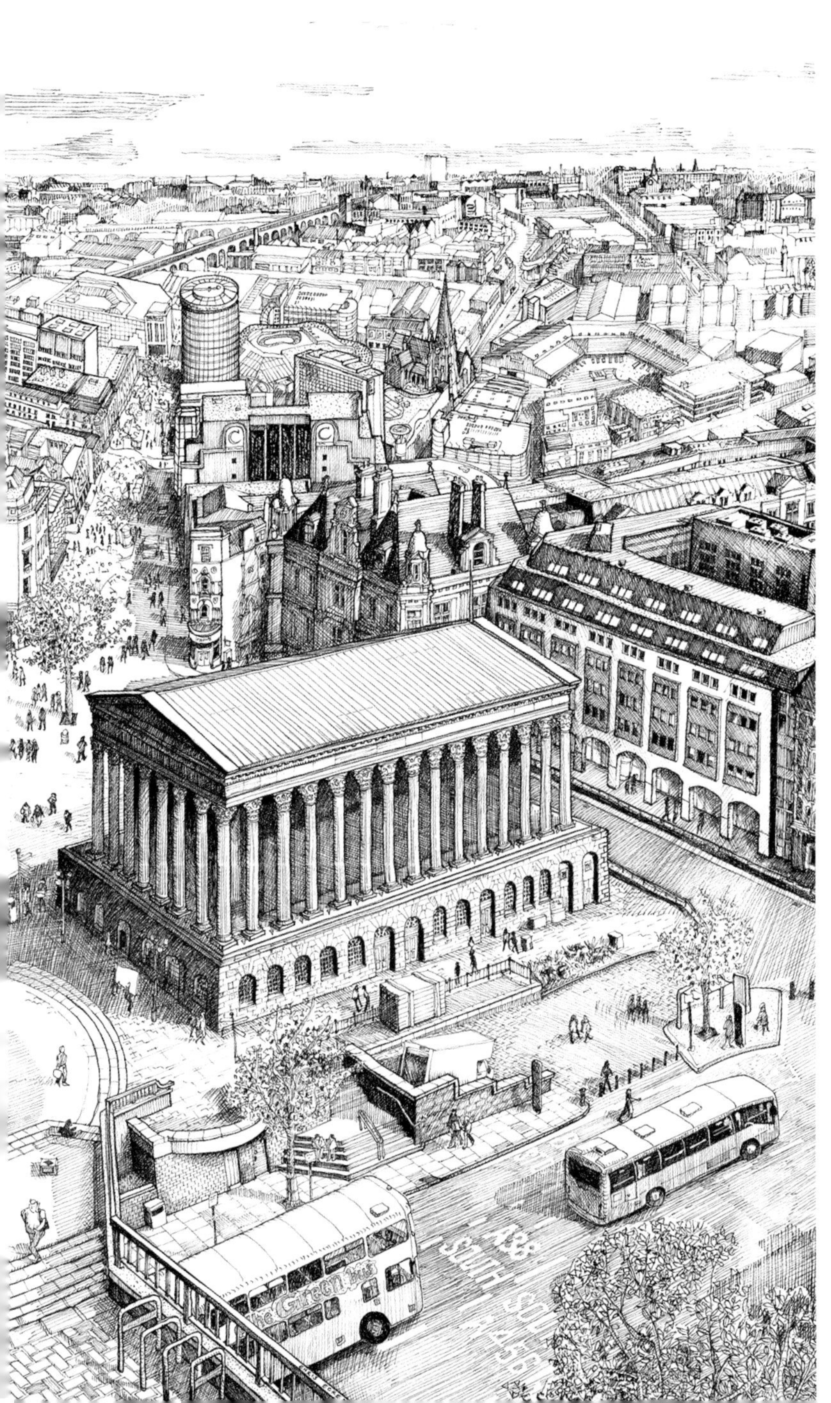

CHRIS ECKERSLEY,
BIRD'S EYE BRUM

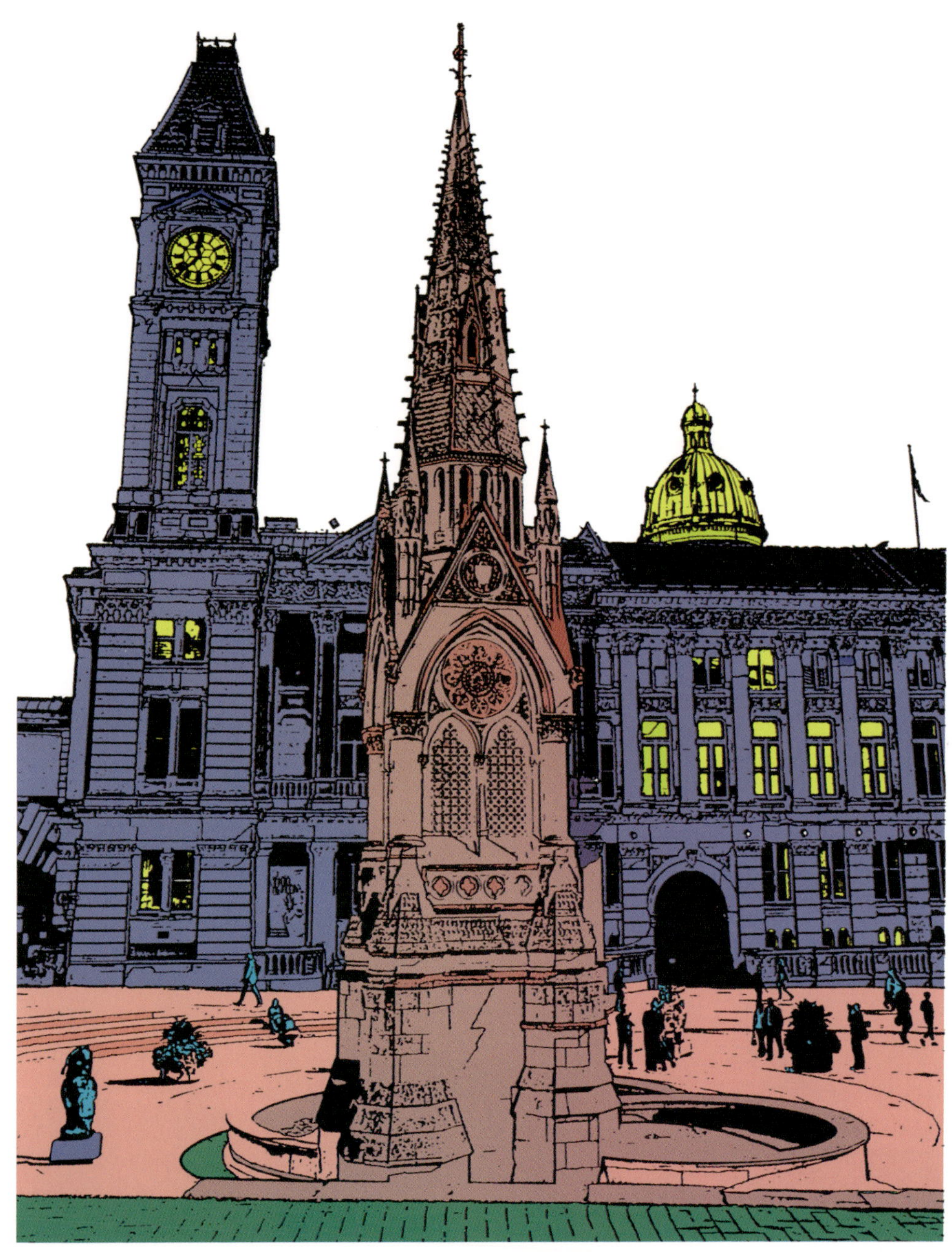

KAREN CROSS, VICTORIA SQUARE

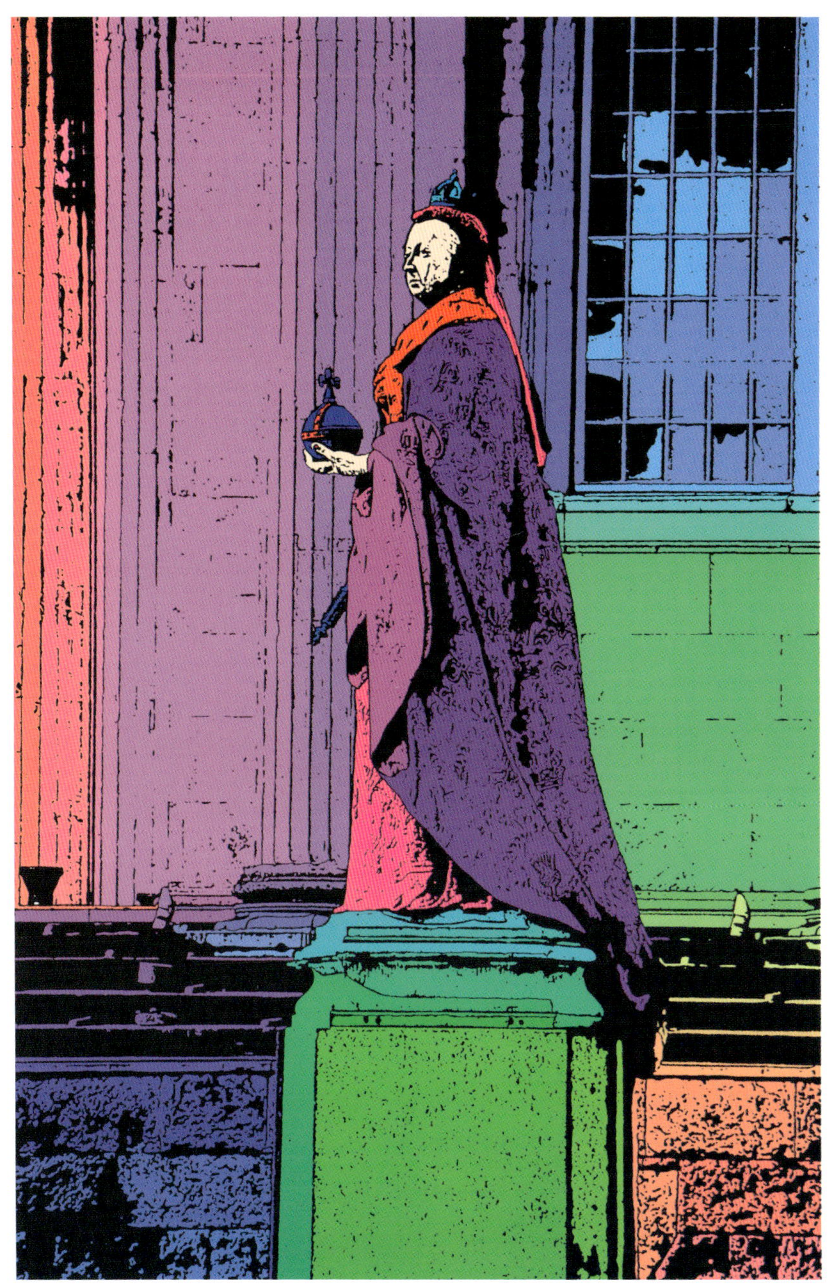

KAREN CROSS, QUEEN VICTORIA

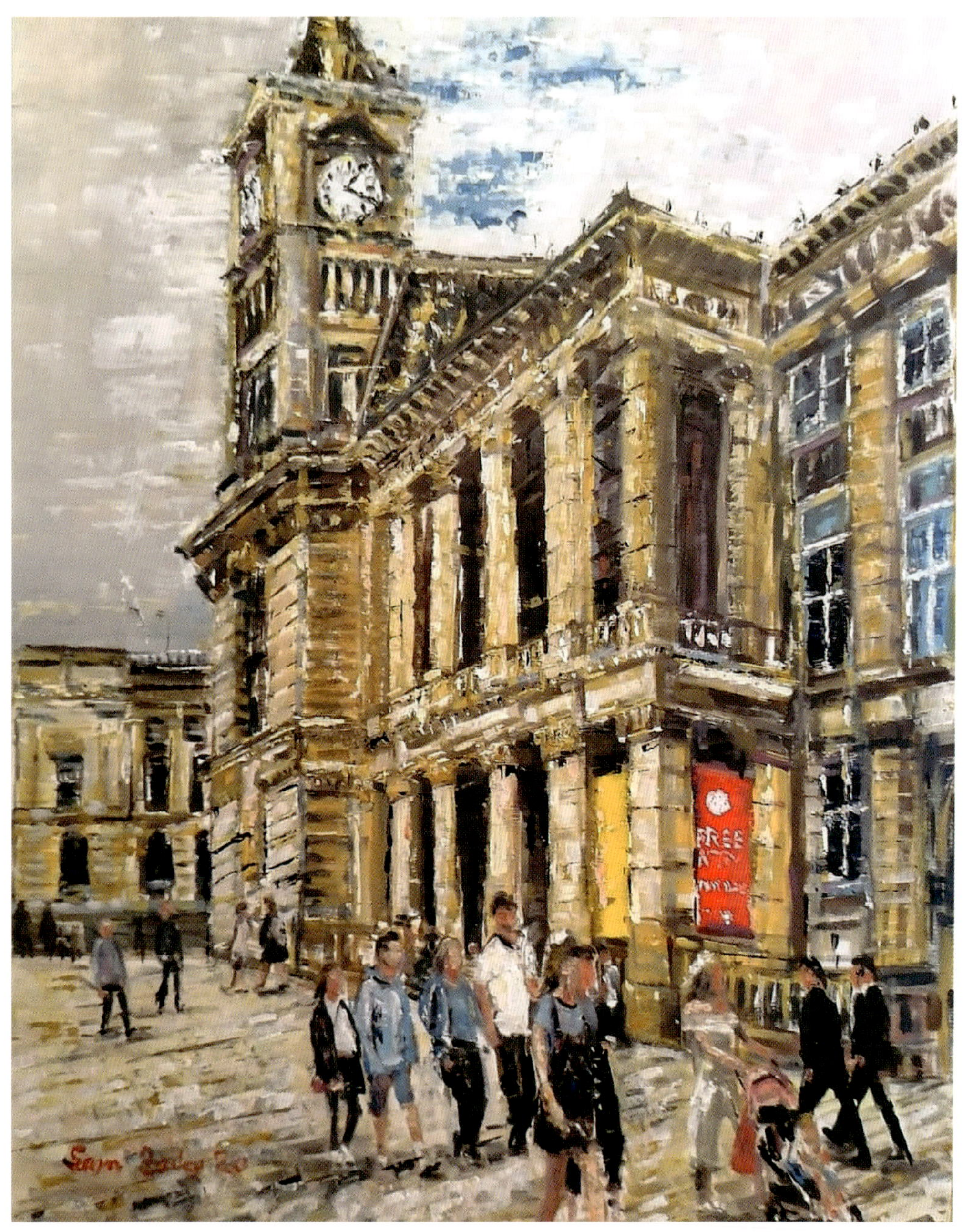

SAM BAILEY, BIRMINGHAM MUSEUM AND ART GALLERY

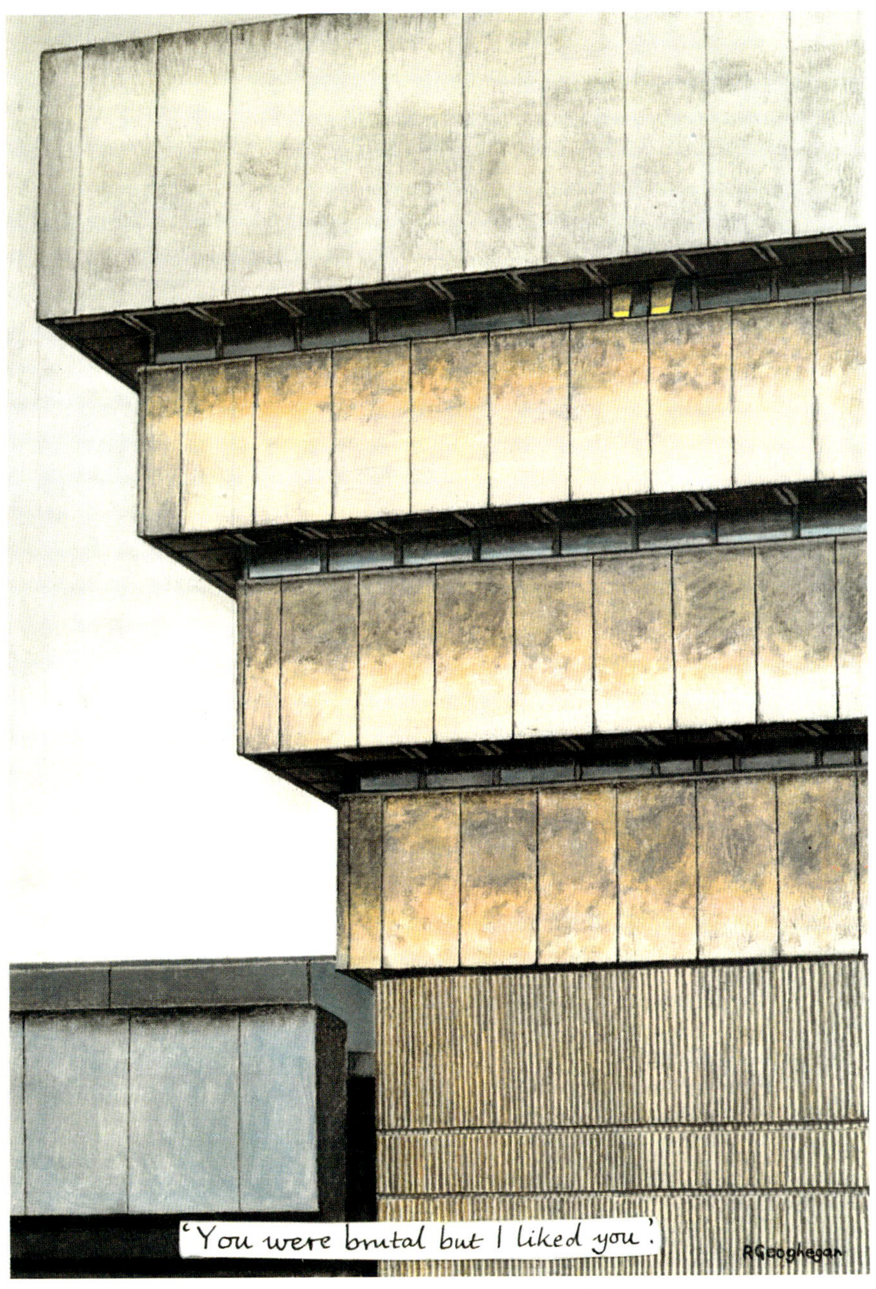

ROBERT GEOGHEGAN, OLD BIRMINGHAM CENTRAL LIBRARY

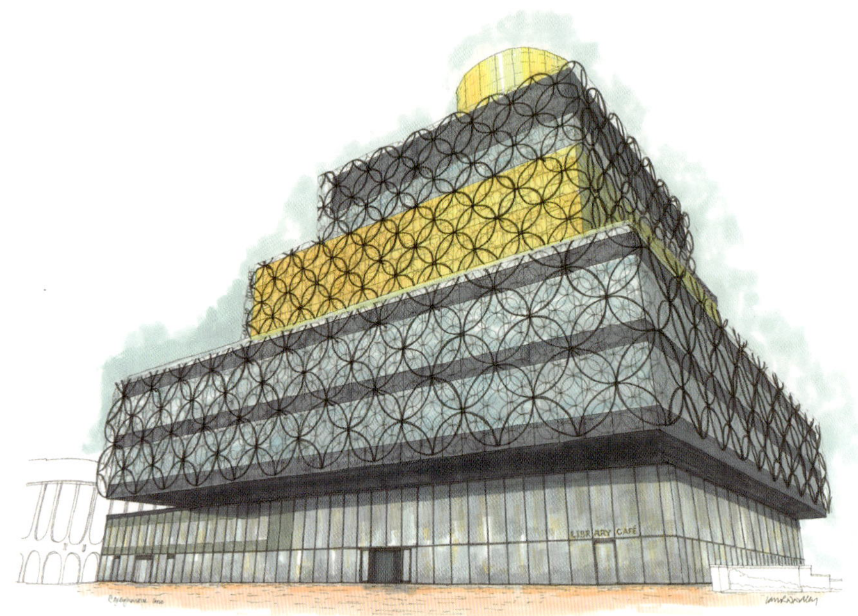

IAN WOODLEY, LIBRARY OF BIRMINGHAM

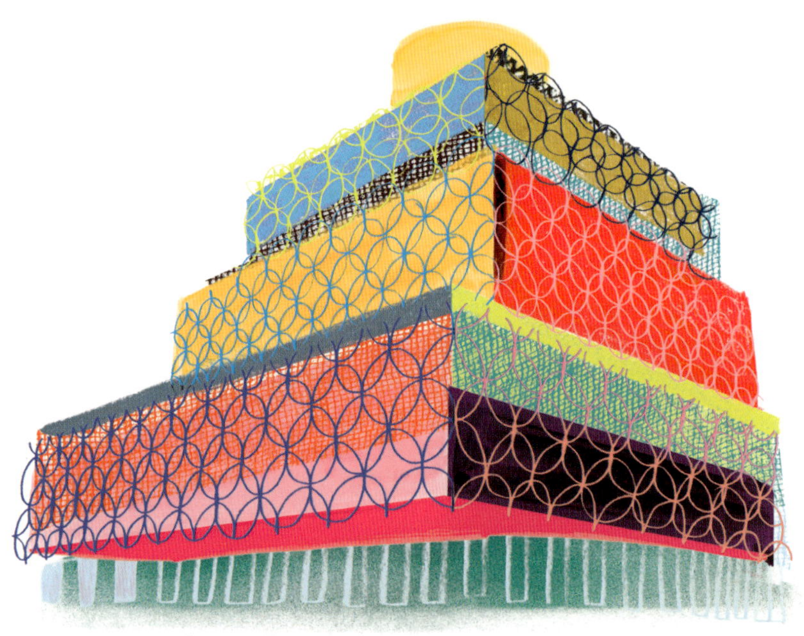

ILONA DREW, LIBRARY OF BIRMINGHAM

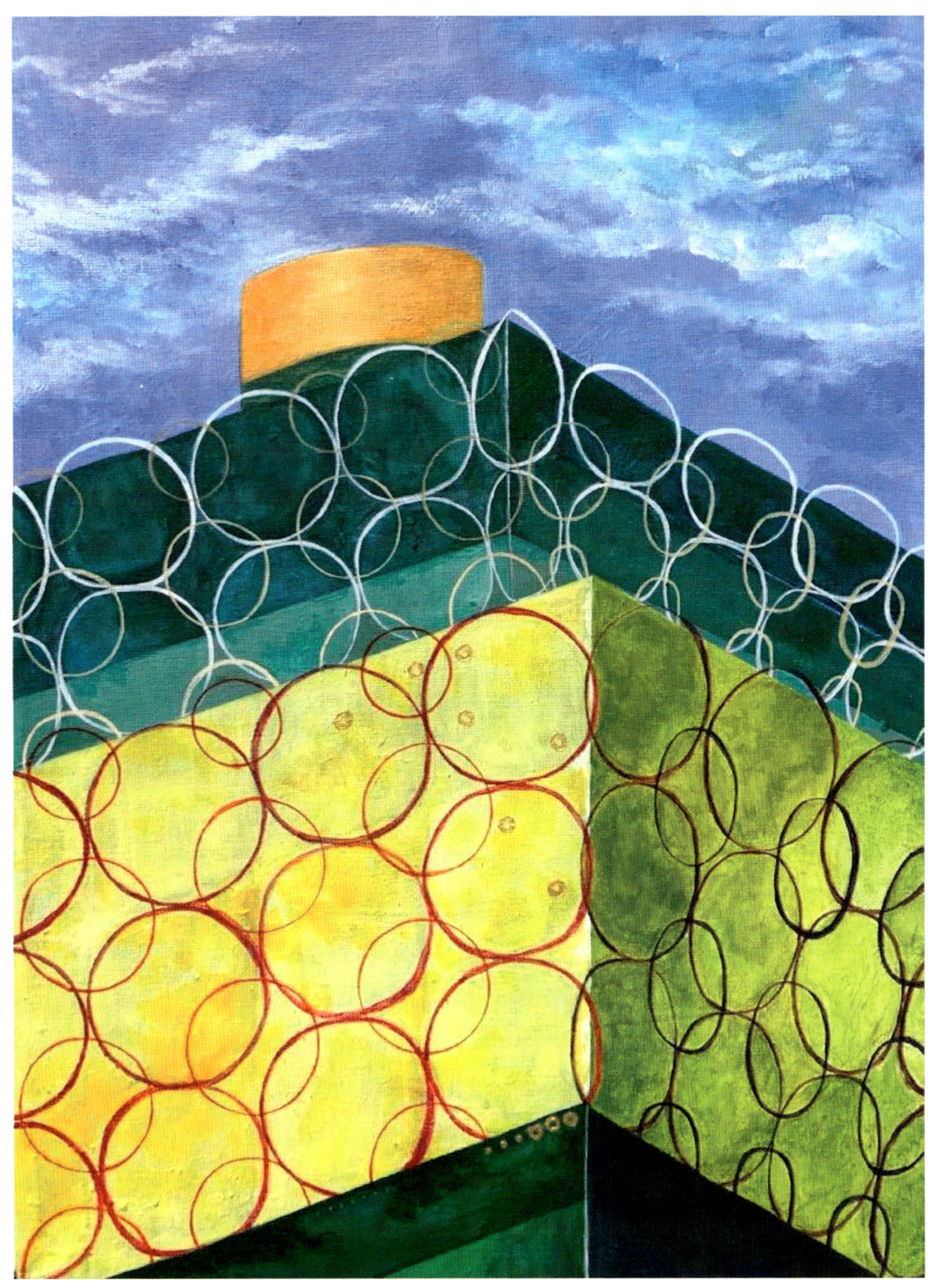

BECCA MOODY, LIBRARY OF BIRMINGHAM

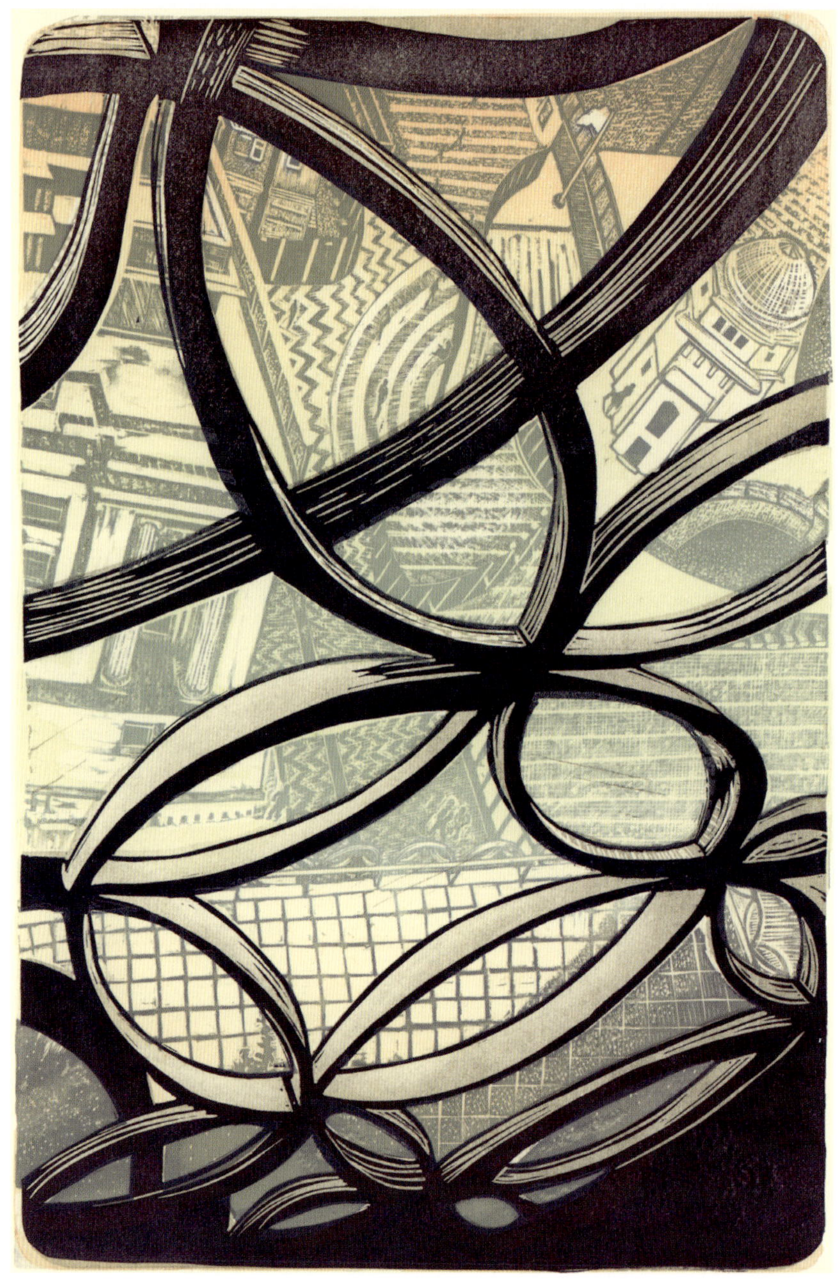

32

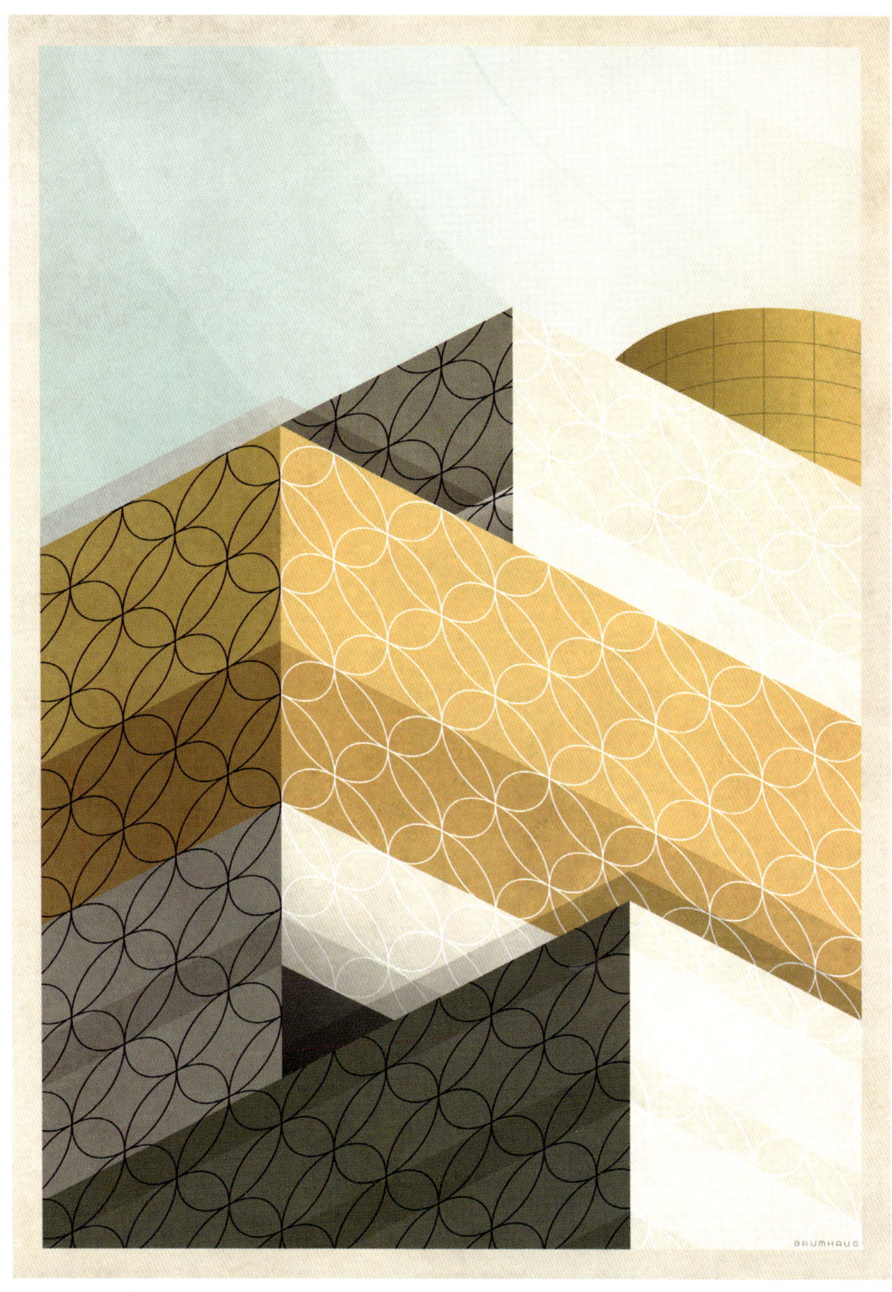

ALEXANDER EDWARDS (BRUMHAUS), LIBRARY IN TANGENT

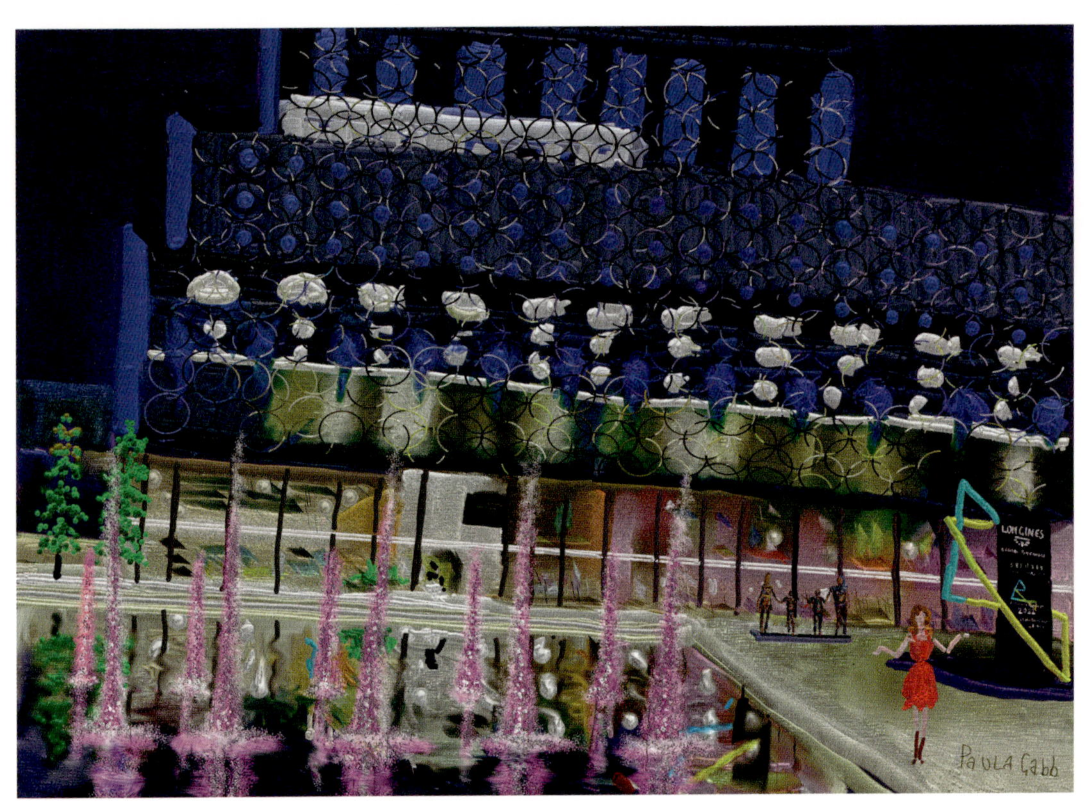

PAULA GABB, LIBRARY OF BIRMINGHAM

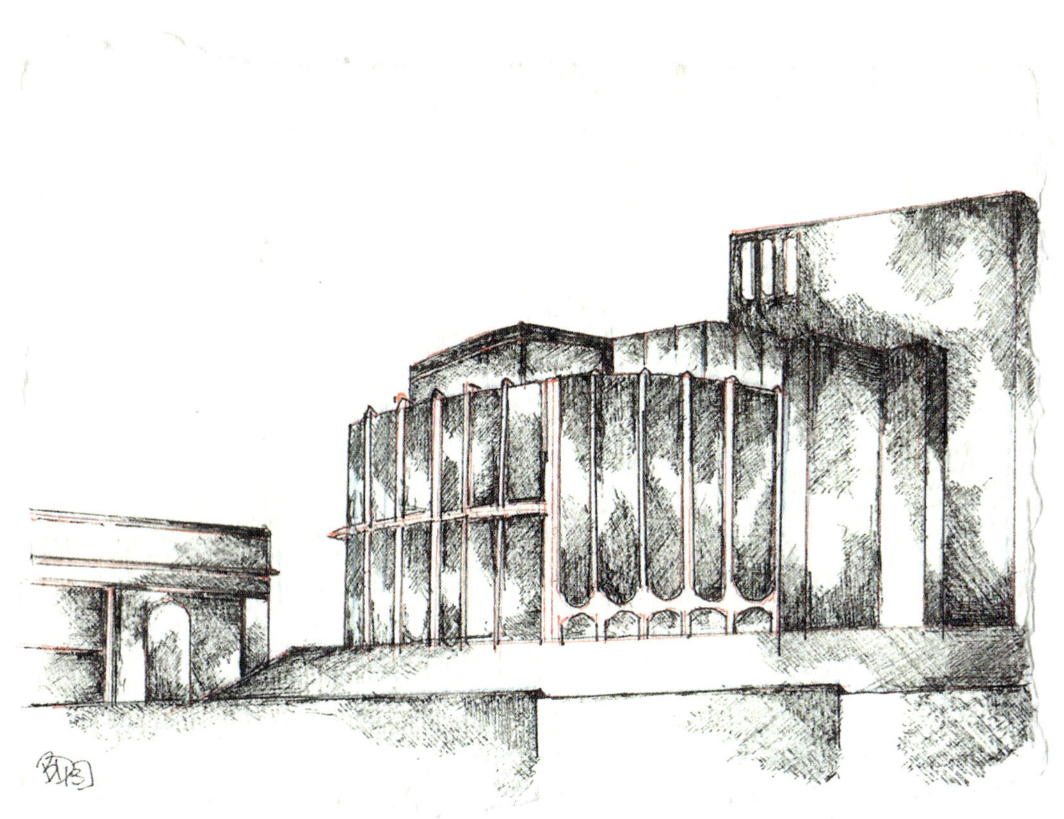

BETHANY DARTNELL, BIRMINGHAM REPERTORY THEATRE

35

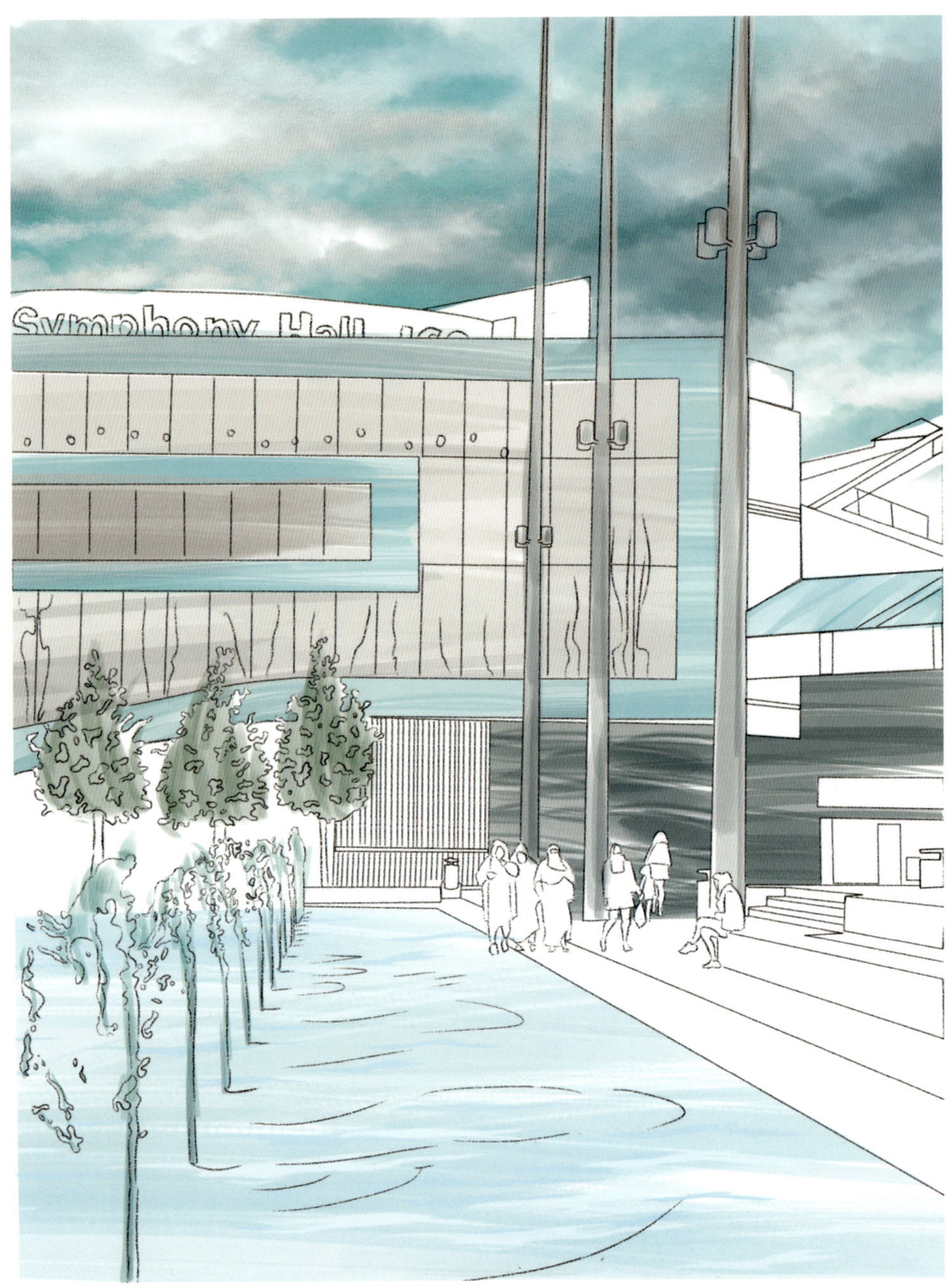

LOIS CHESHIRE, SYMPHONY HALL

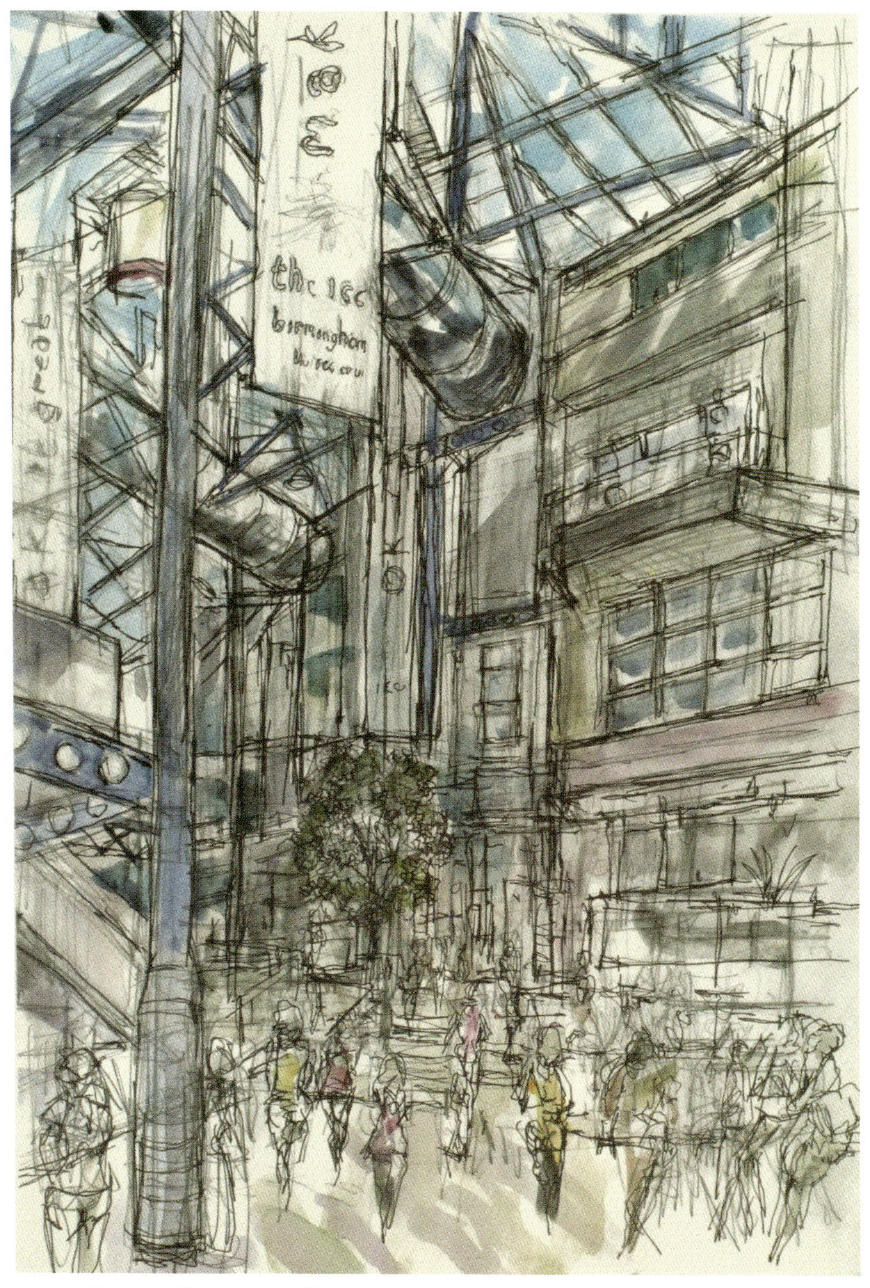
love
the icc
birmingham
theicc.co.uk
icc

DANIEL STEDMAN, THE INTERNATIONAL CONVENTION CENTRE

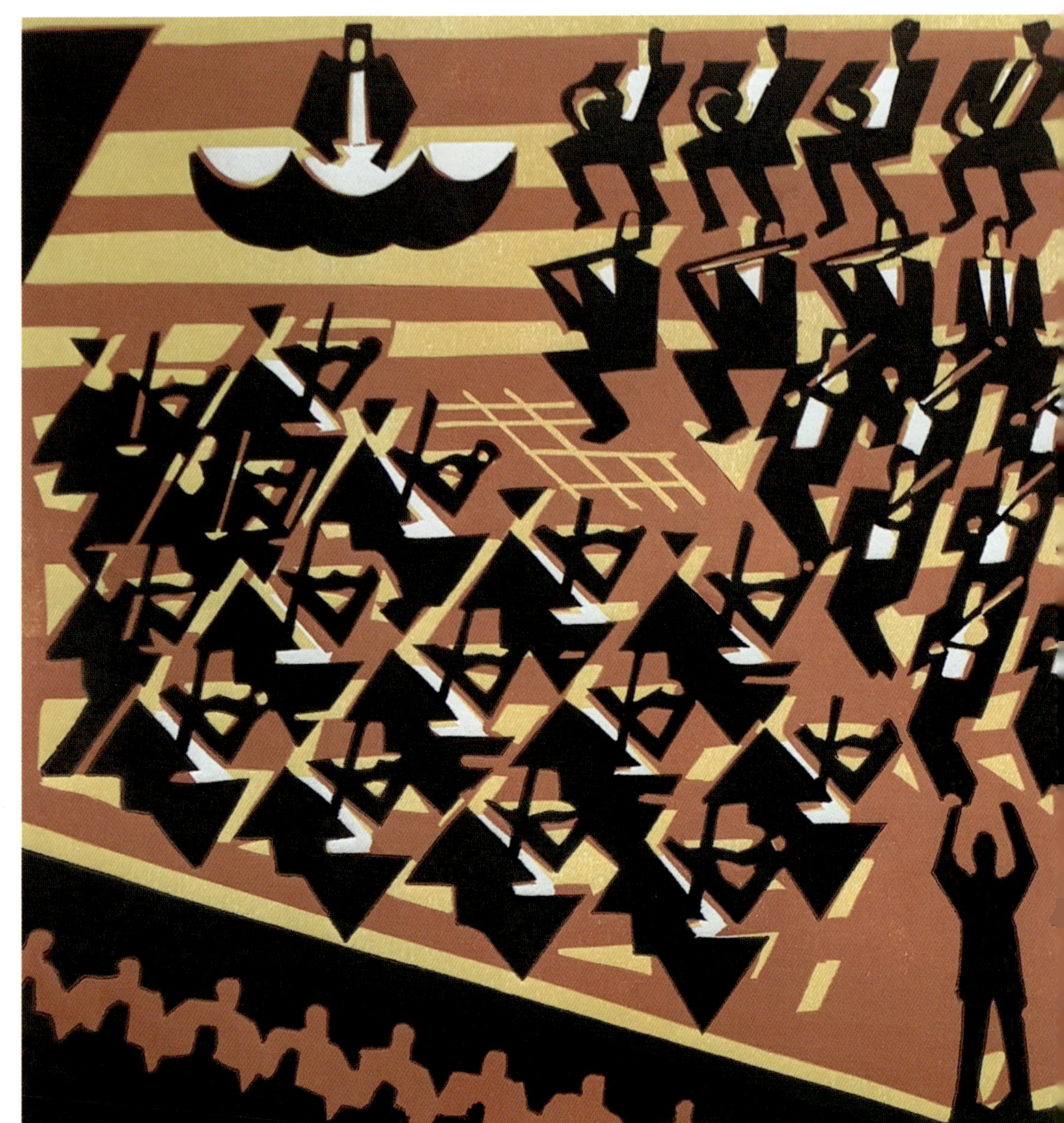

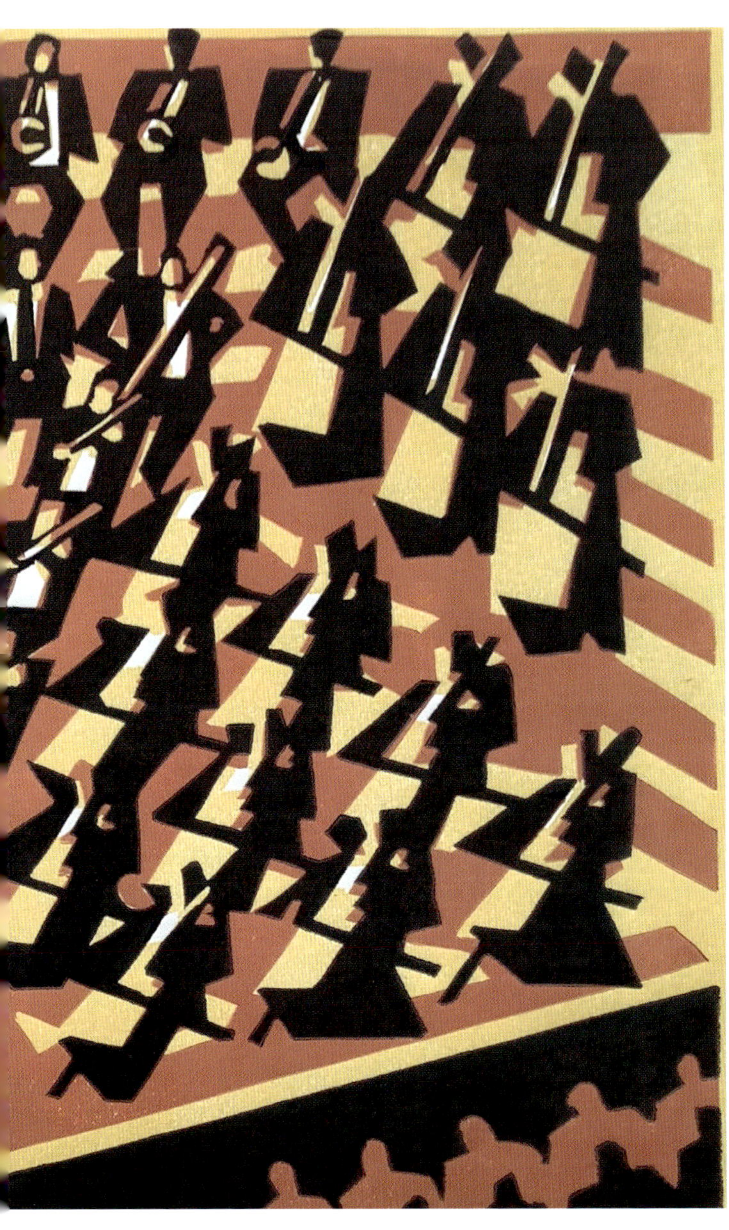

PETER SHREAD,
ORCHESTRA, SYMPHANY HALL

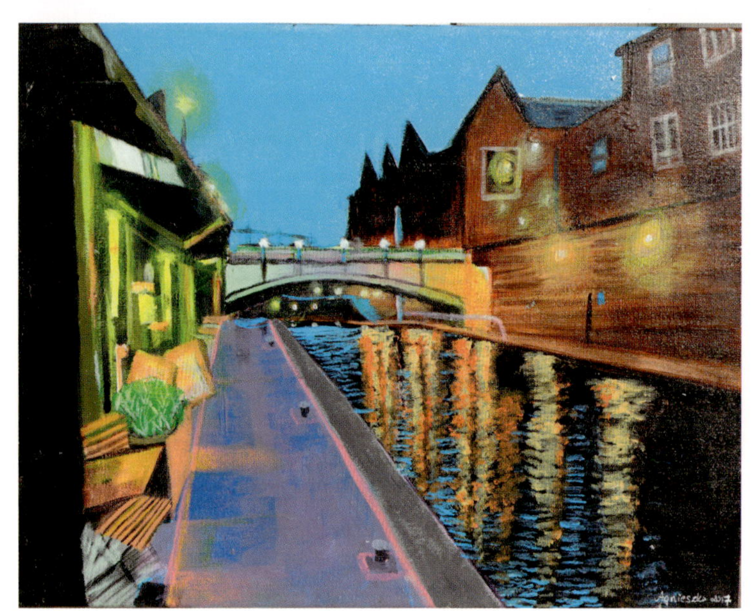

AGNIESZKA KLIMASZEWSKA, BRINDLEY PLACE

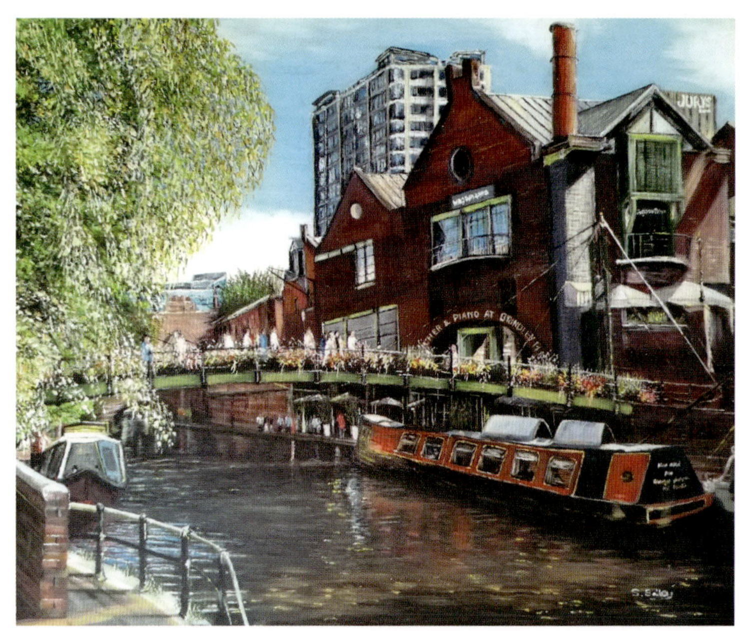

SAM BAILEY, BRINDLEY PLACE

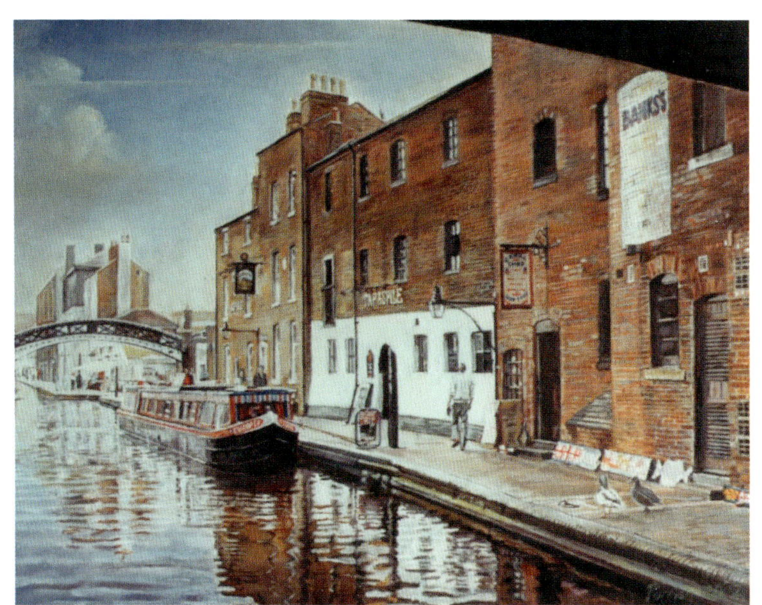

Kevin Parrish, Gas Street Basin

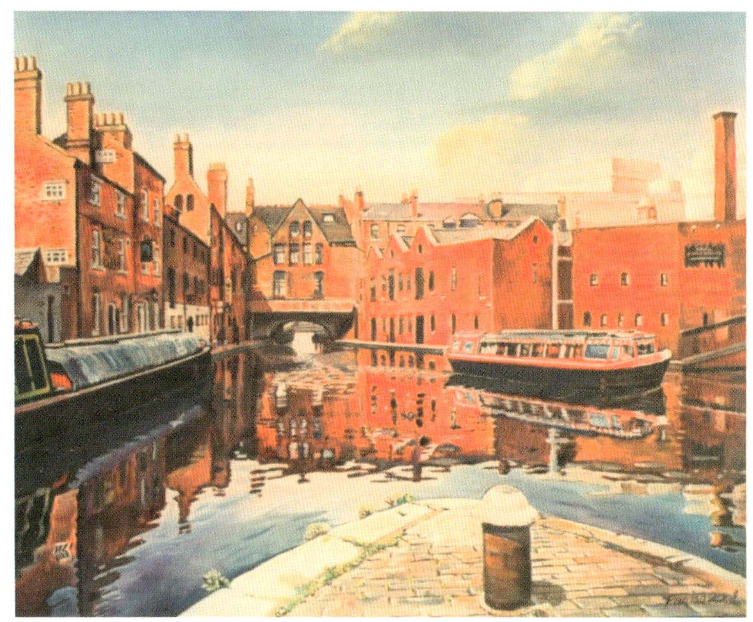

Kevin Parrish, Gas Street Basin

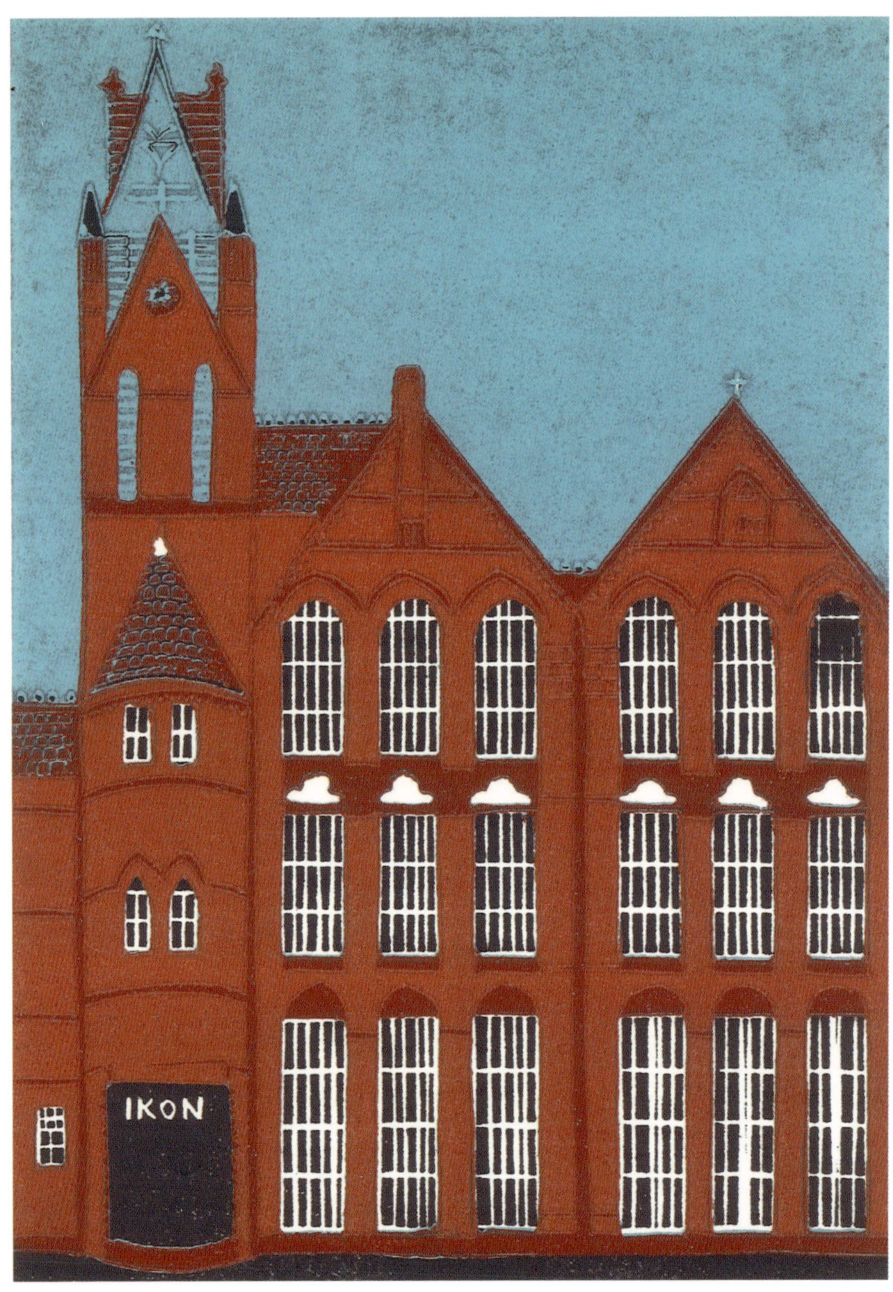

JENNIE ING, IKON GALLERY

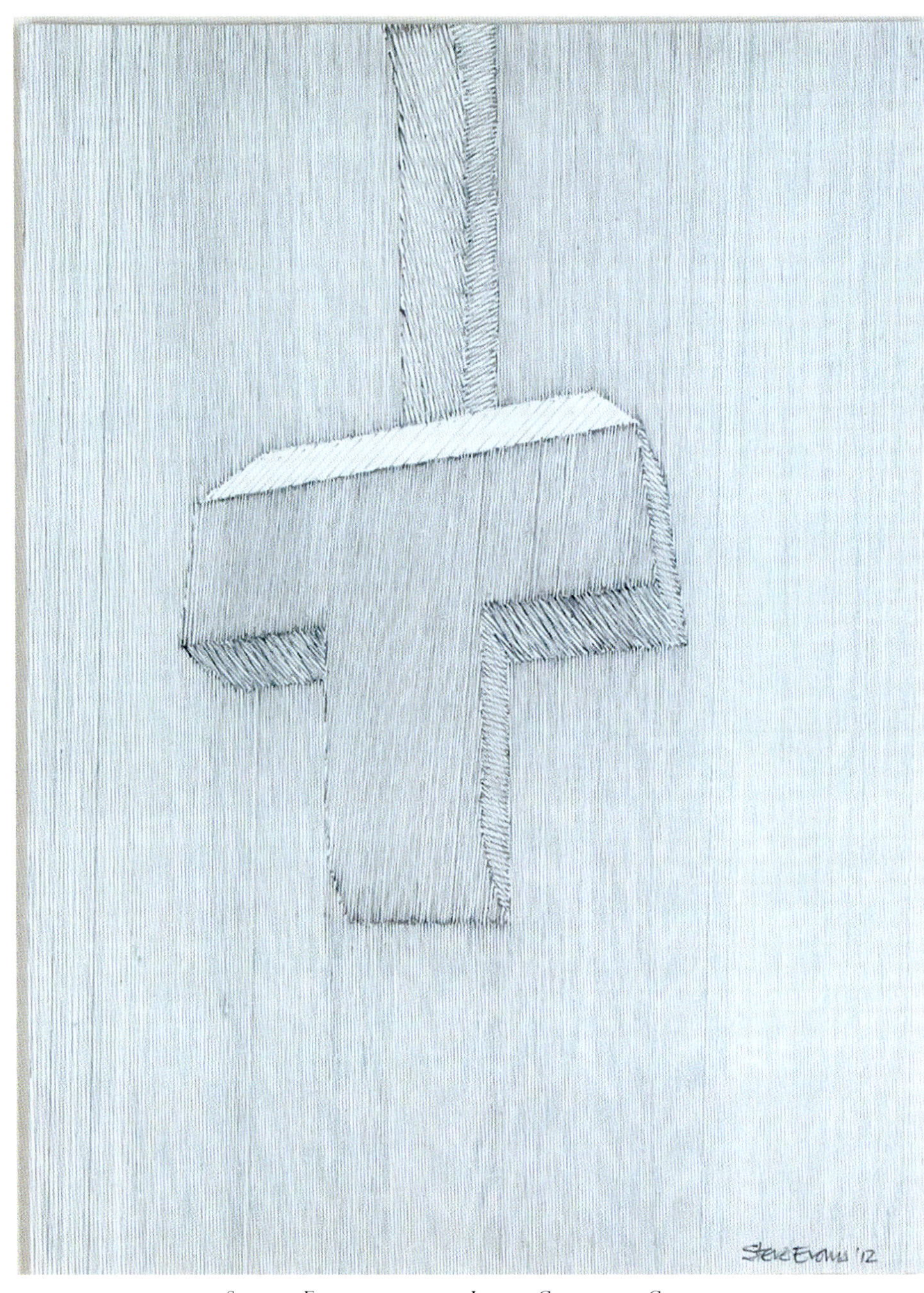

Steve Evans prbsa, Ikon Gallery Corbel

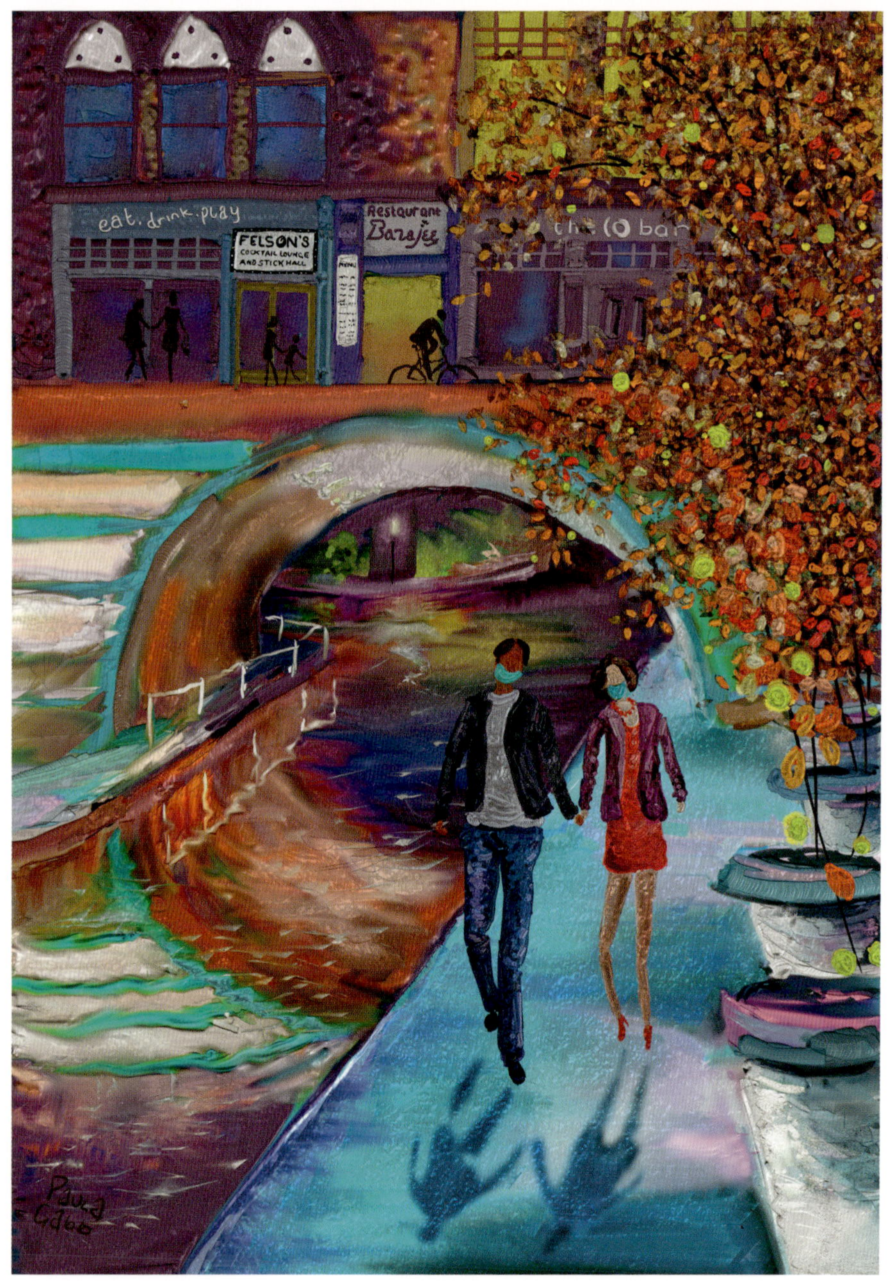

PAULA GABB, CANAL AT BROAD STREET

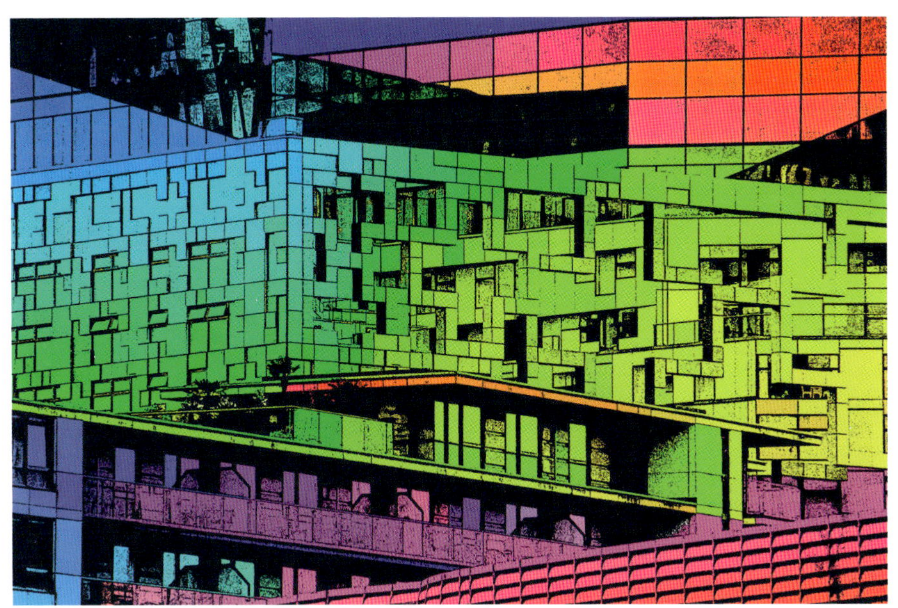

KAREN CROSS, THE CUBE

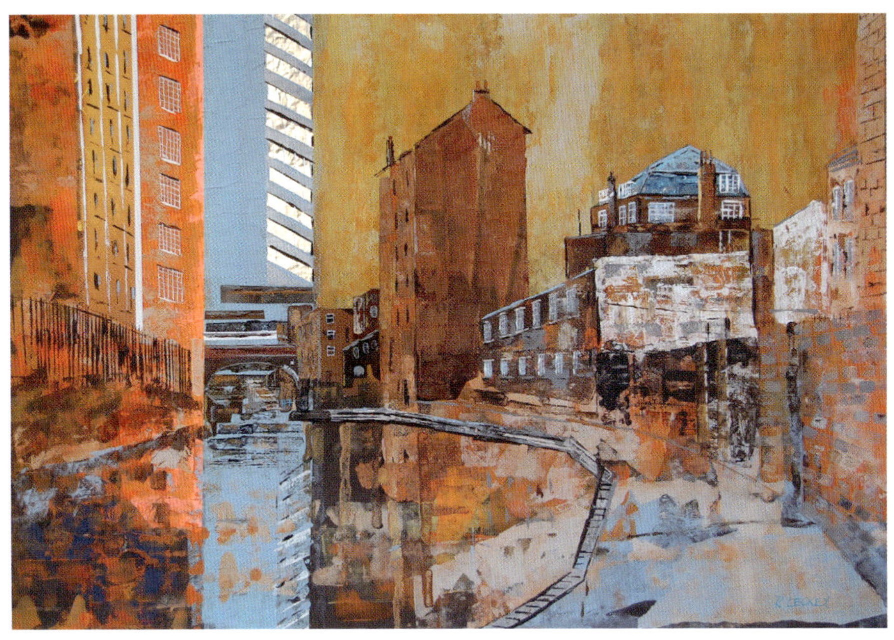

ROB LECKEY, BIRMINGHAM CANAL

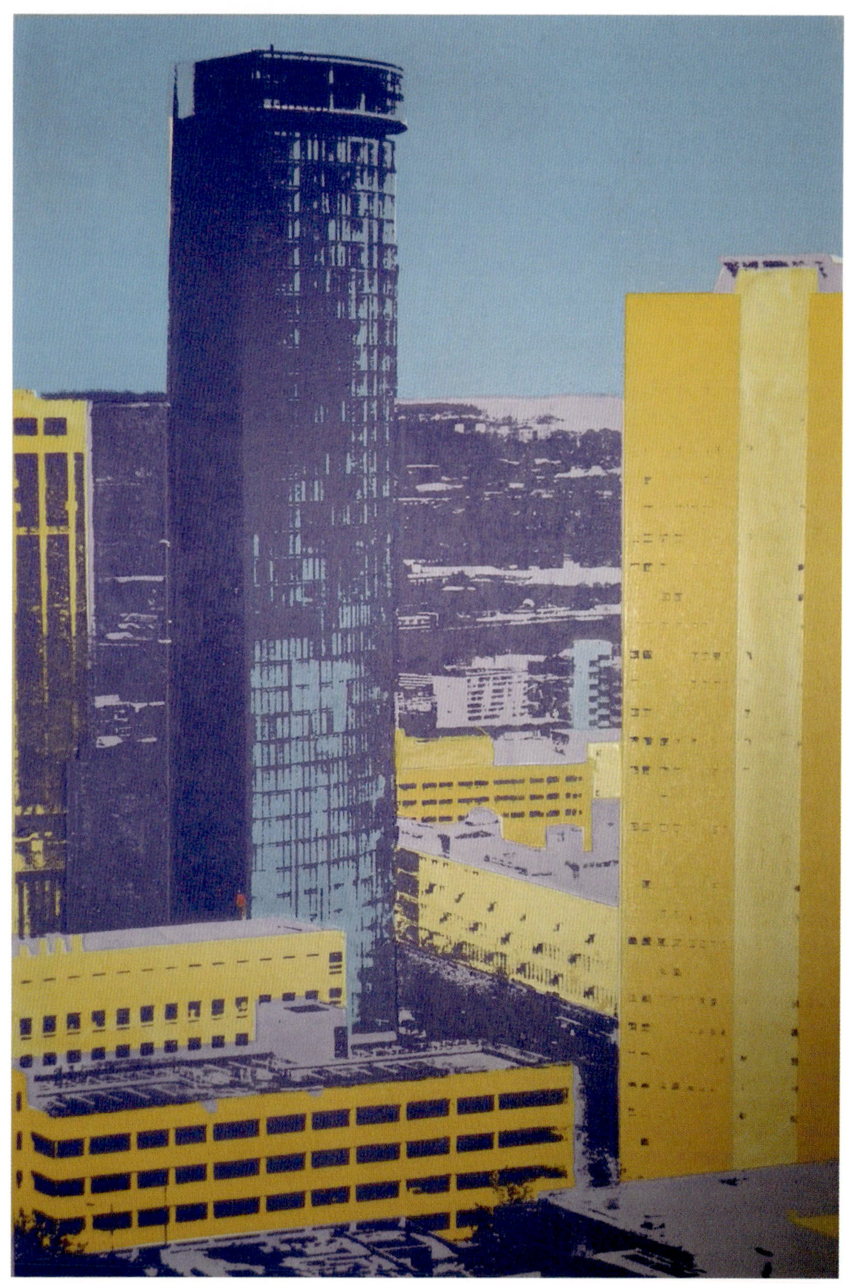

Lynn Jeffery rbsa, View from The Cube

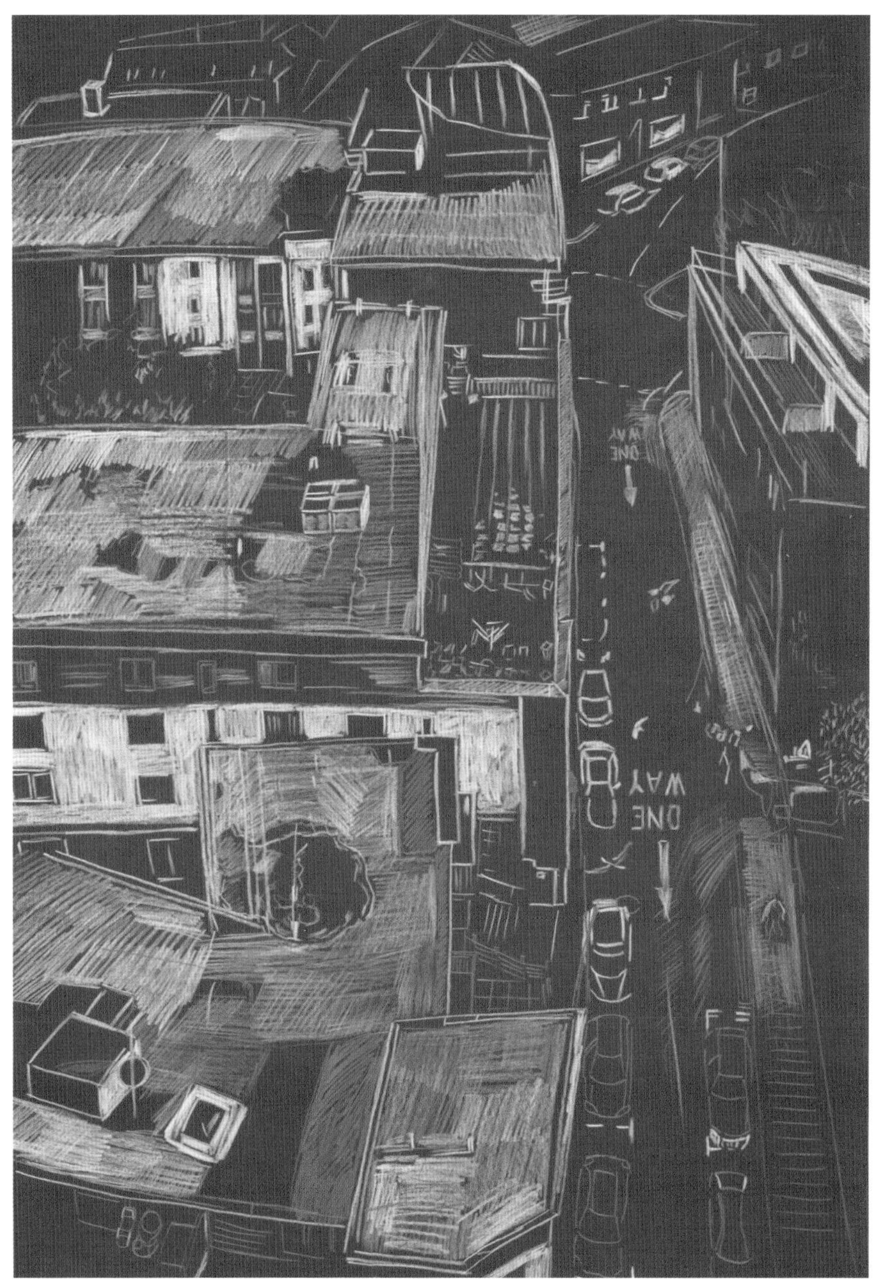

NICHOLAS SIMS, VIEW FROM THE TOP OF THE CUBE

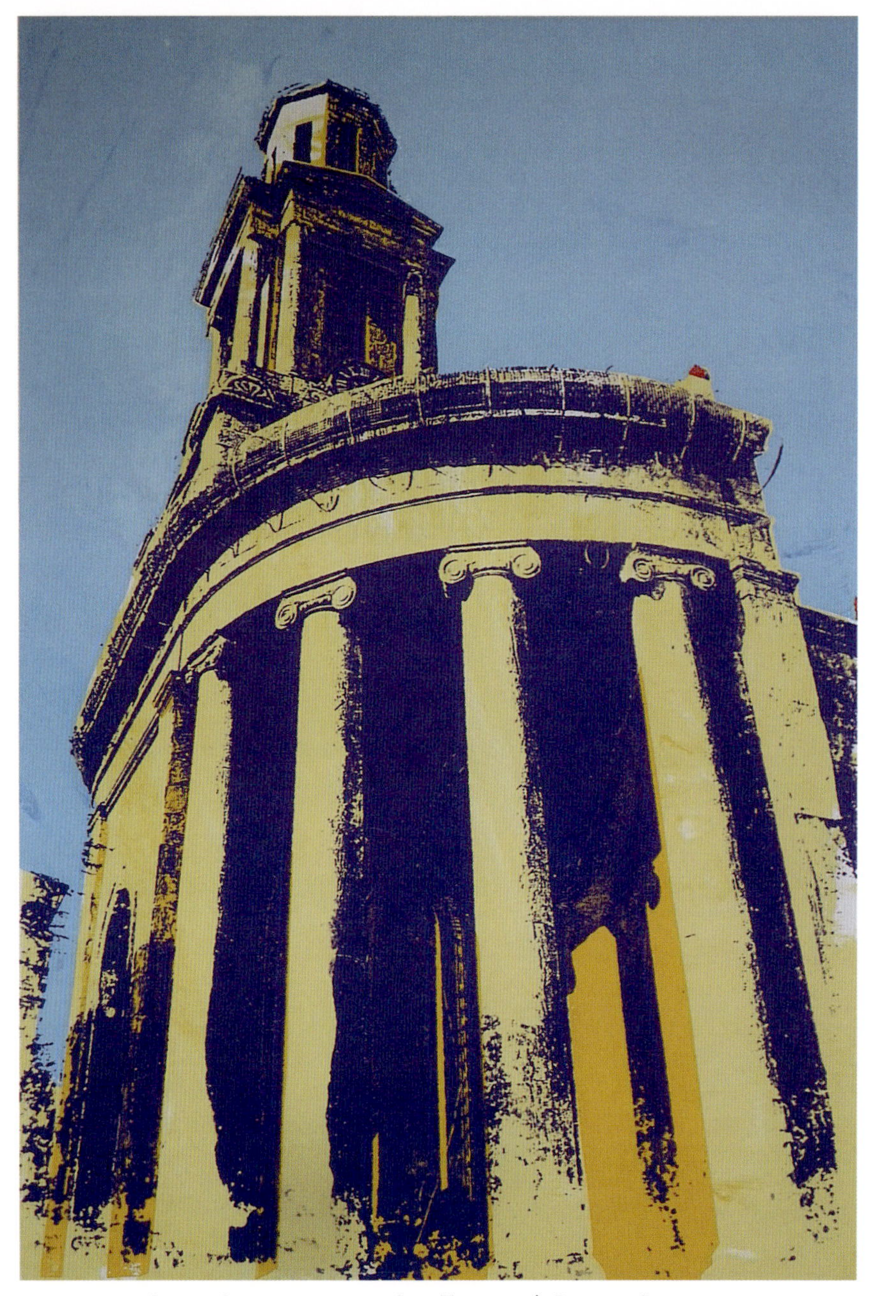

Lynn Jeffery rbsa, St. Thomas' Peace Garden

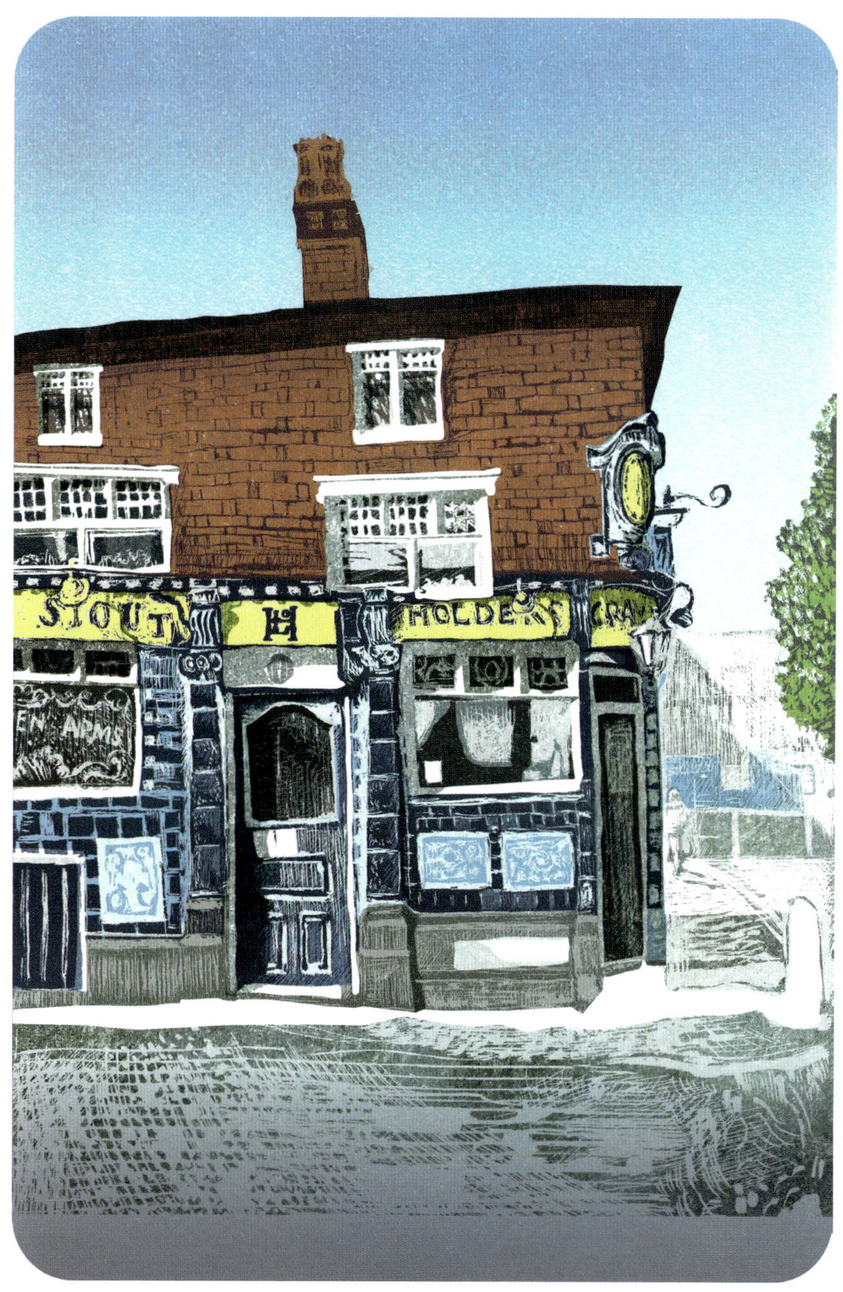

MIKE ALLISON, THE CRAVEN ARMS

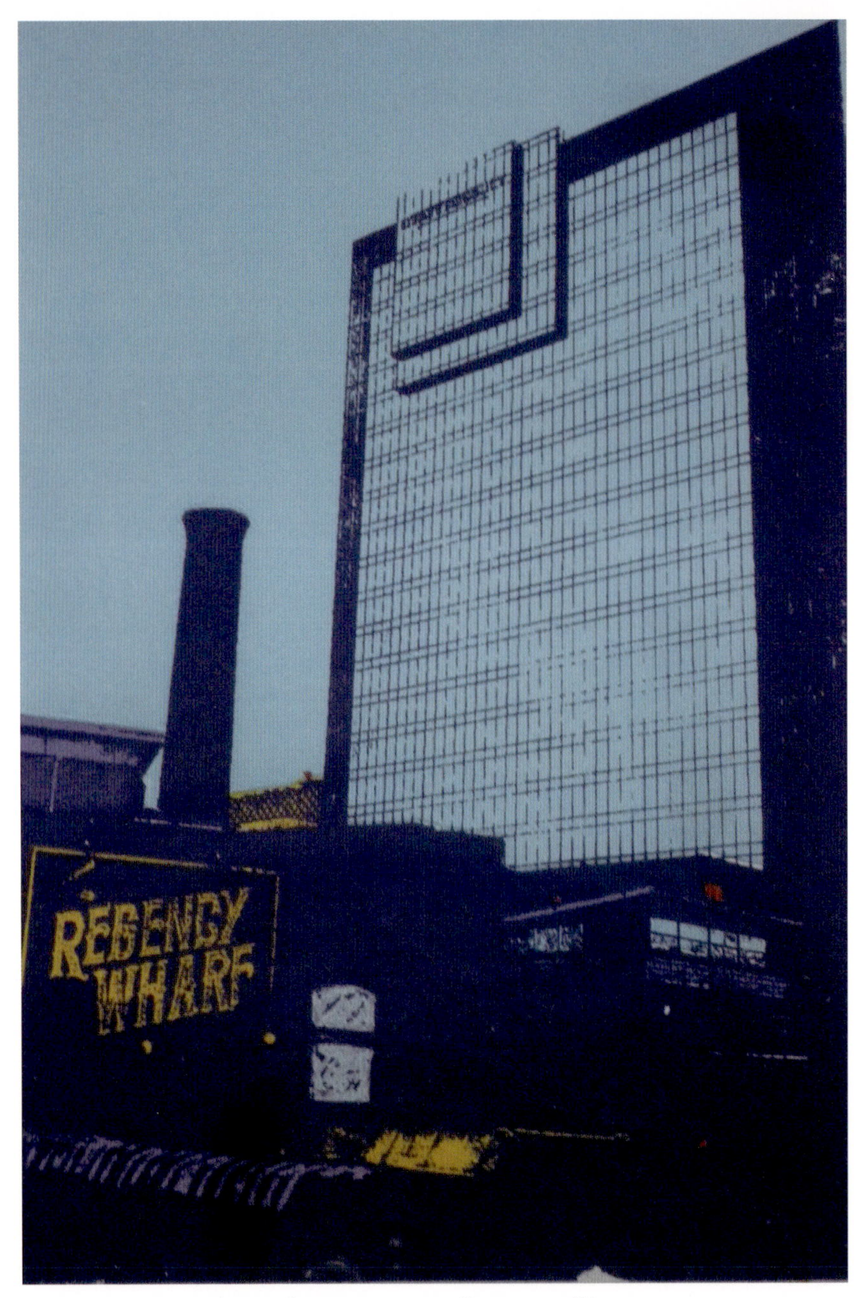

LYNN JEFFERY RBSA, REGENCY WHARF

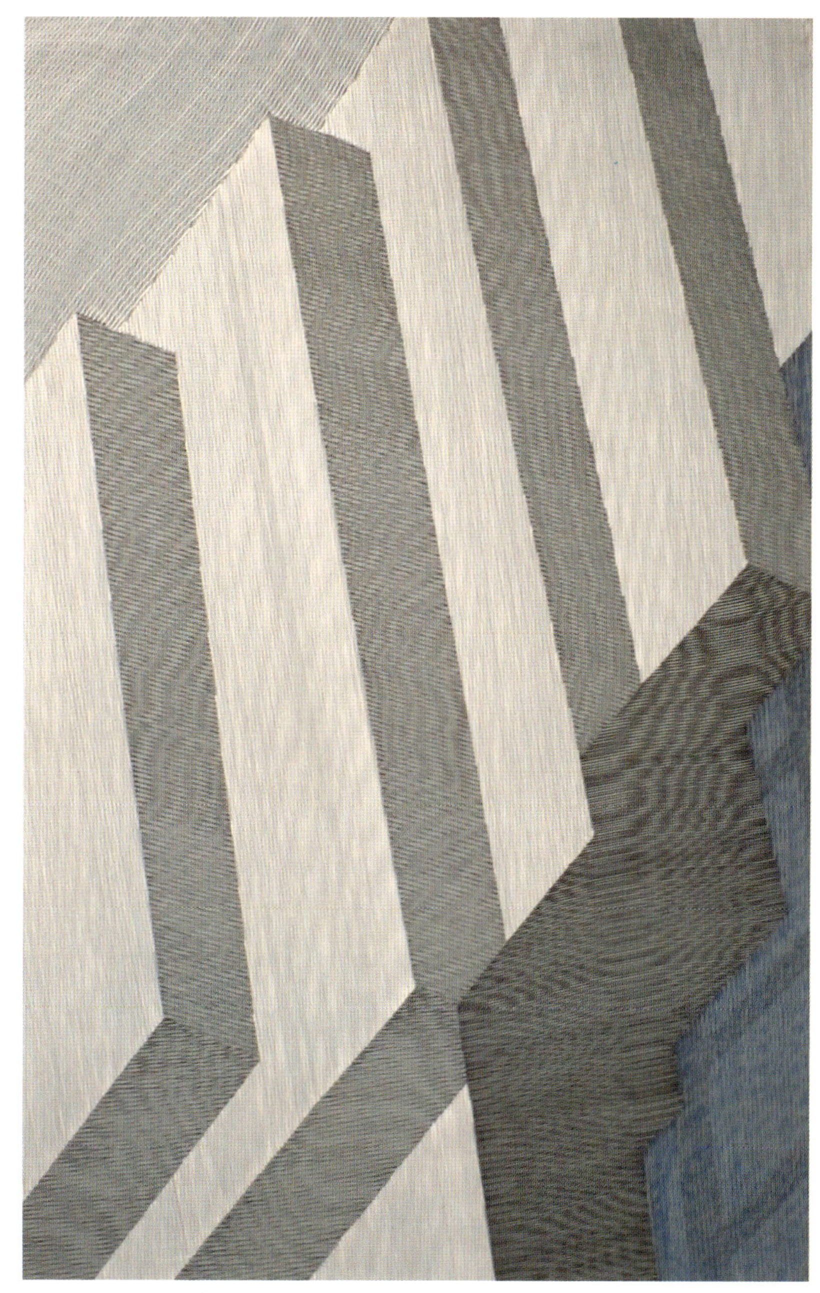

STEVE EVANS PRBSA, HYATT REGENCY

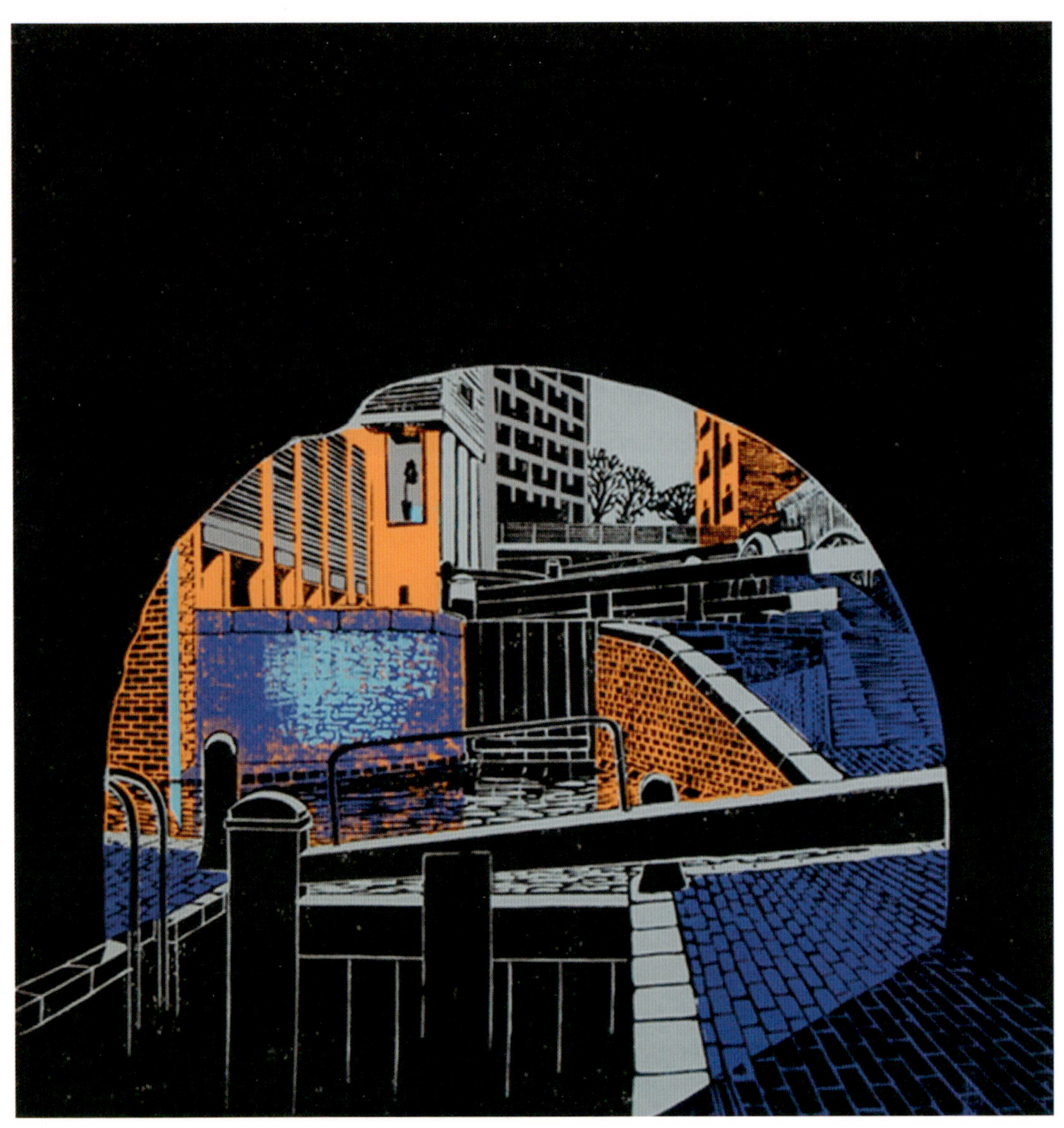

Paul Hipkiss rbsa, Farmers Bridge locks

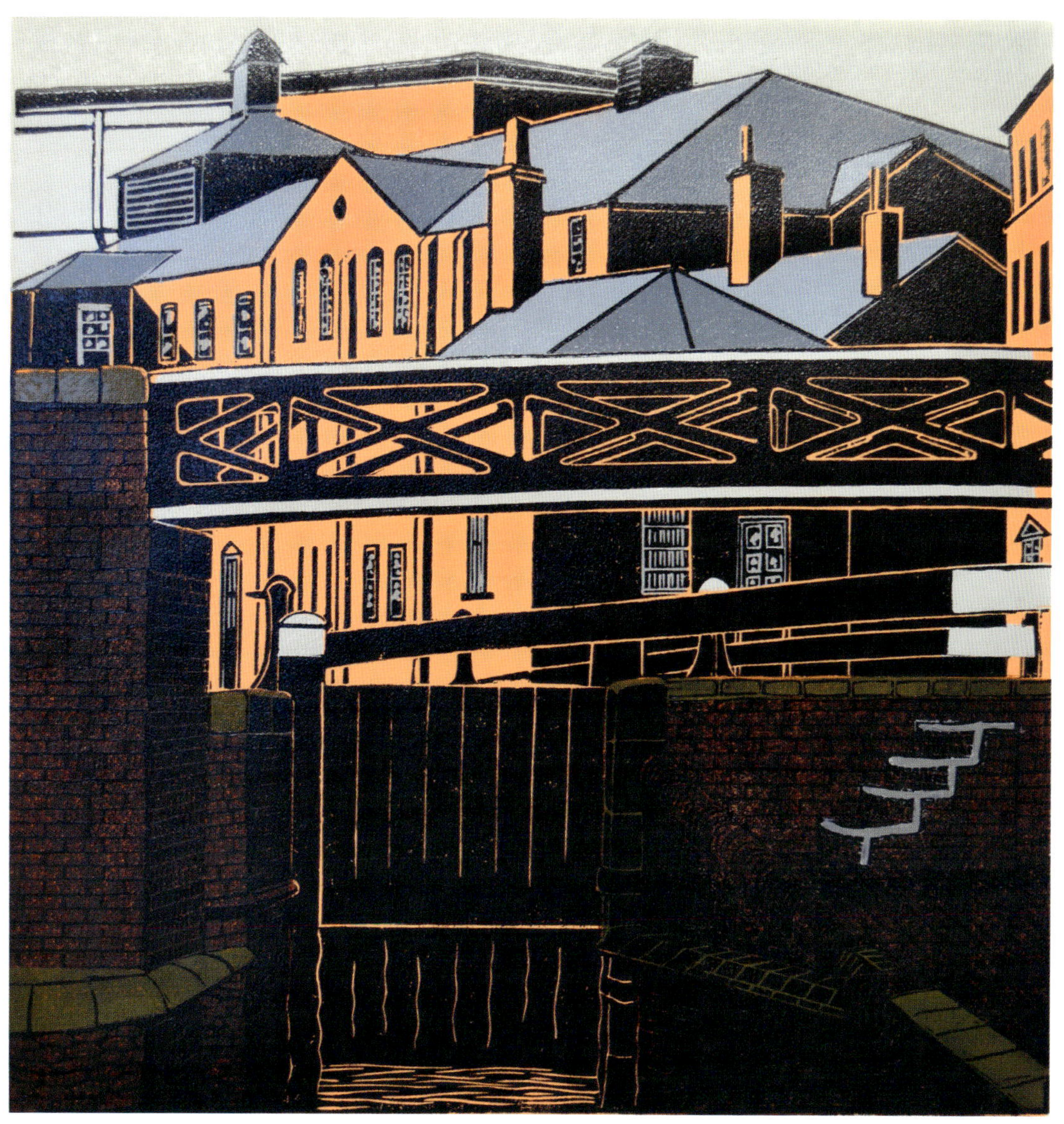

Paul Hipkiss rbsa, Farmers Bridge top lock

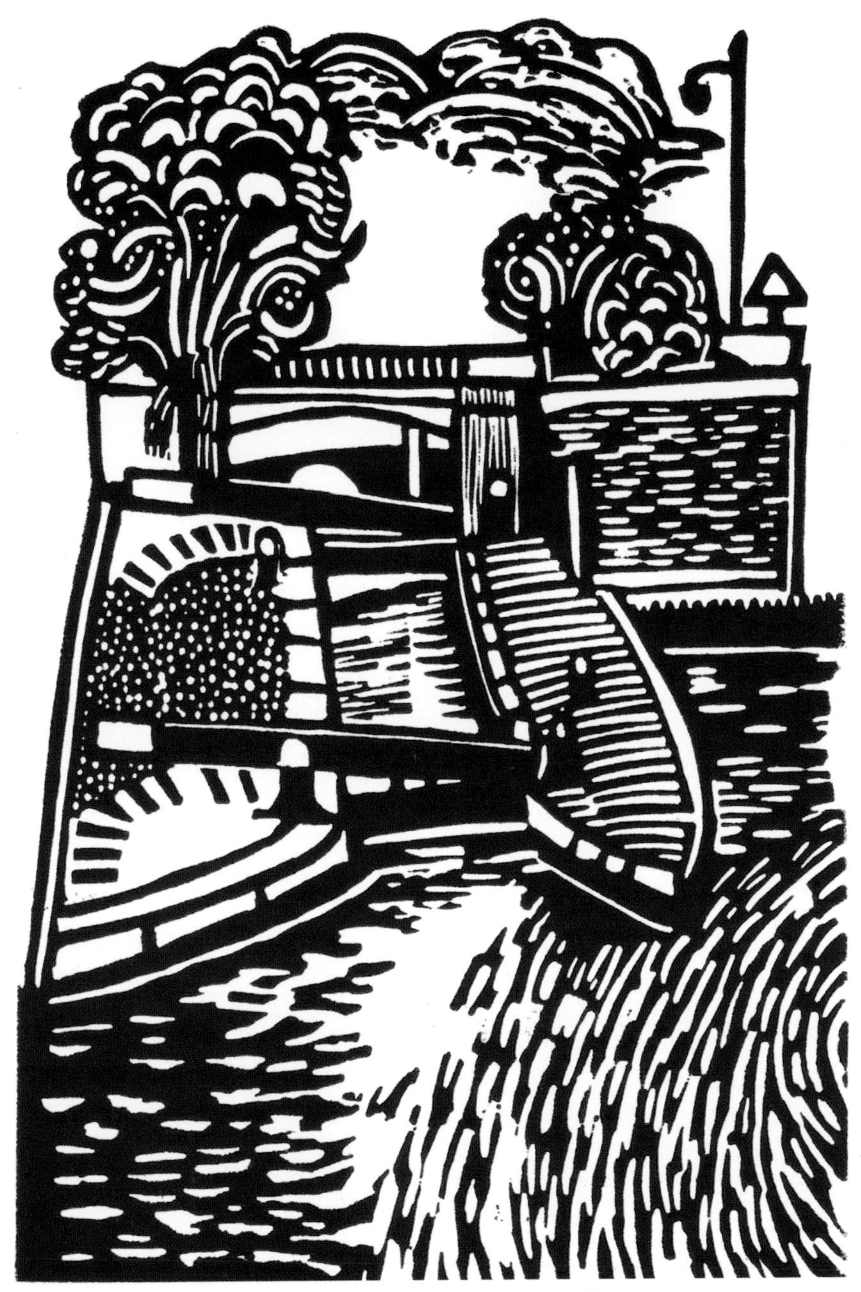

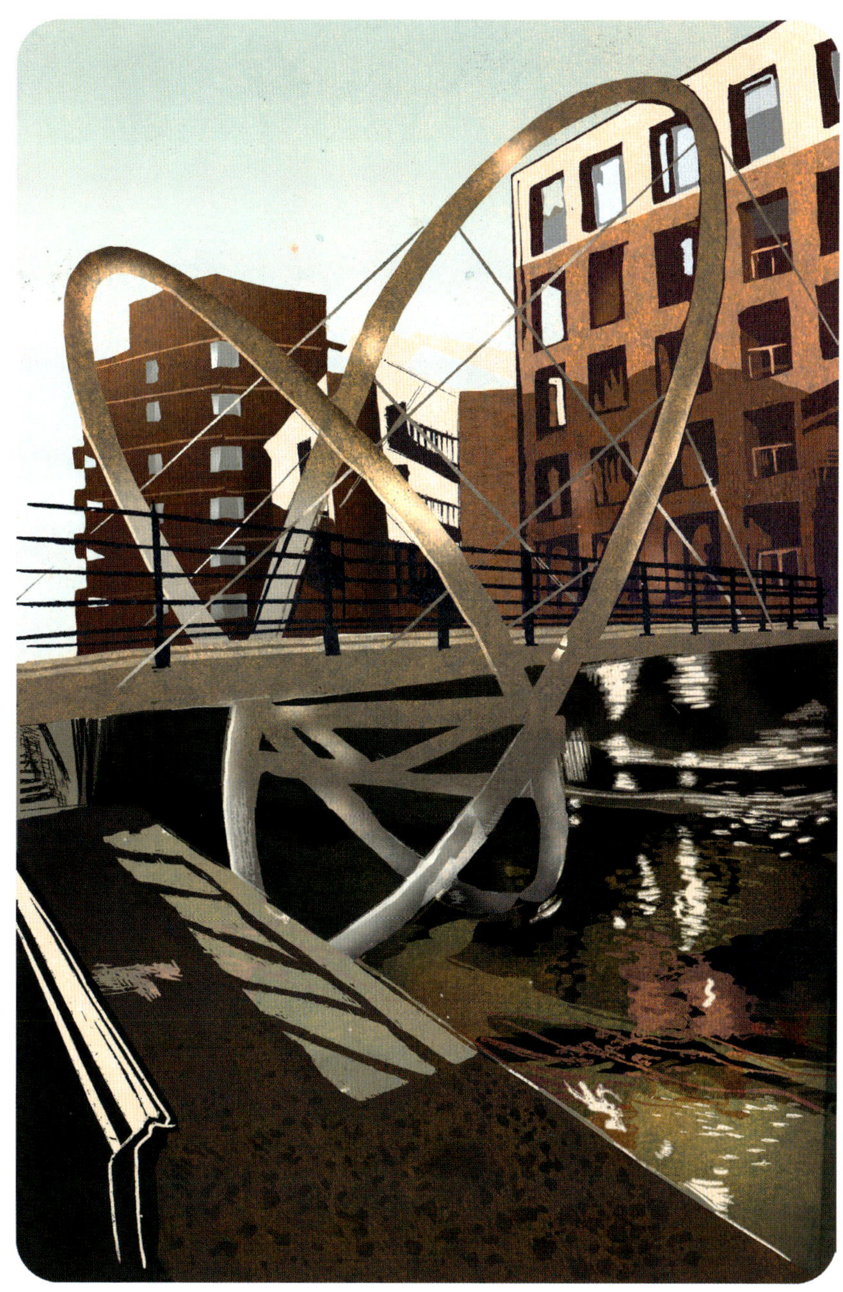

Mike Allison, Fleet Street Footbridge

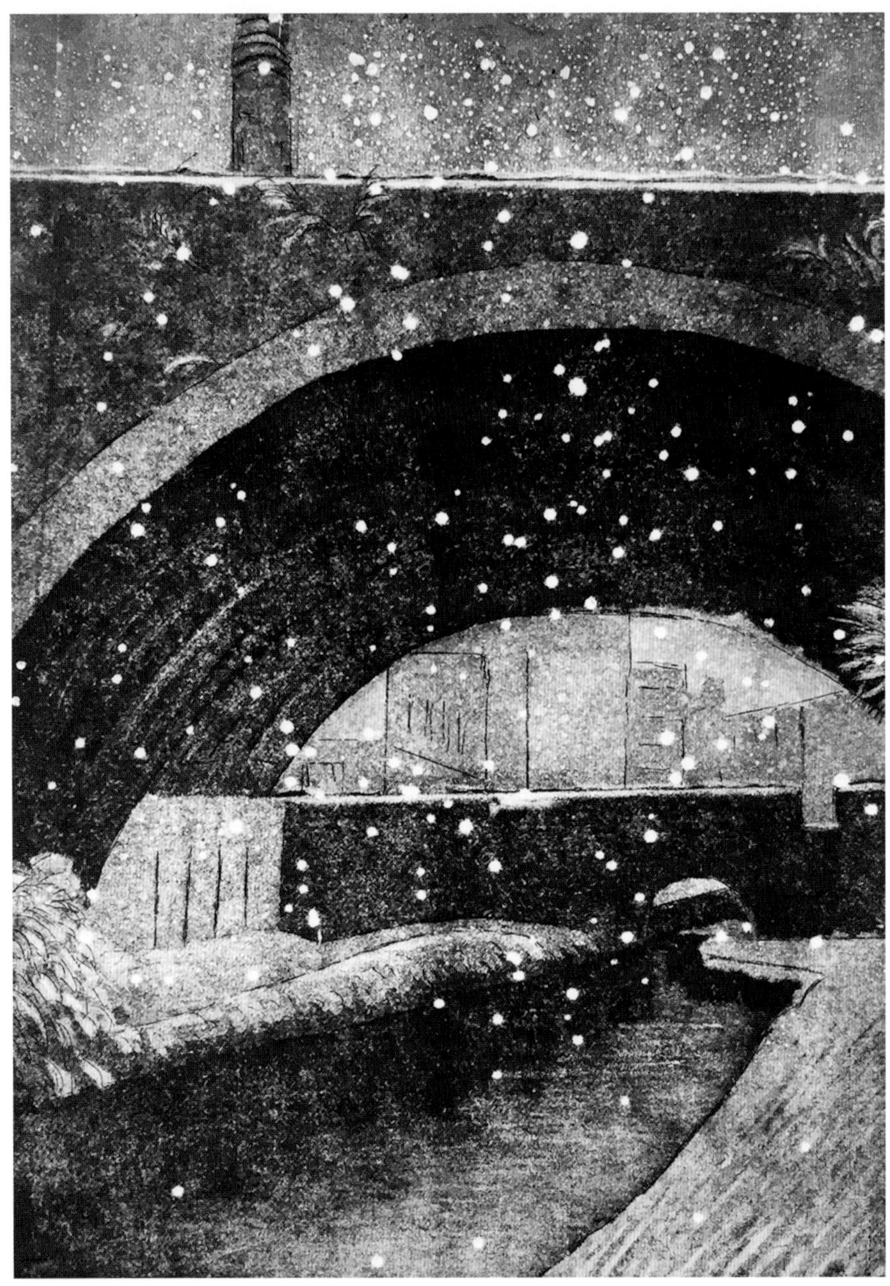

LINDA NEVILL, *SNOWFALL WITH BT TOWER*

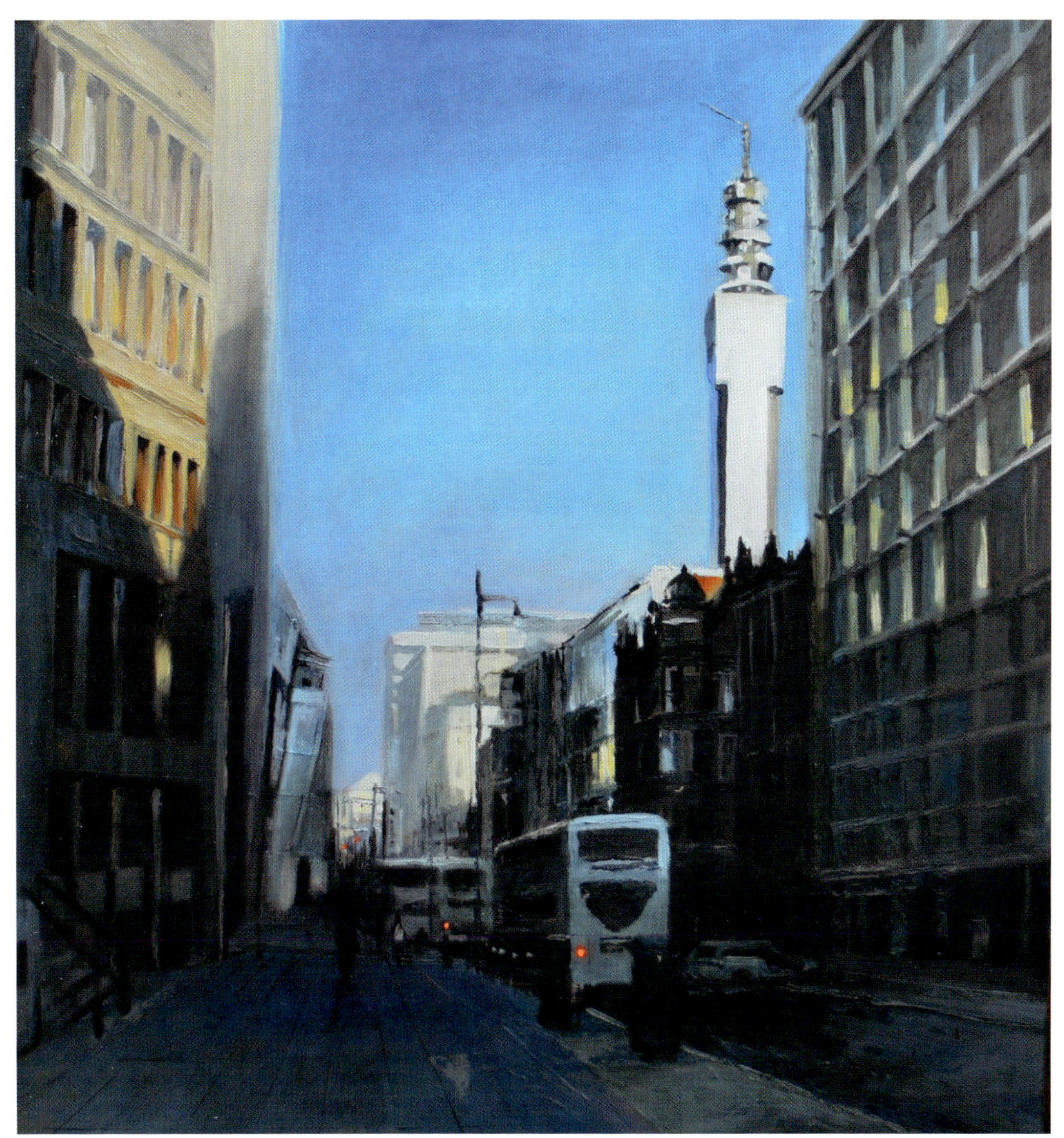

CARRICK SIDDELL, NEWHALL STREET

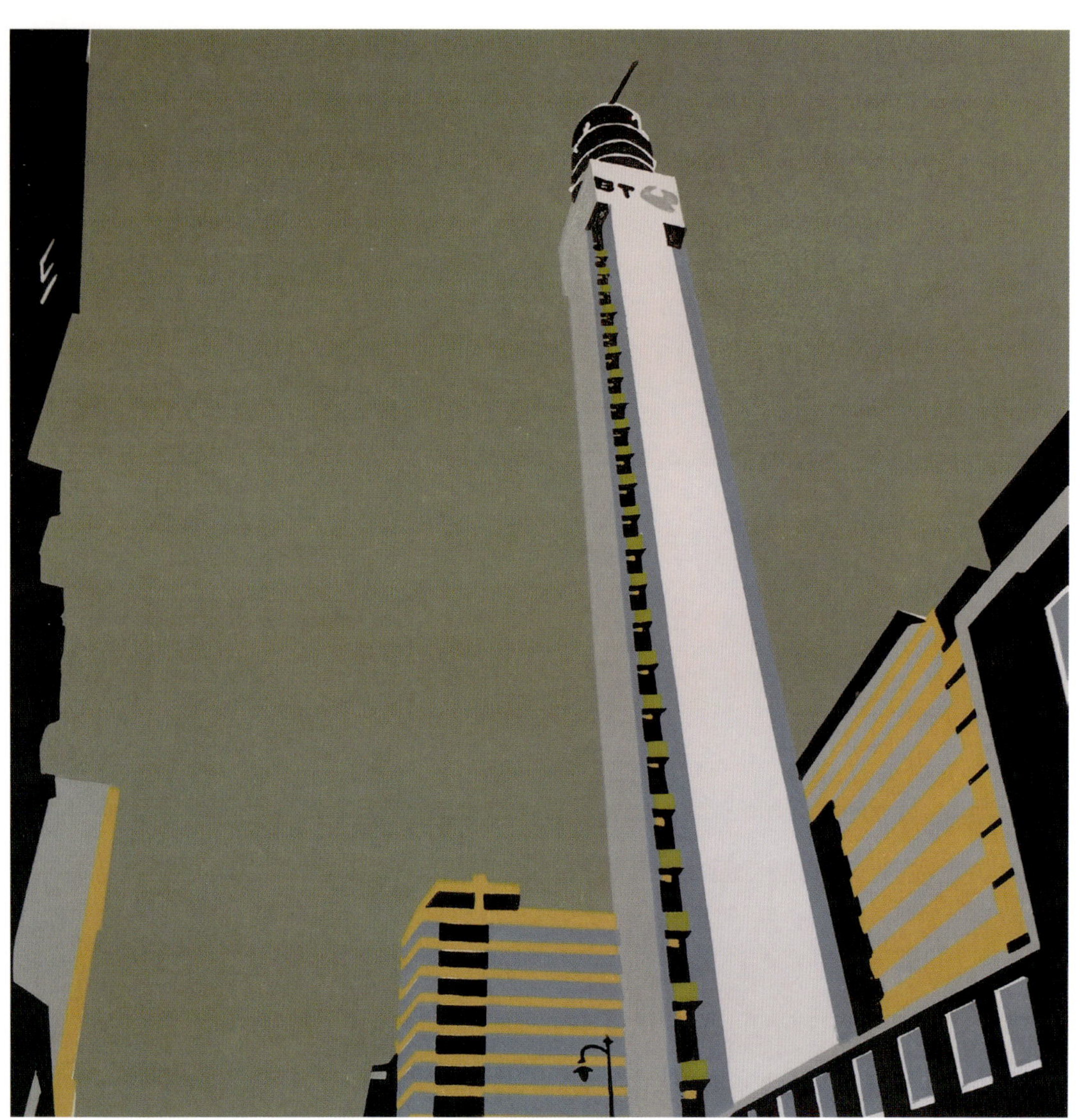

STEVE MILLWARD, BT TOWER

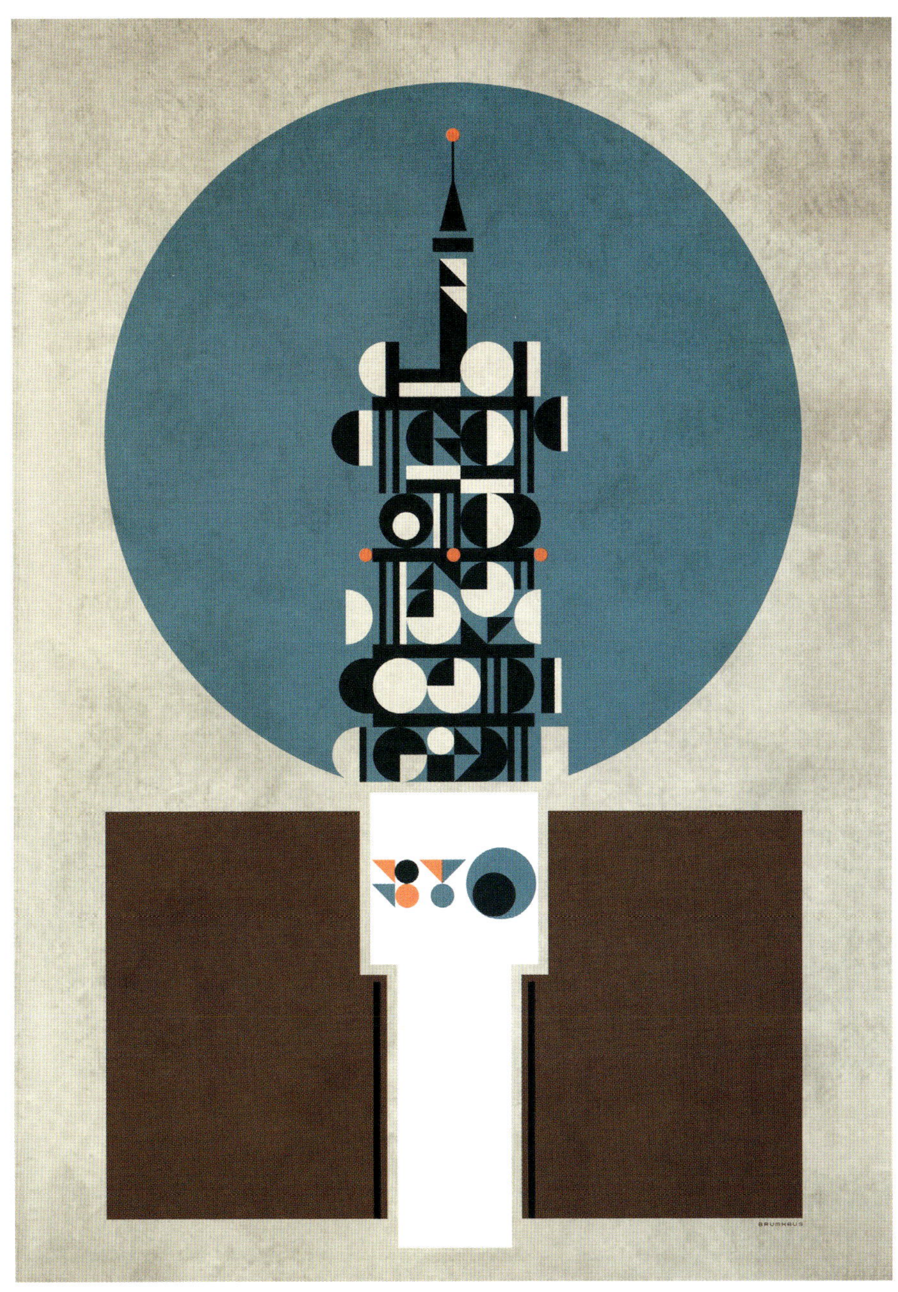

A L E X A N D E R   E D W A R D S   (B R U M H A U S) ,   B T   T O W E R

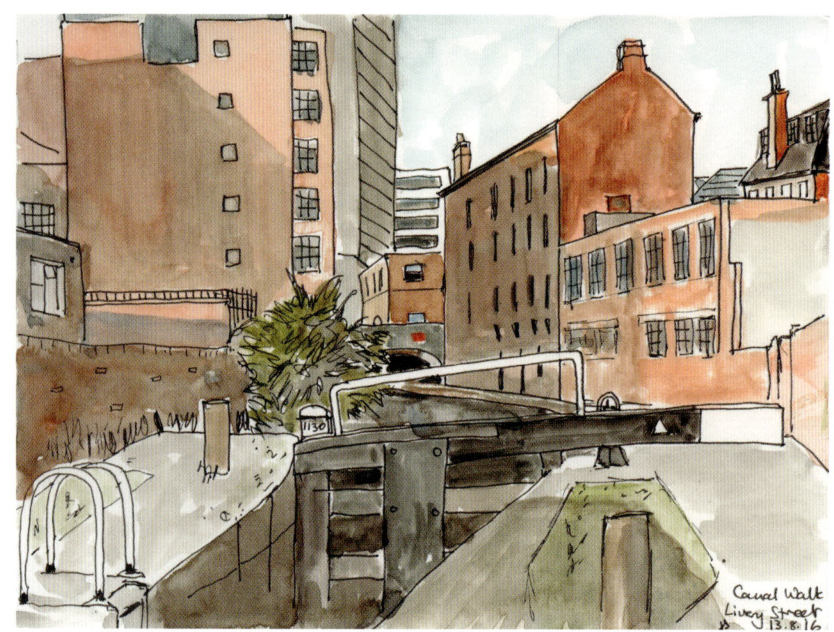

JANET SCOTT, CANAL WALK, LIVERY STREET

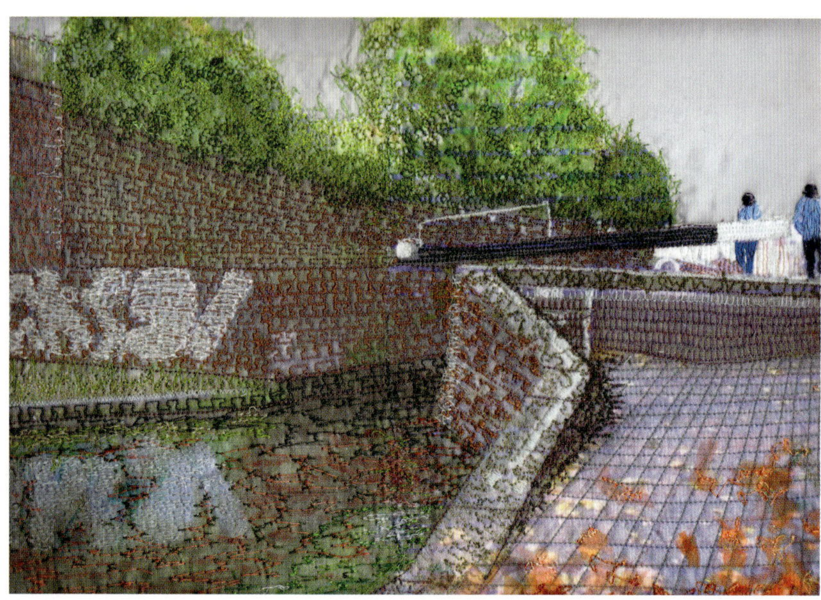

MARGARET FAIRHEAD RBSA, LOCK 3, BIRMINGHAM & FAZELEY CANAL

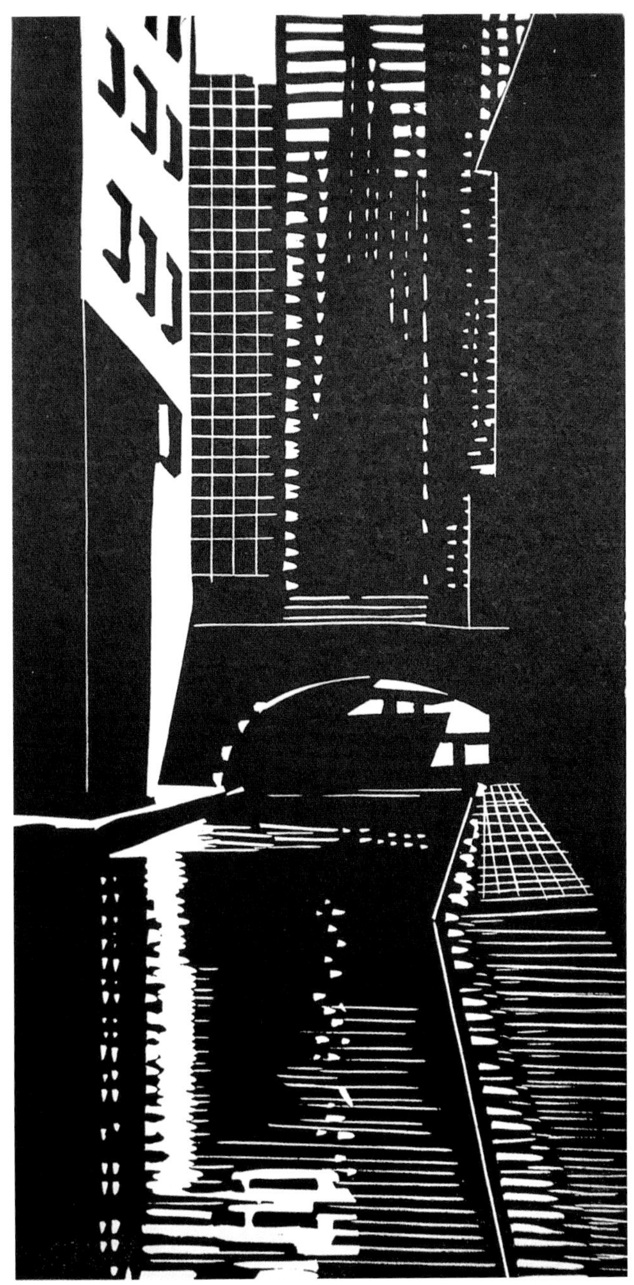

PETER SHREAD, BIRMINGHAM CANAL IN THE 1990s

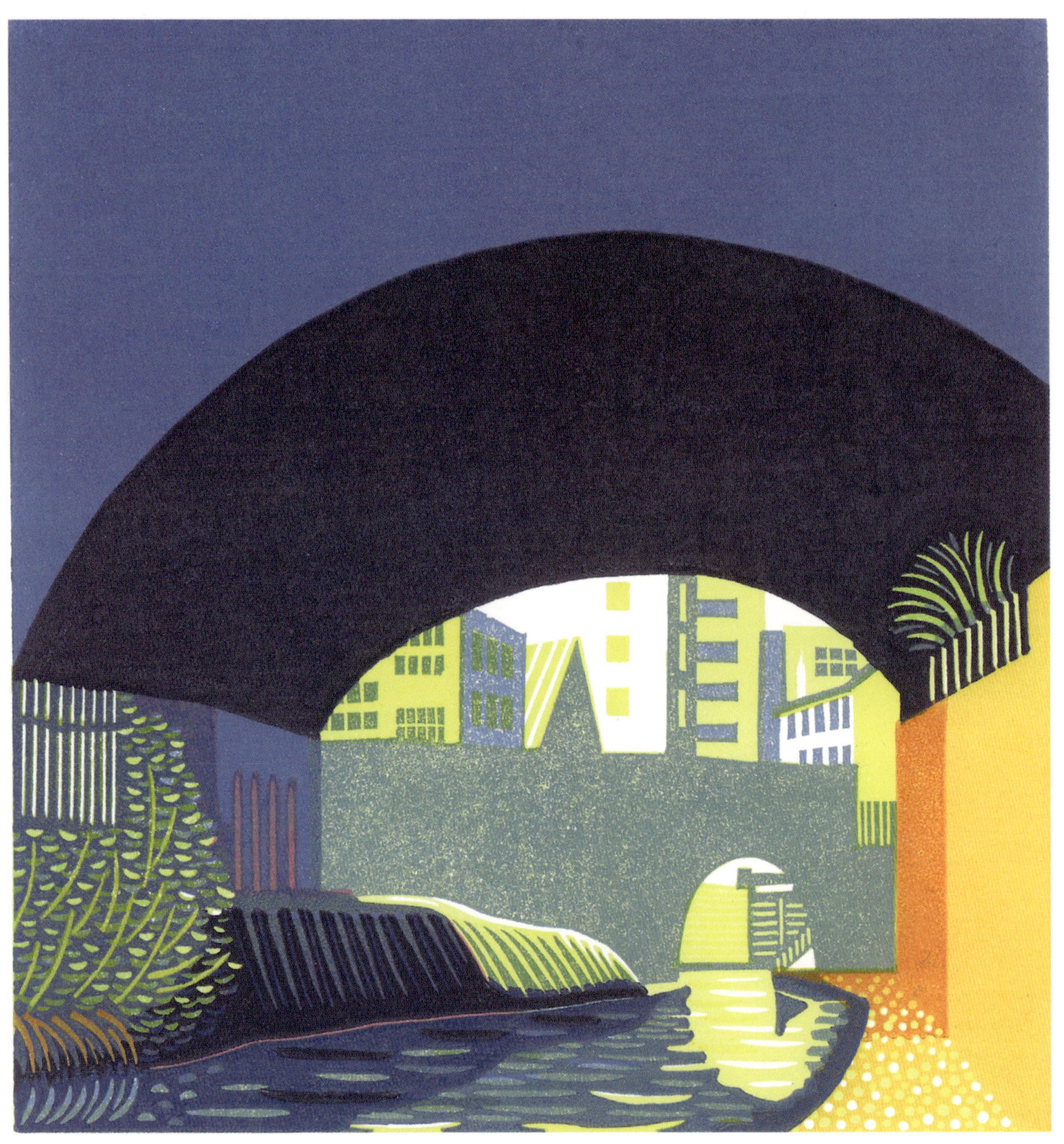

ERIC GASKELL, SNOWHILL BRIDGE

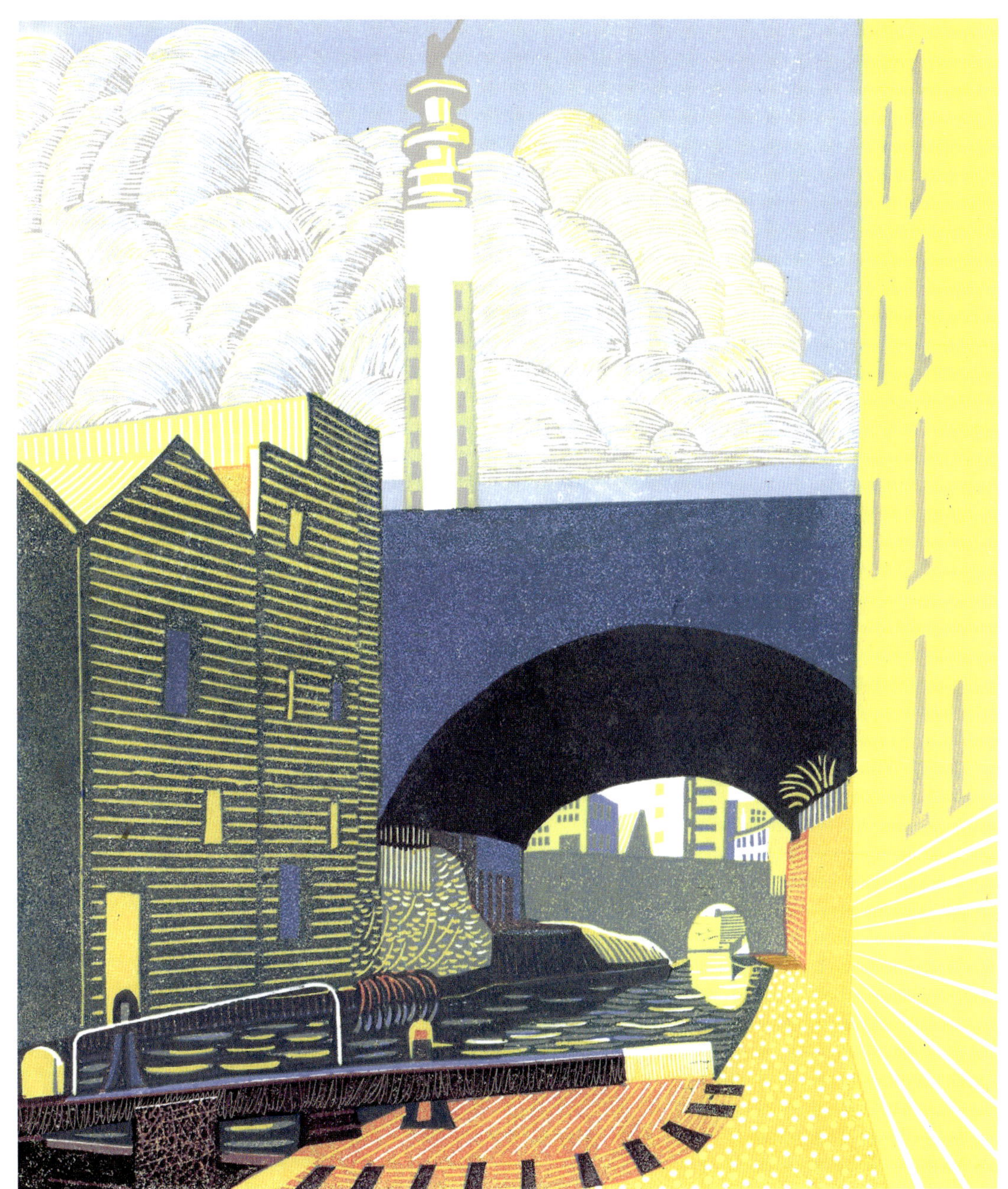

Eric Gaskell, Snowhill Bridge and BT Tower

63

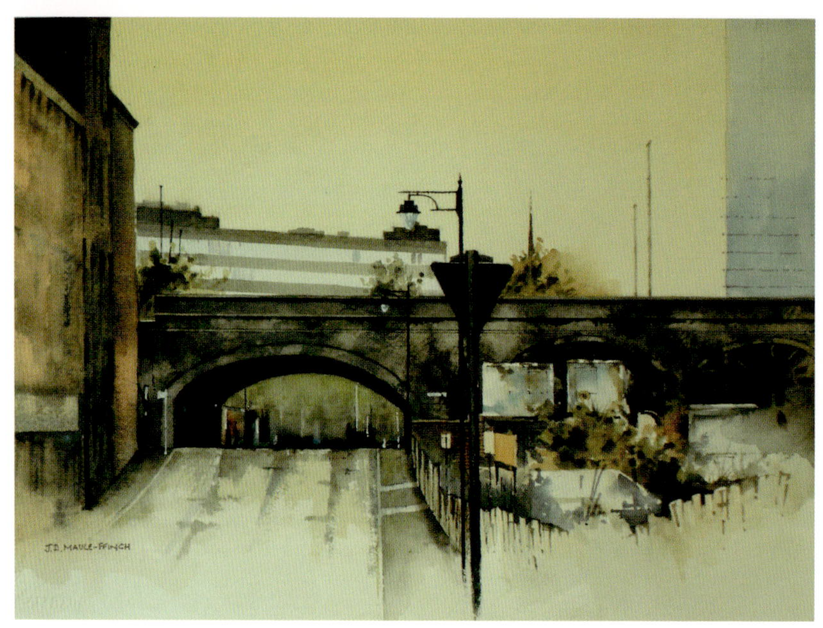

John Maule-ffinch, Railway bridge crossing Lionel Street

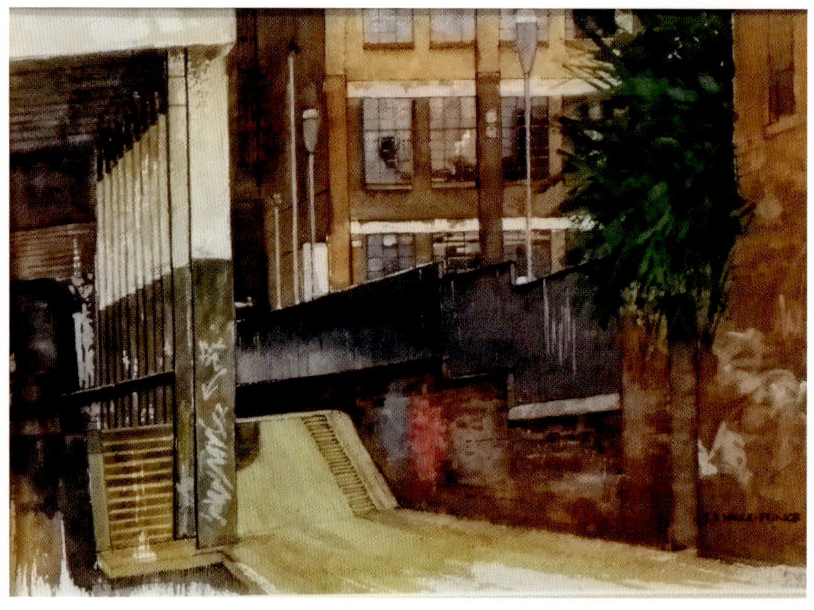

John Maule-ffinch, Canal access, Ludgate Hill

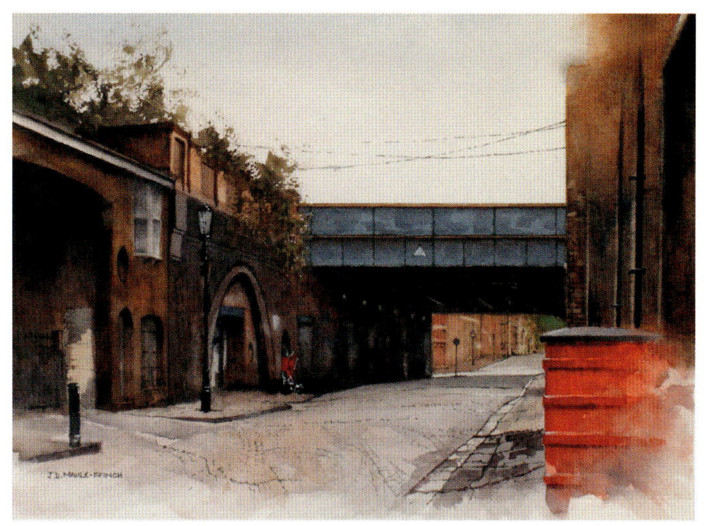

J OHN M AULE -FFINCH , M ARY A NN S TREET INTO S T . P AUL ' S S QUARE

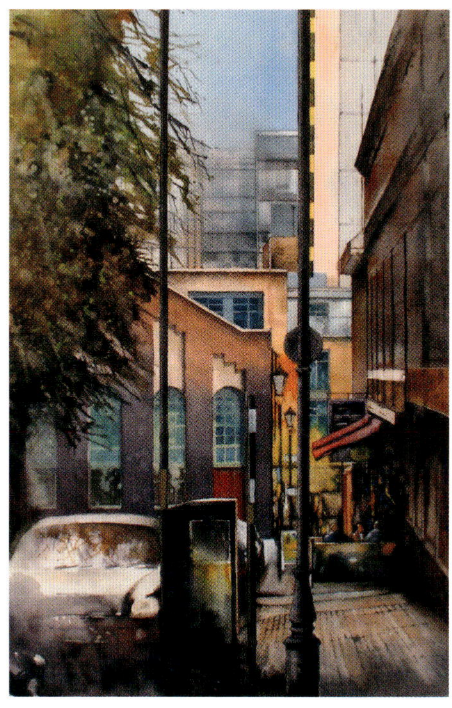

J OHN M AULE -FFINCH , T HE R ECTORY , S T . P AUL ' S S QUARE

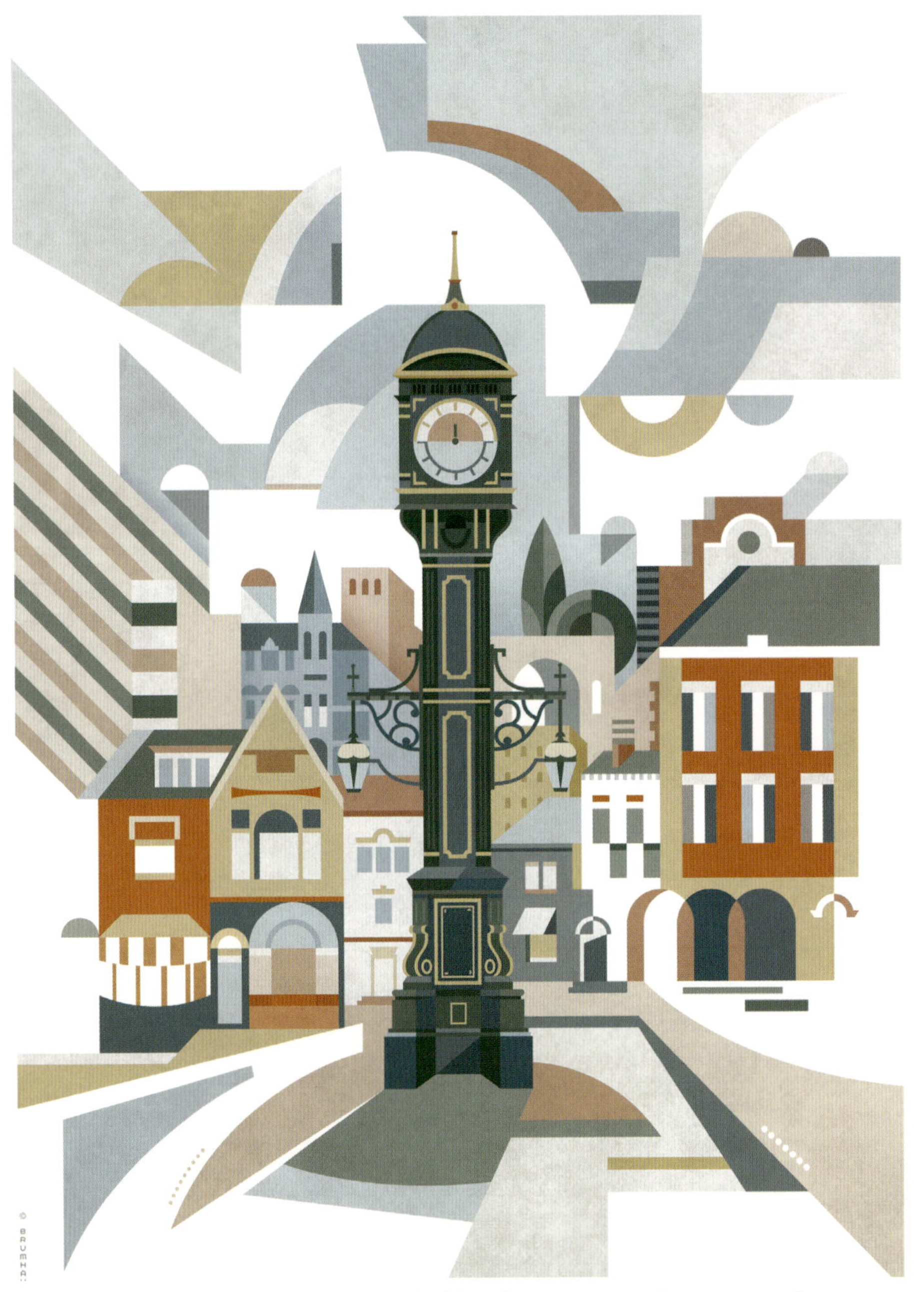

ALEXANDER EDWARDS (BRUMHAUS), THE BIRMINGHAM JEWELLERY QUARTER

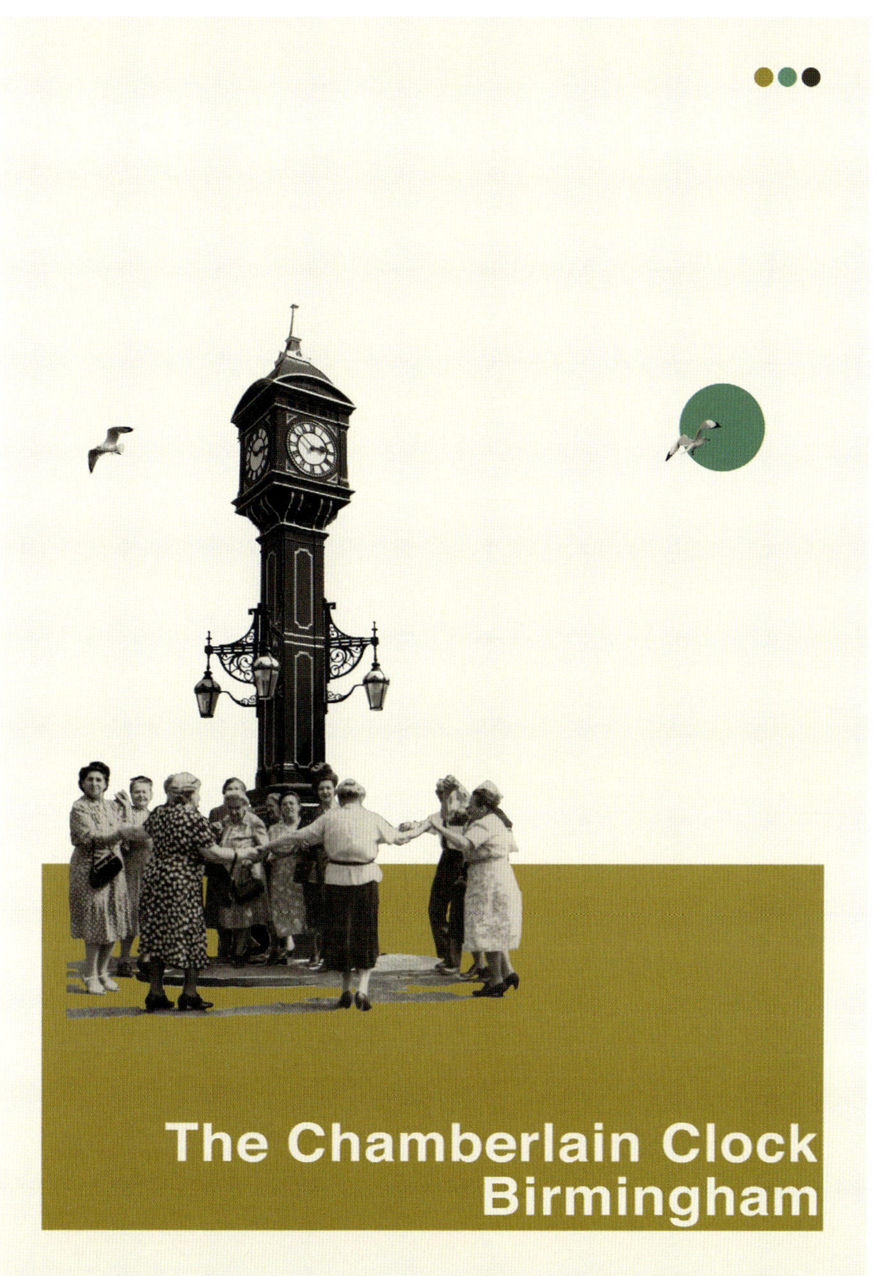

BARBARA GIBSON, THE JOSEPH CHAMBERLAIN MEMORIAL CLOCK TOWER

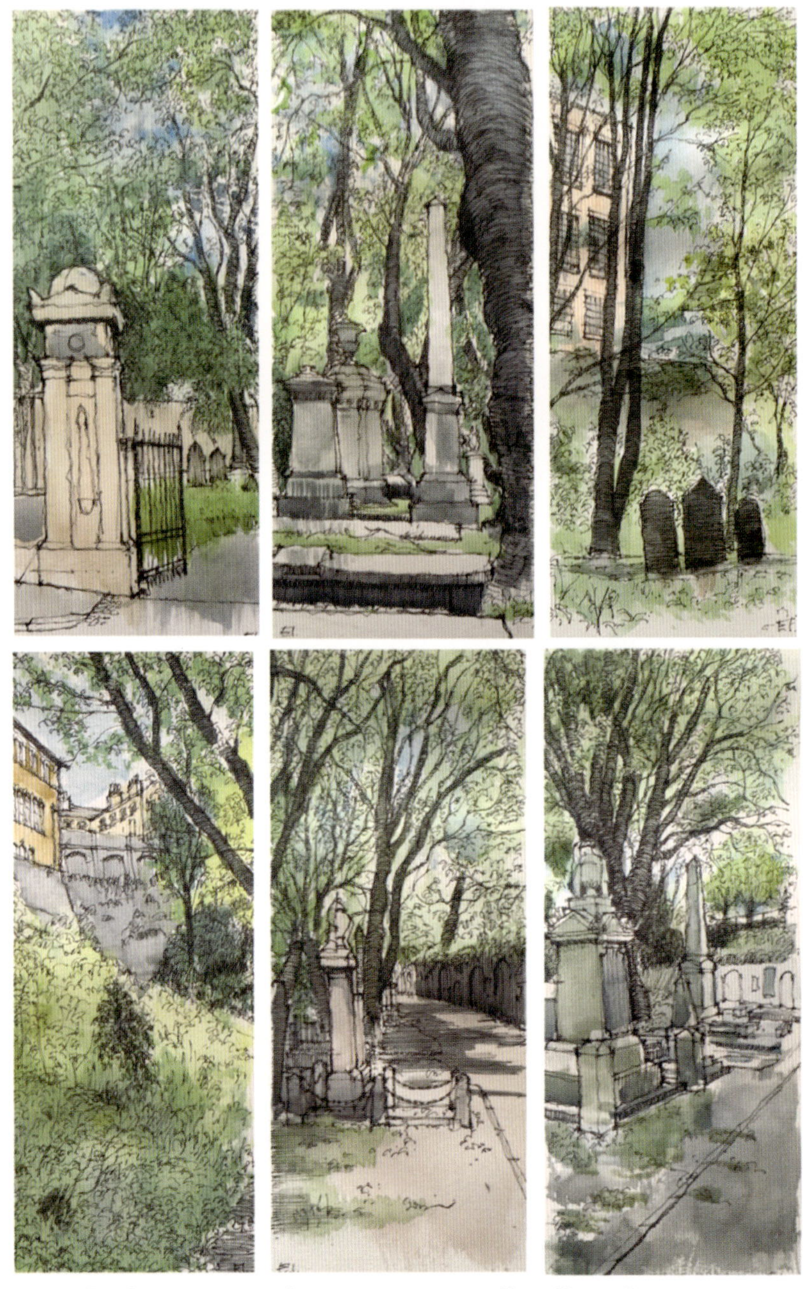

Ed Isaacs rbsa, A walk through Key Hill Cemetery

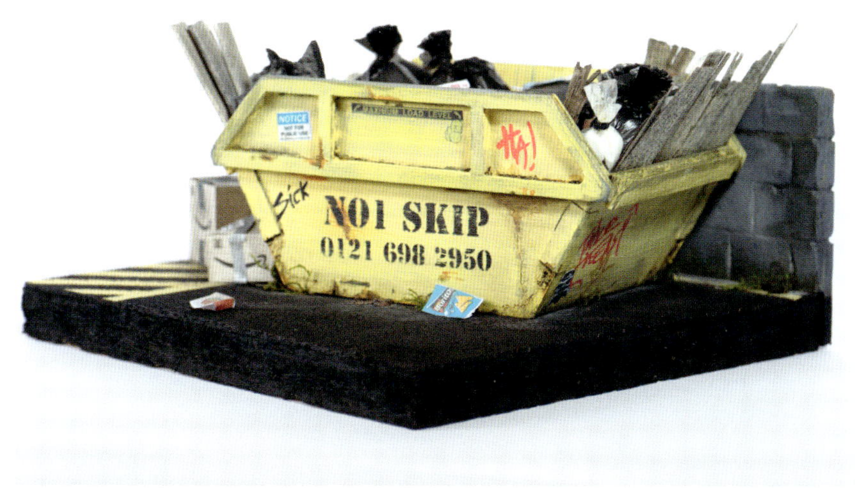

MARTA KOCHANEK, 0121 BIRMINGHAM SKIP

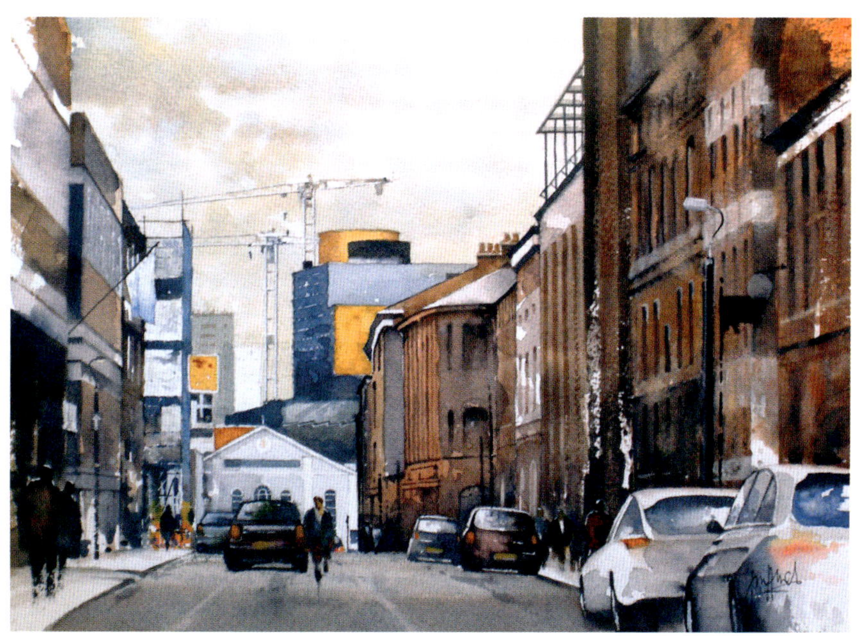

JOHN MAULE-FFINCH, VITTORIA STREET

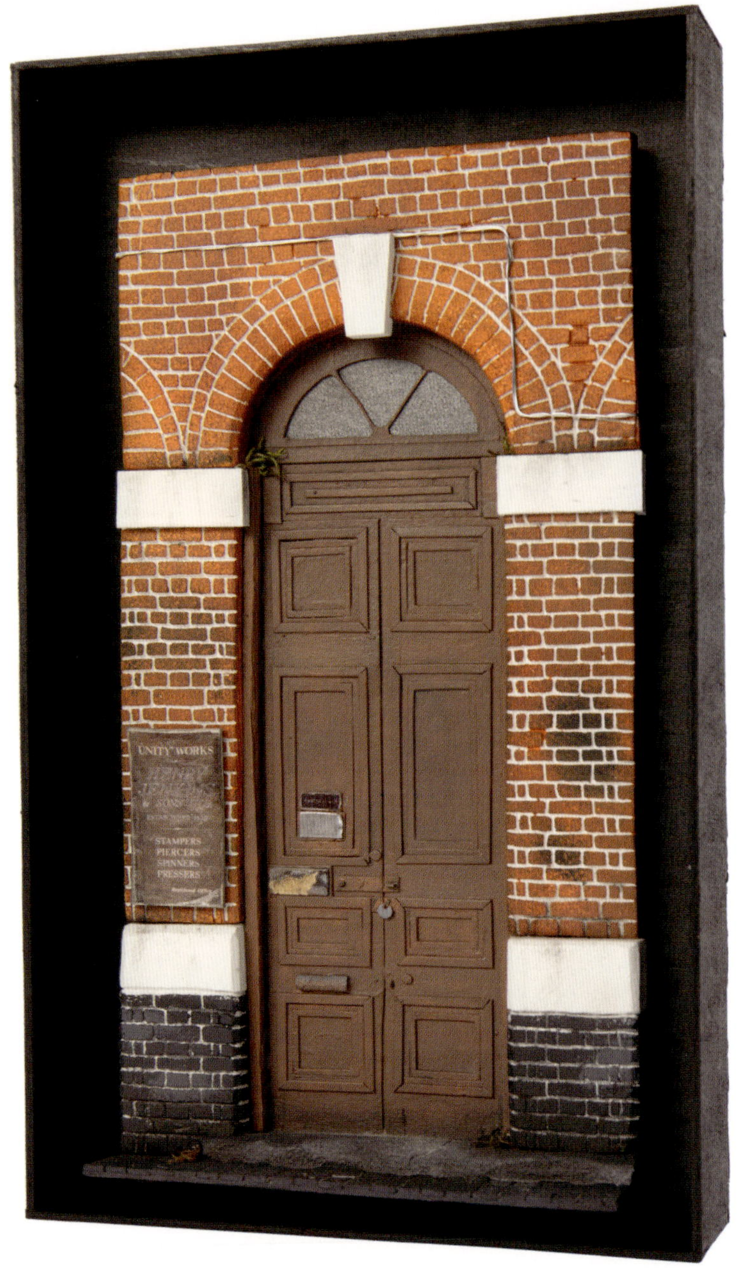

MARTA KOCHANEK, 40 VITTORIA STREET

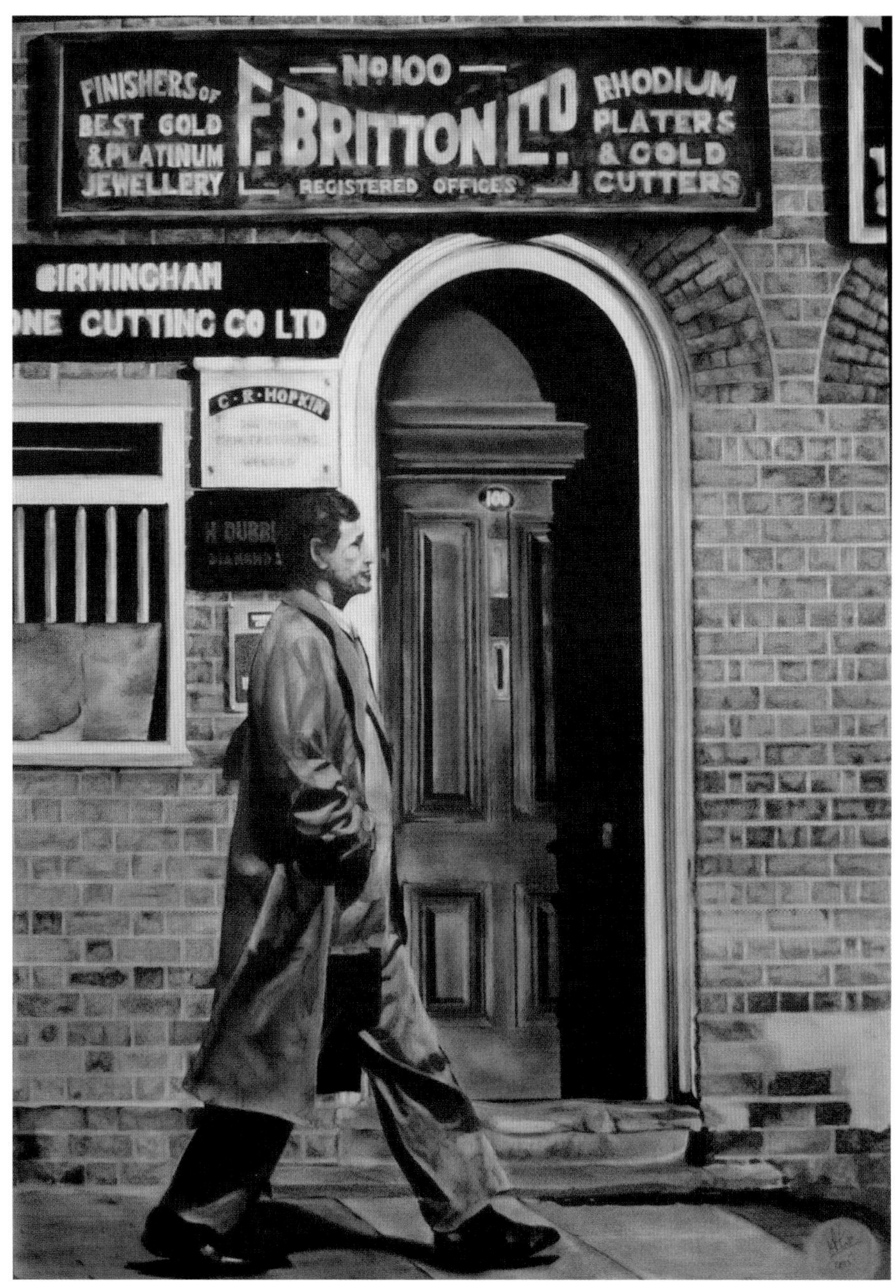

Kevin Line rbsa, Vyse Street

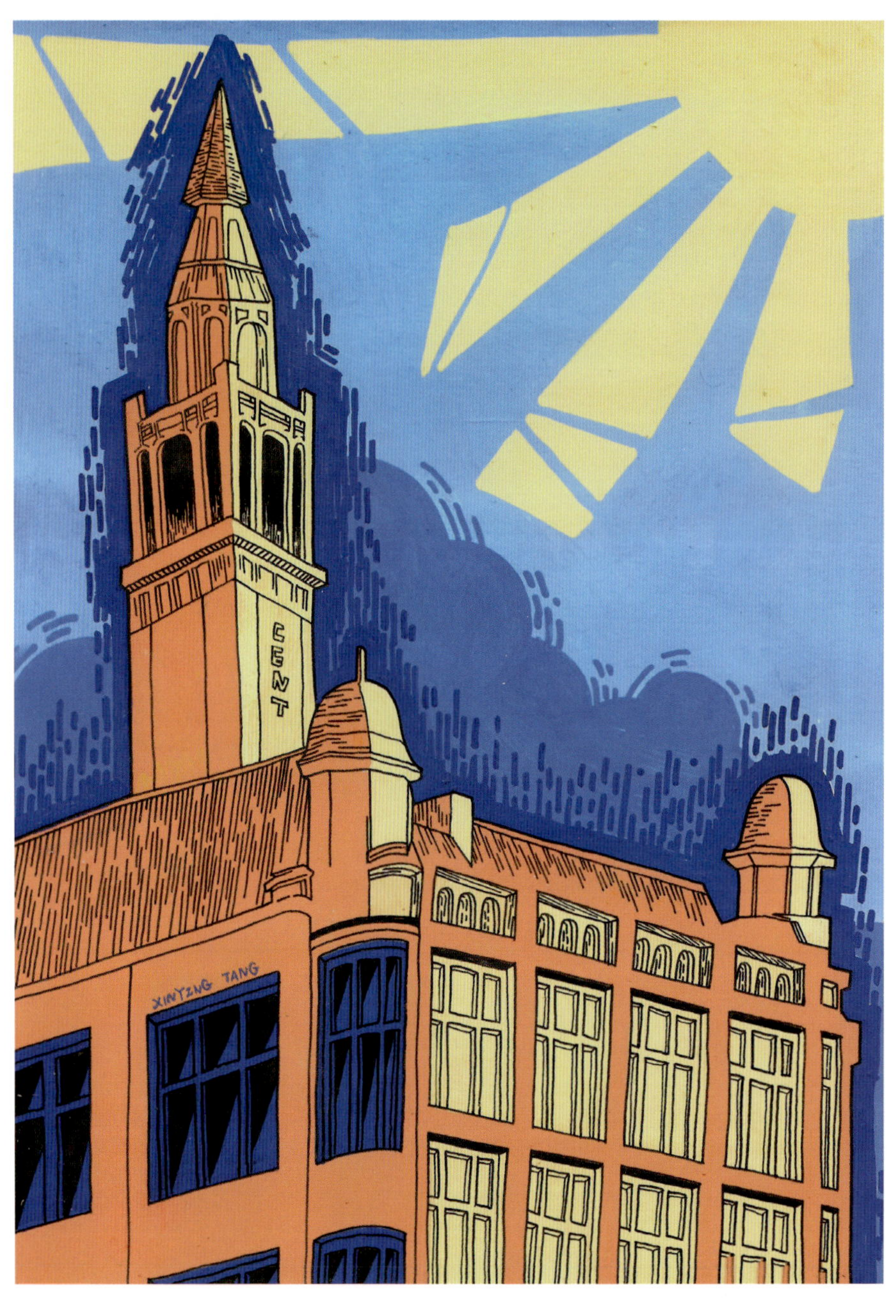

XINYING TANG, METHODIST CENTRAL HALL

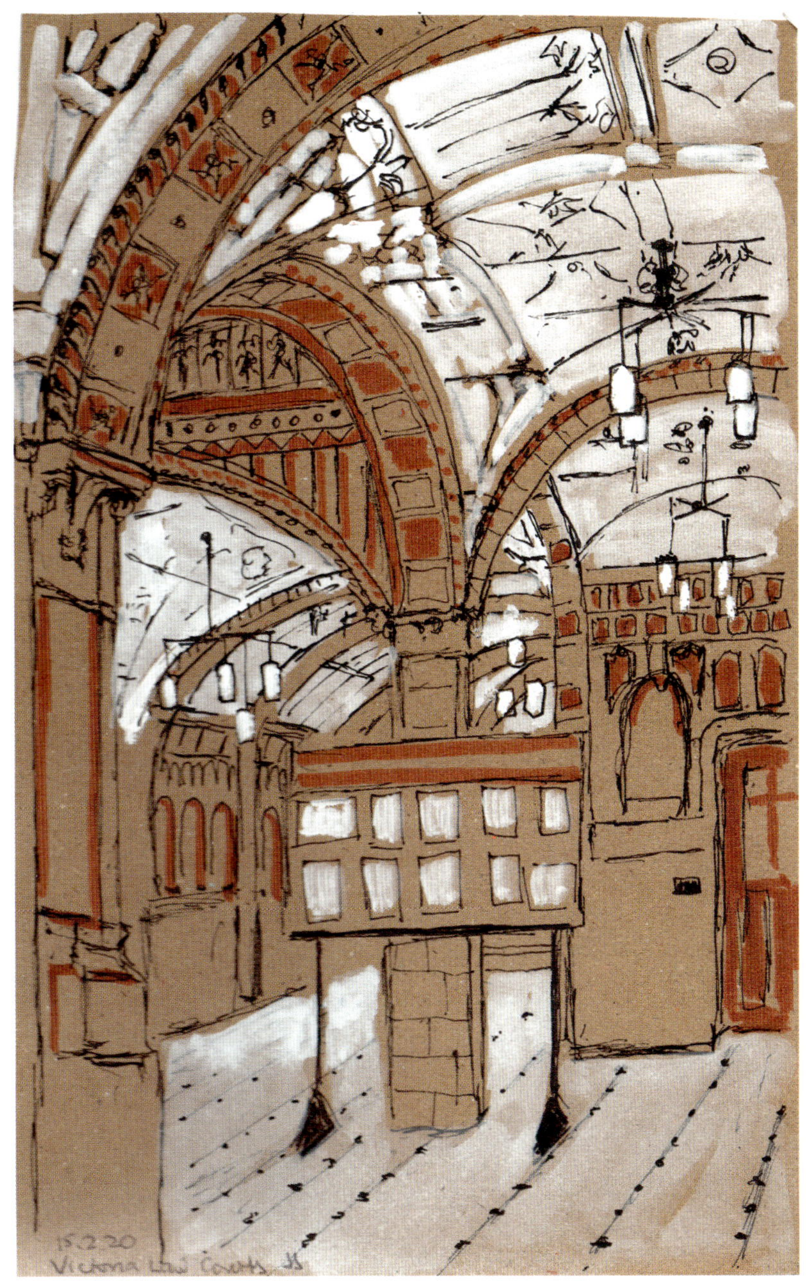

Janet Scott, Victoria Law Courts

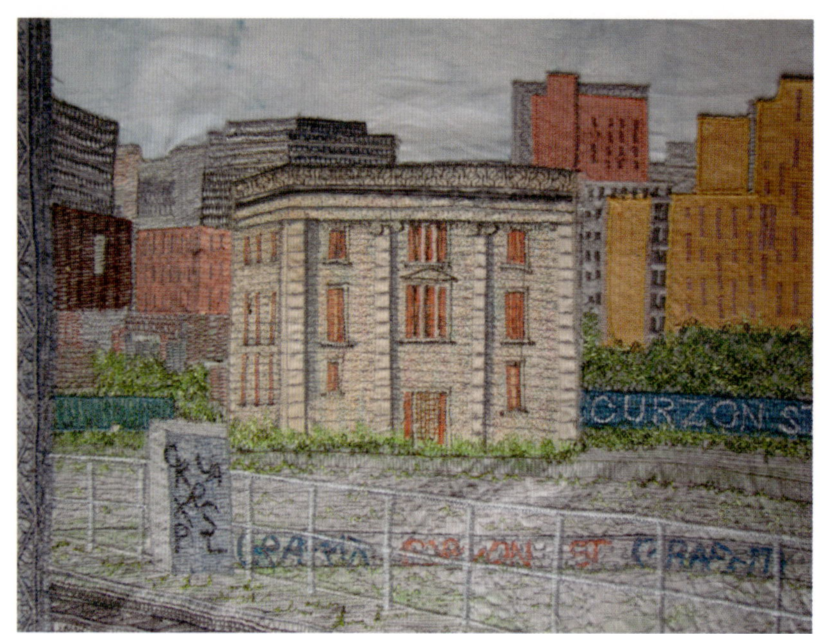

Margaret Fairhead rbsa, Curzon Street Railway Station

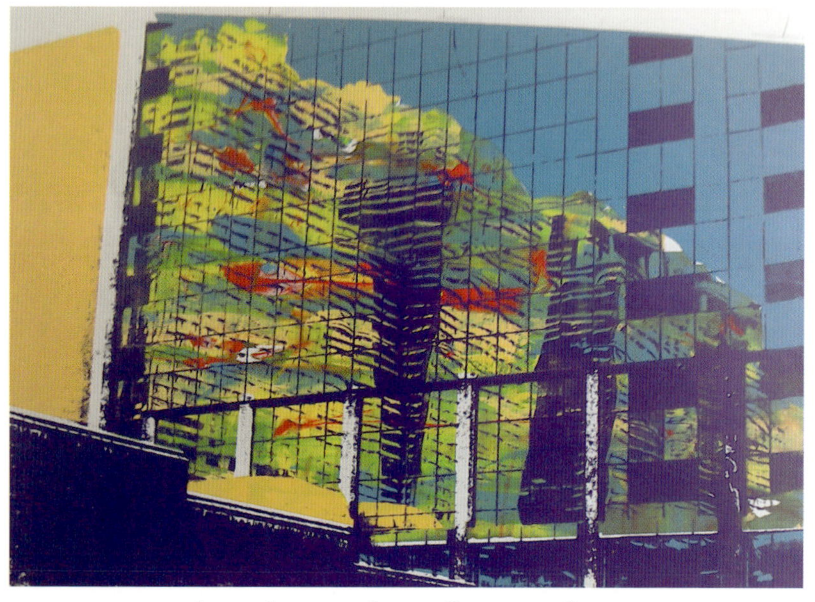

Lynn Jeffery Rbsa, Colmore Row

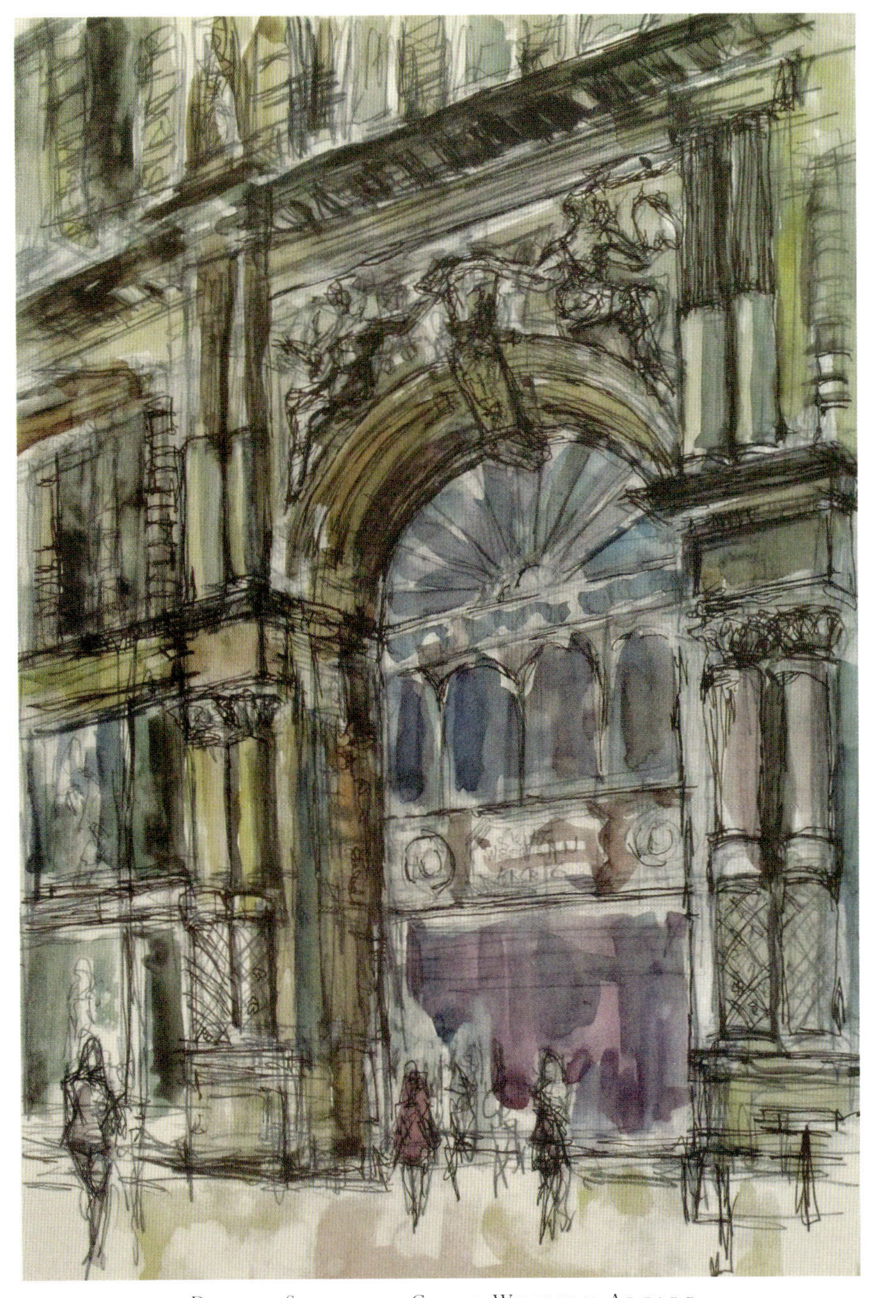

Daniel Stedman, Great Western Arcade

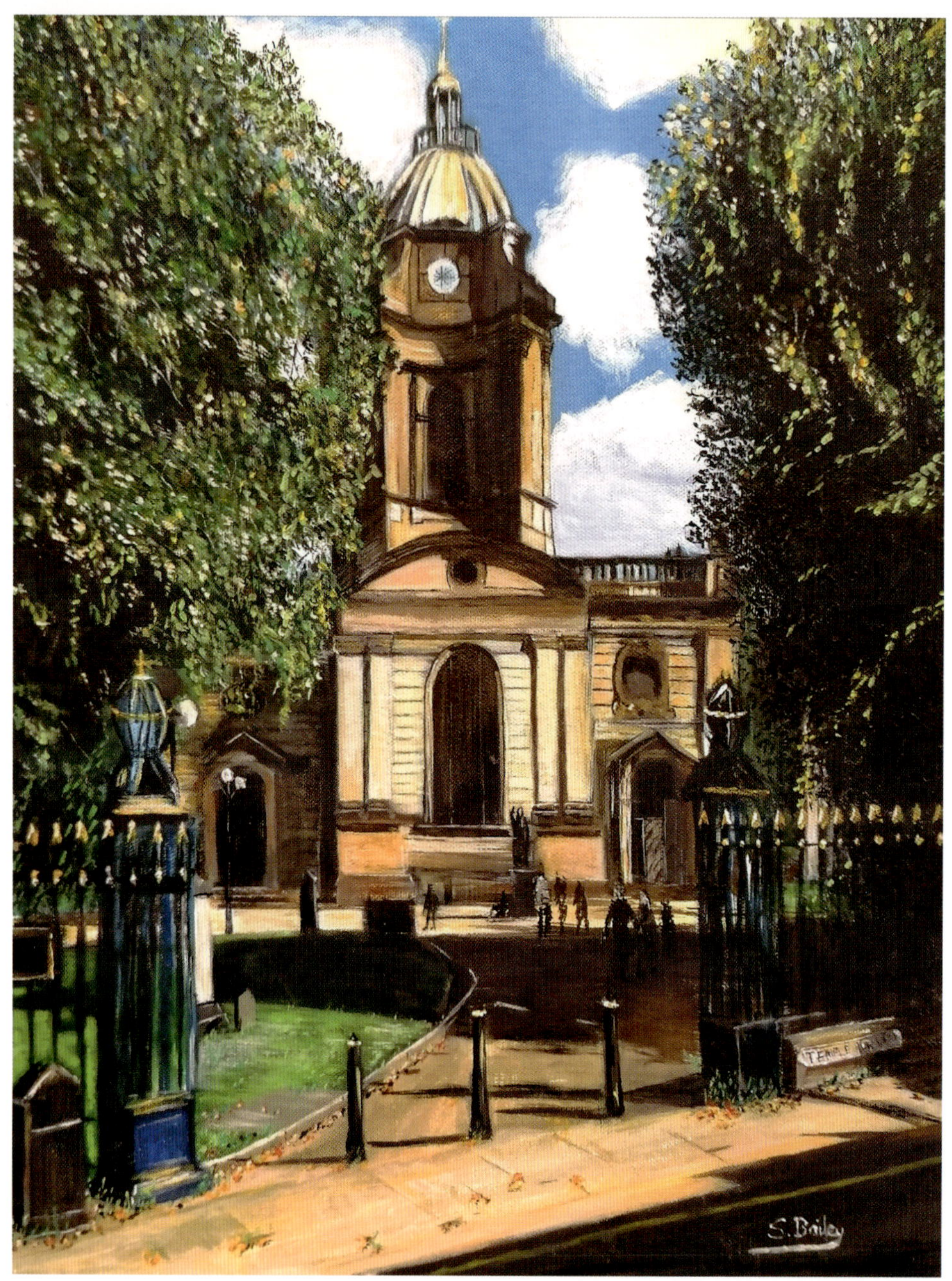

SAM BAILEY, BIRMINGHAM CATHEDRAL

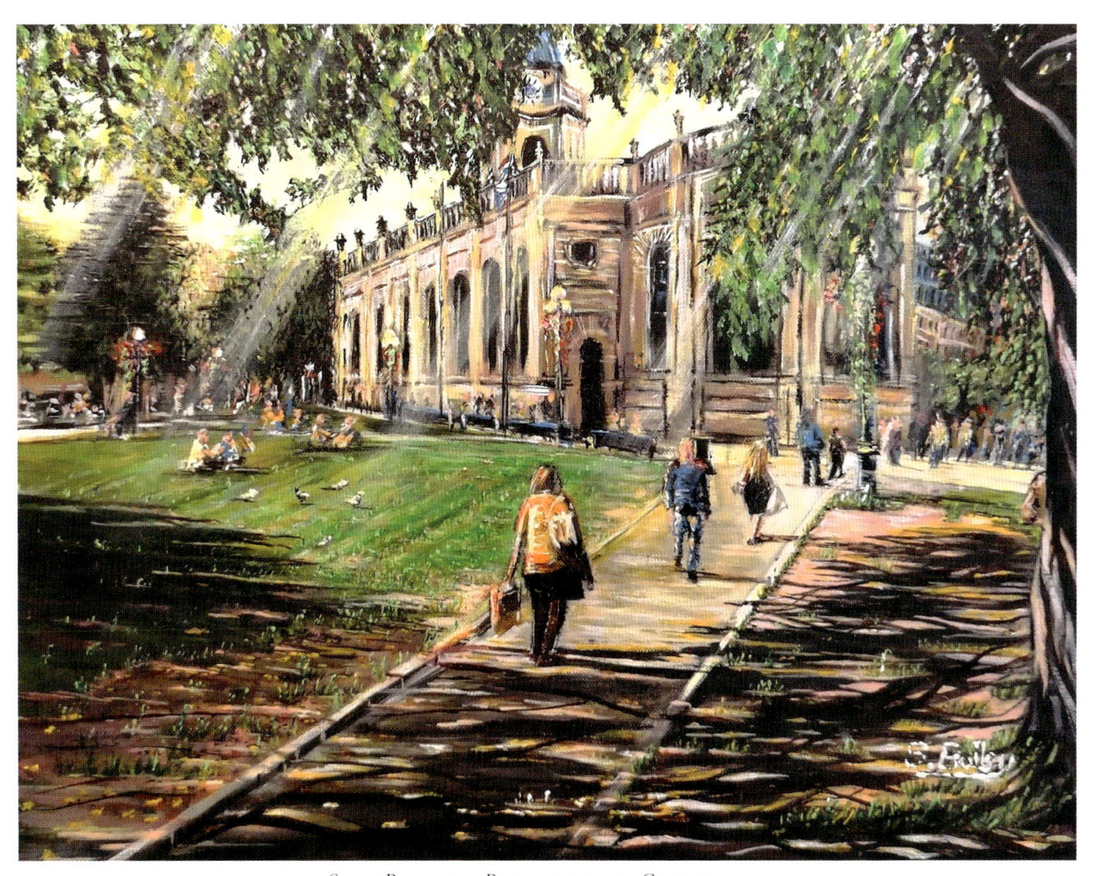

SAM BAILEY, BIRMINGHAM CATHEDRAL

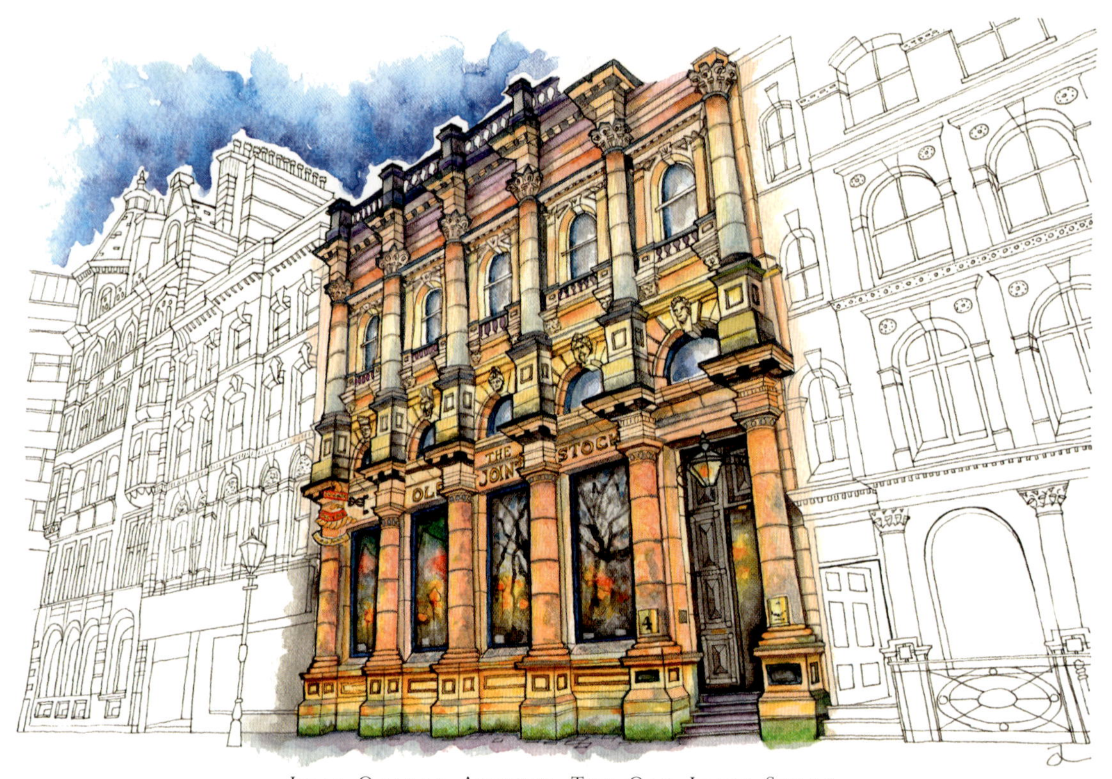

JILLY OXLADE-ARNOTT, THE OLD JOINT STOCK

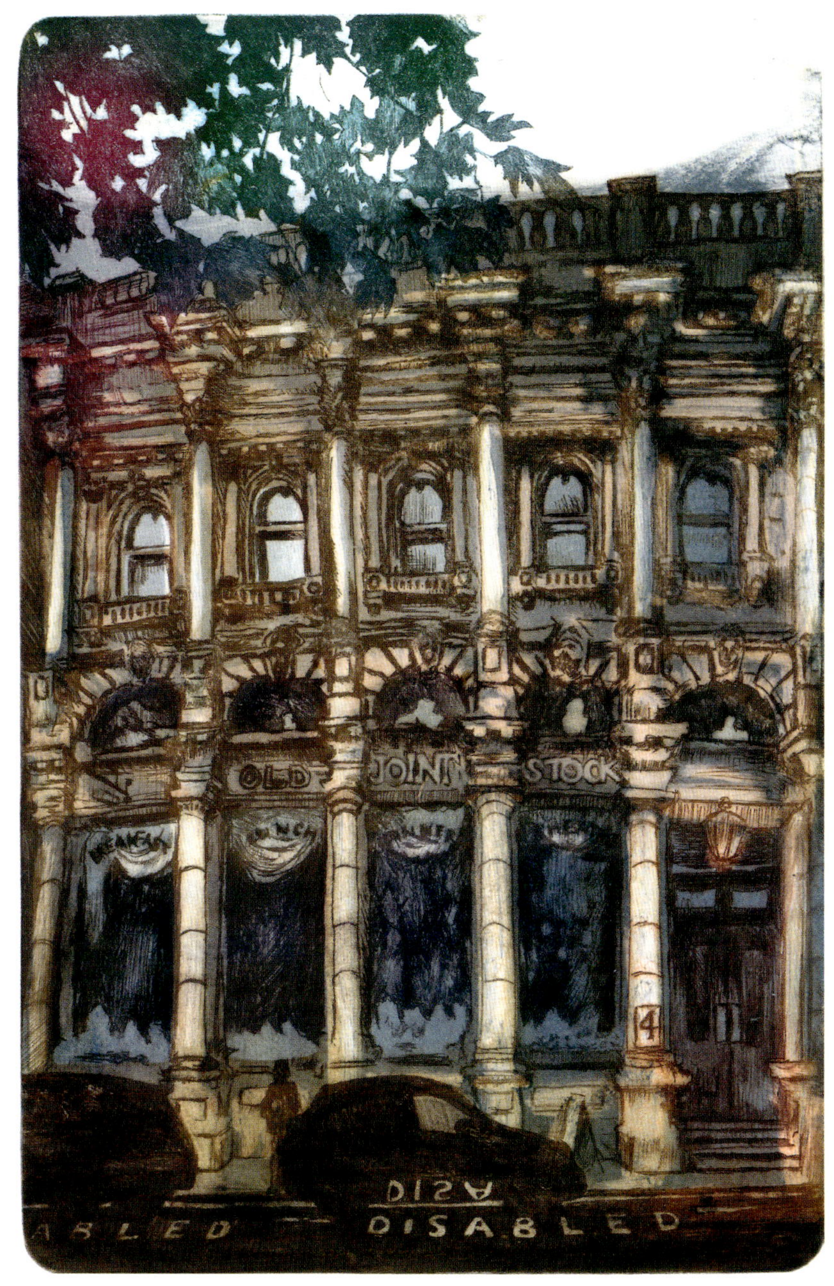

Mike Allison, The Old Joint Stock

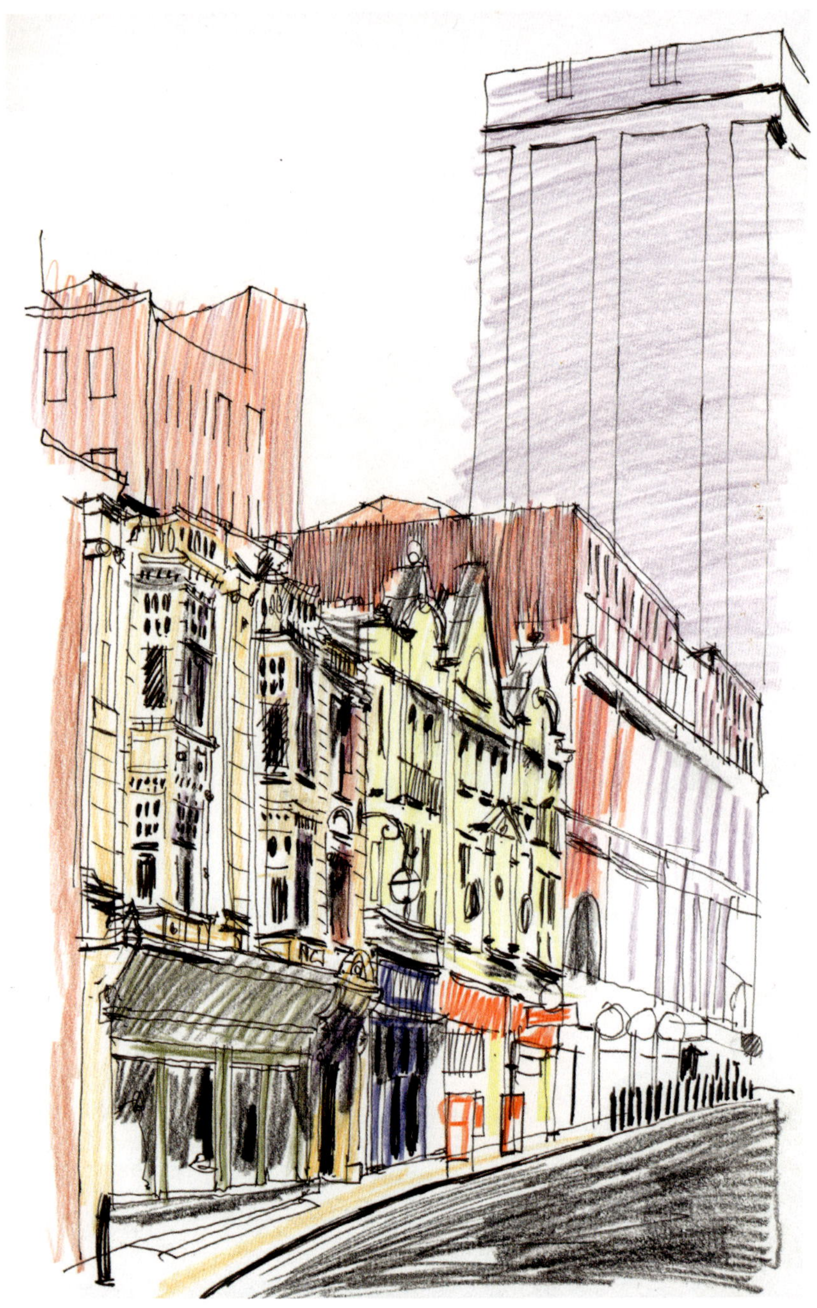

Eric Gaskell, Cannon Street

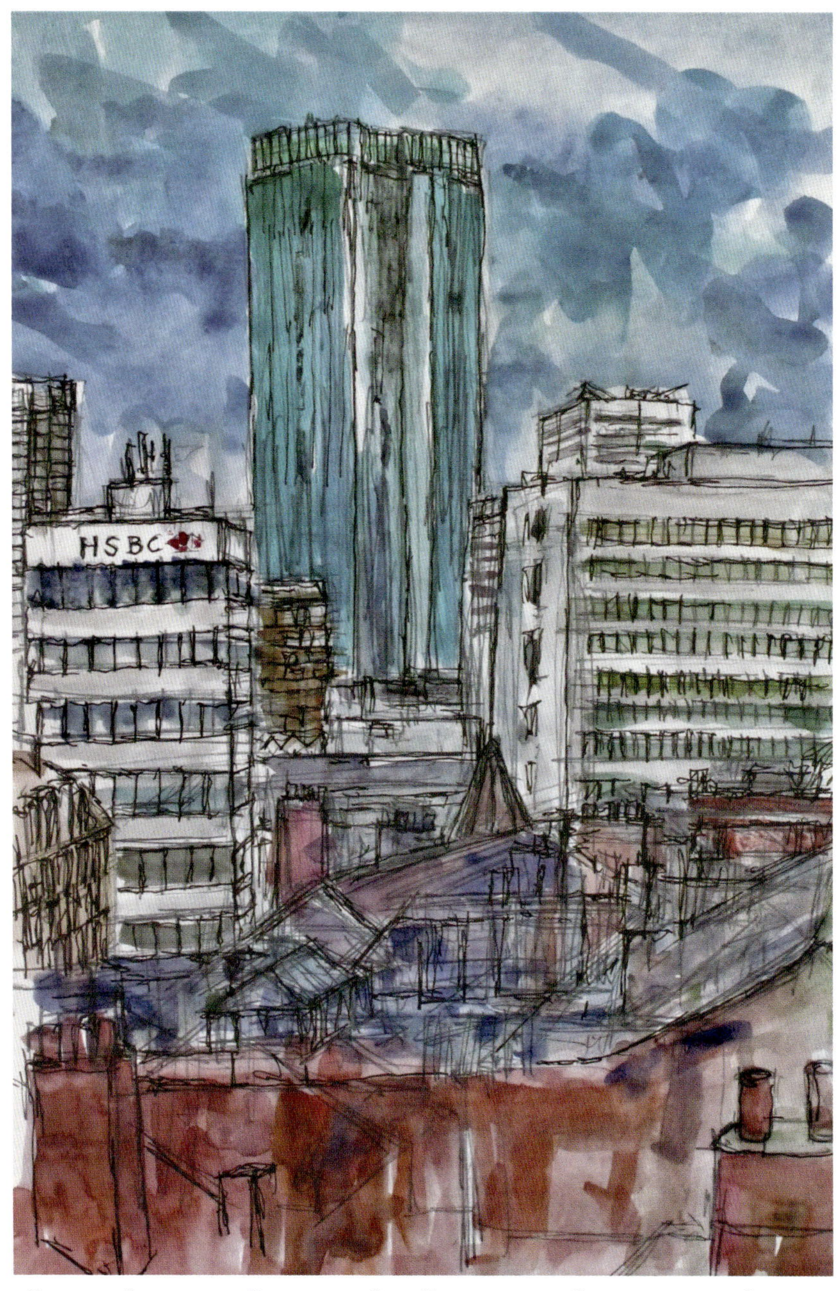

DANIEL STEDMAN, RADISSON BLU TOWER AND CORPORATION STREET

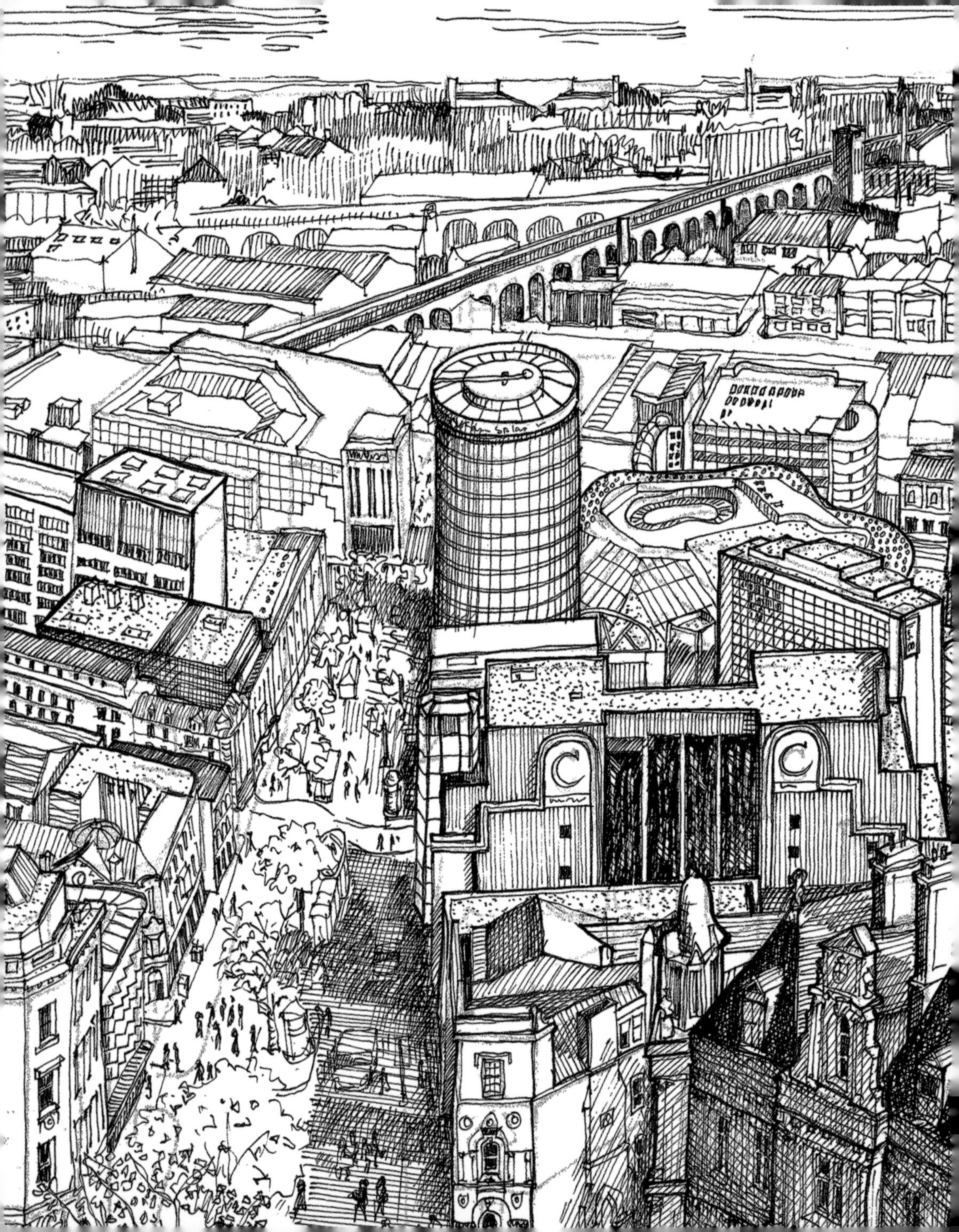

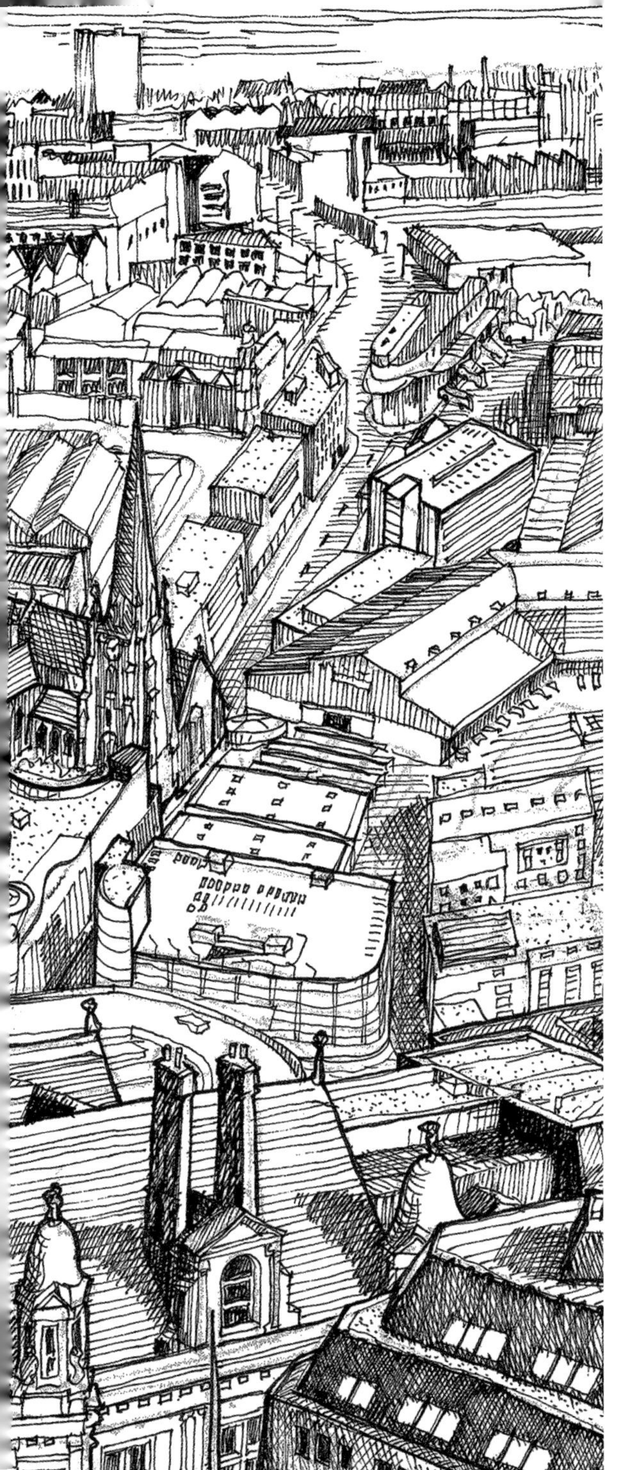

CHRIS ECKERSLEY,
BIRD'S EYE NEW STREET

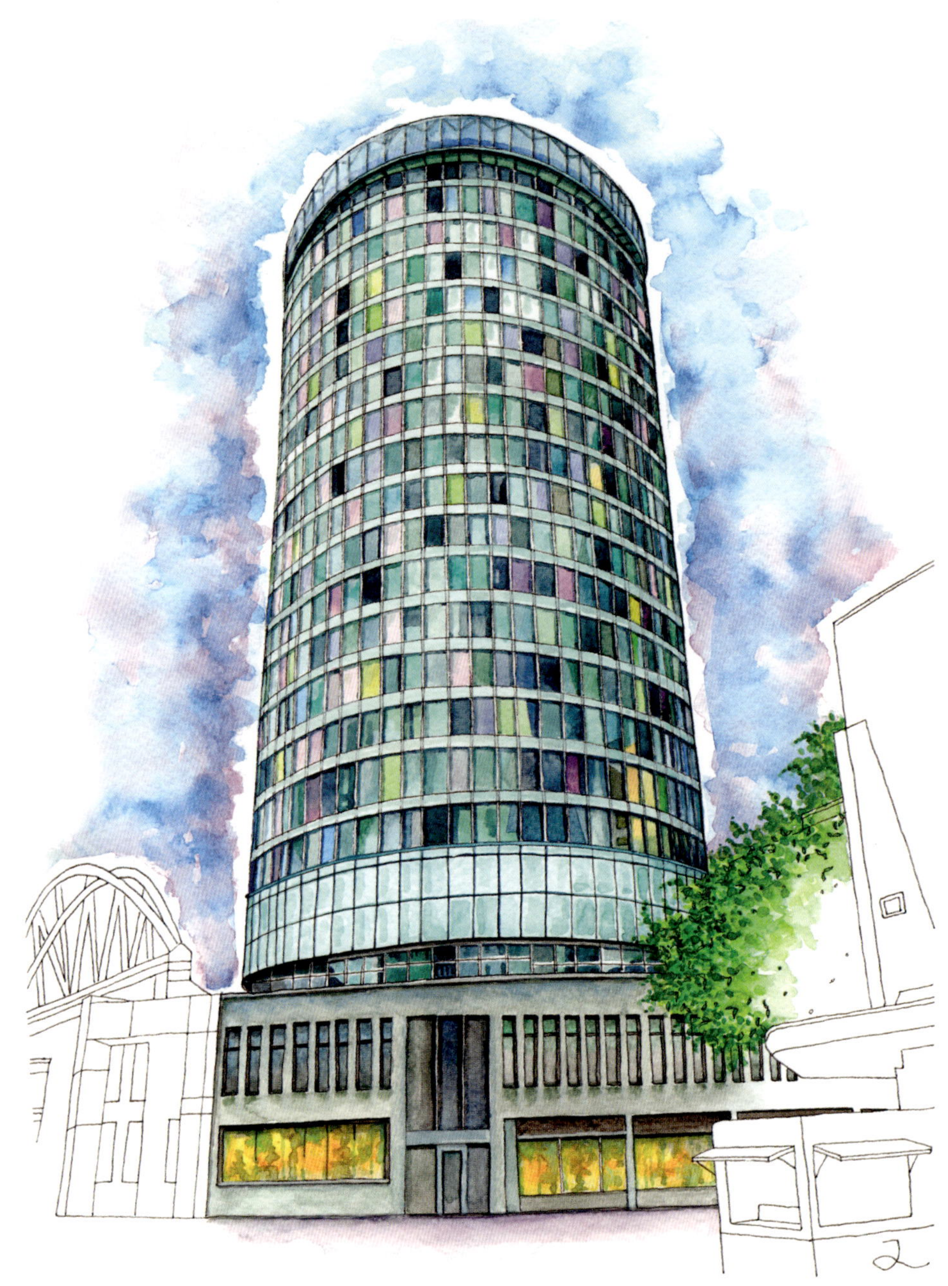

84

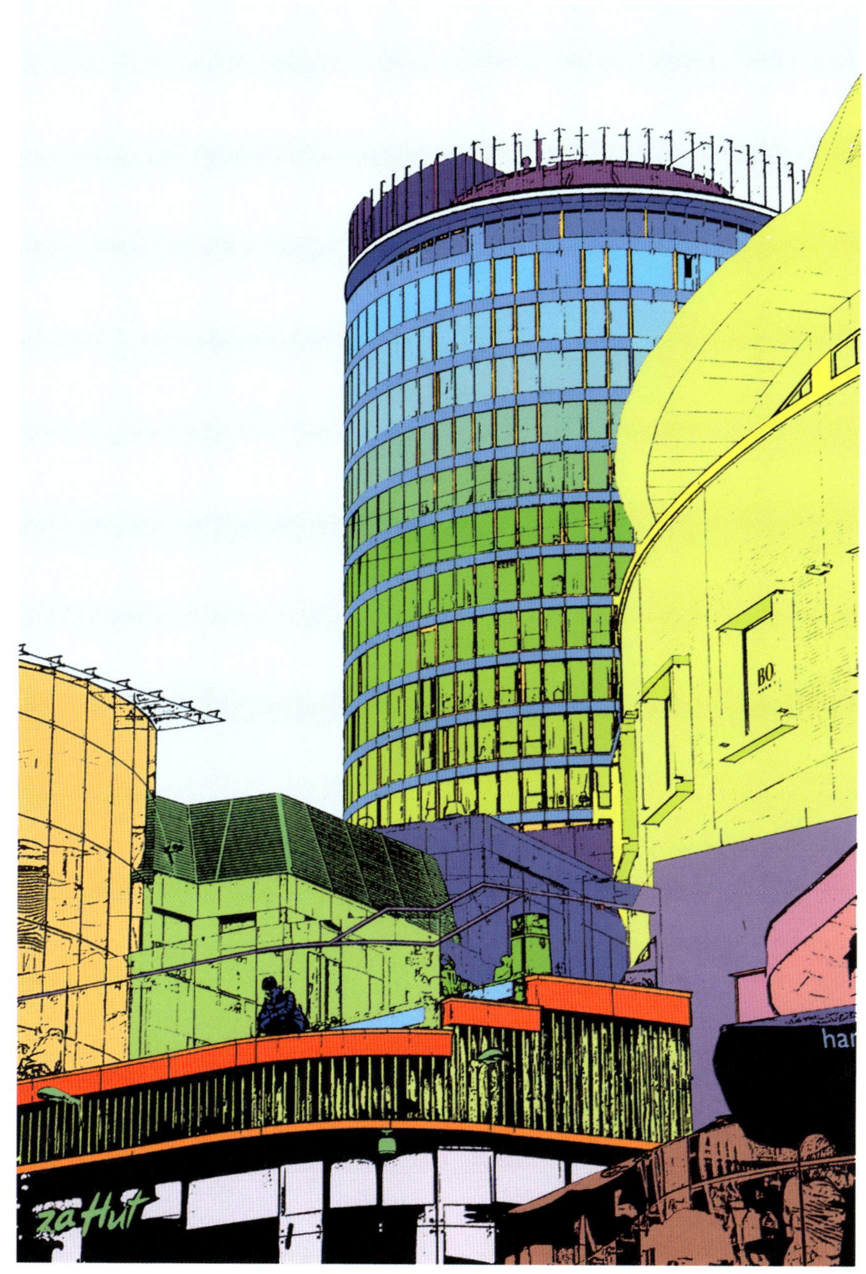

KAREN CROSS, ROTUNDA

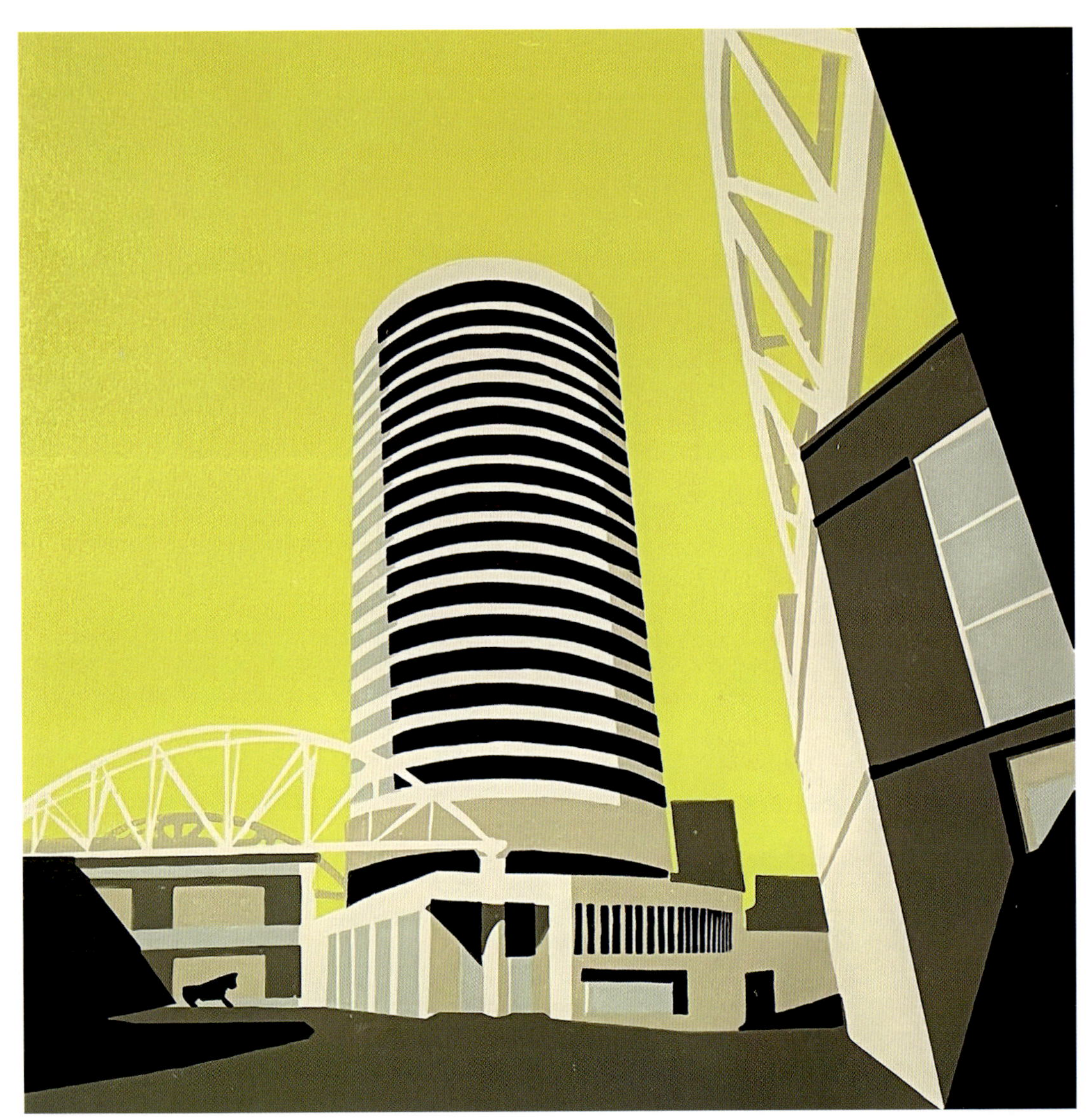

STEVE MILLWARD, BULLRING

86

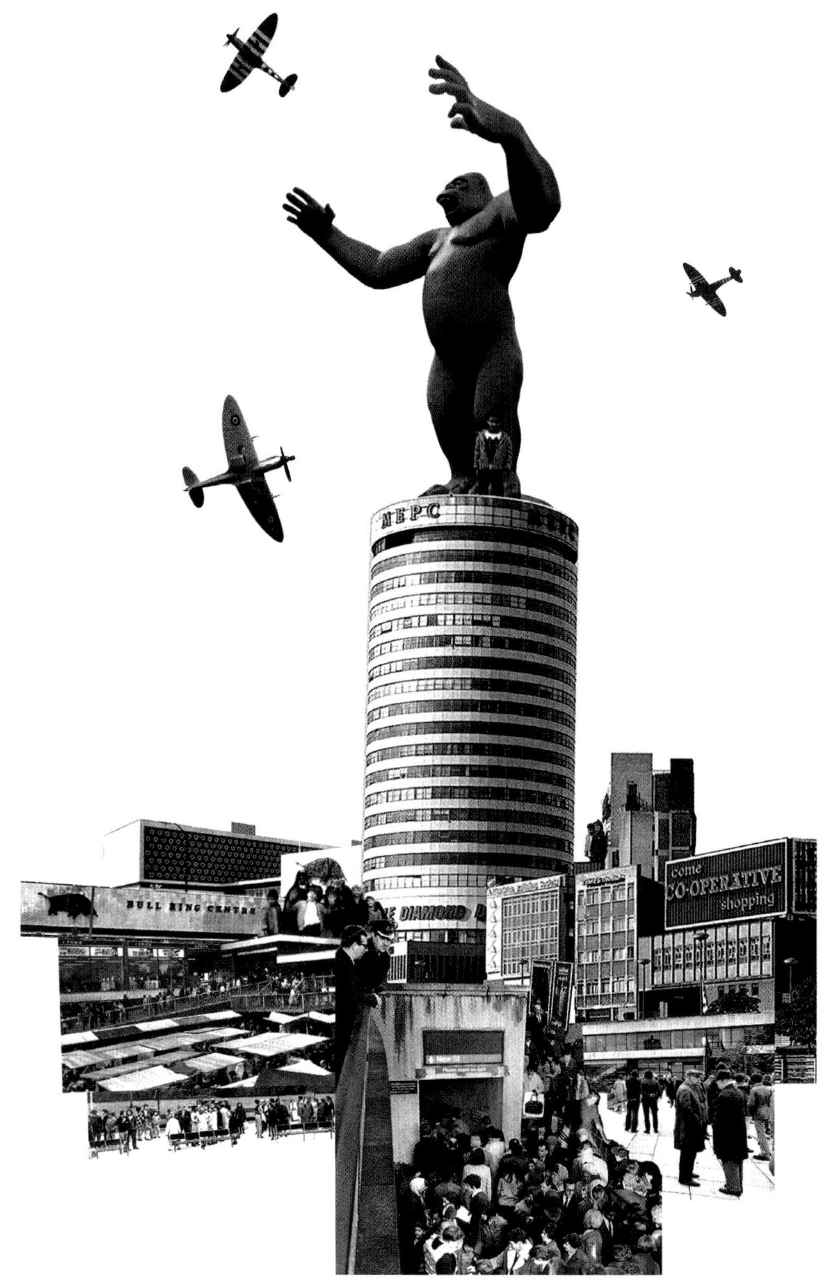

T O M   T E B B Y ,   T H E   K O N G   A N D   I

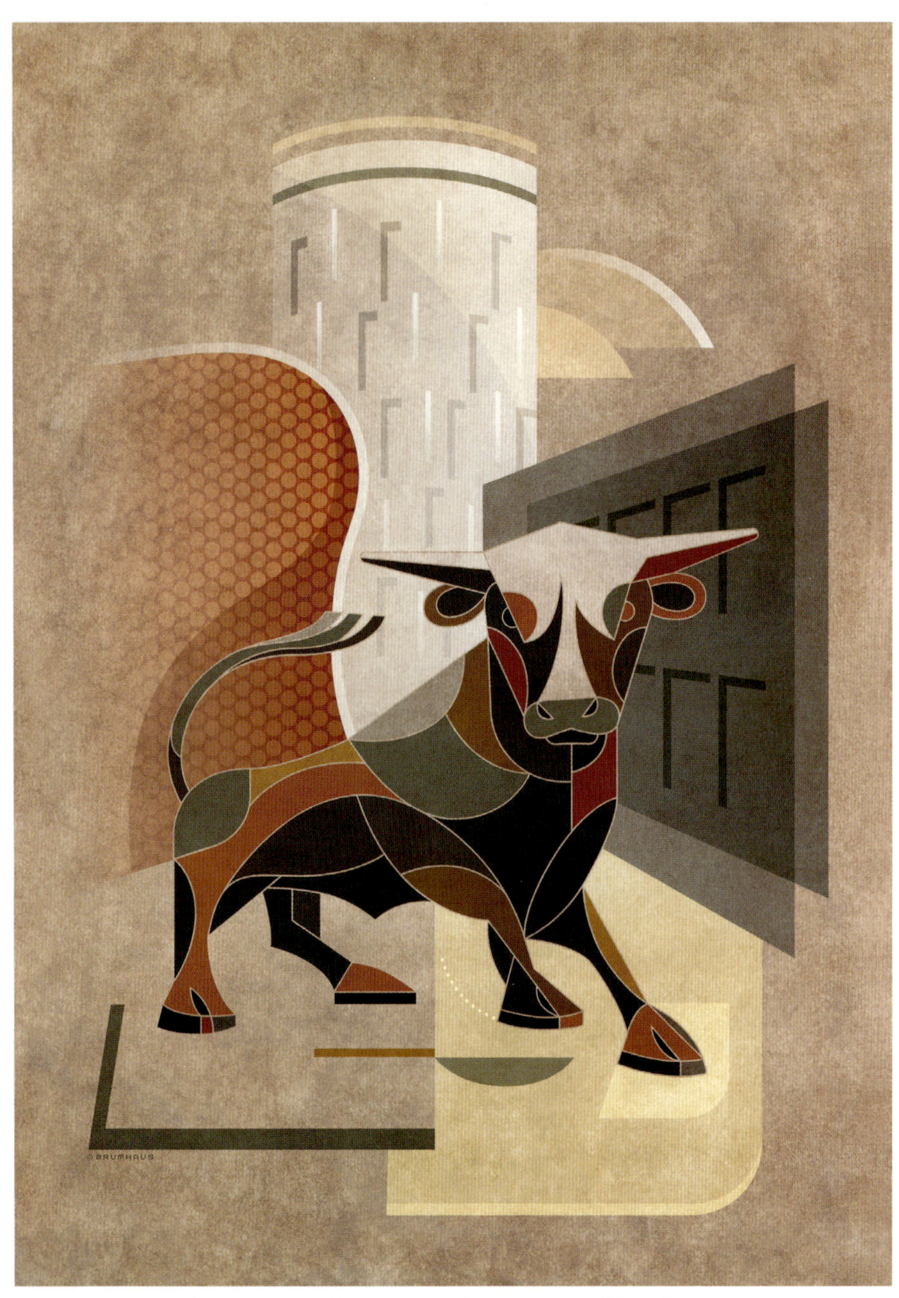

ALEXANDER EDWARDS (BRUMHAUS), THE BULL

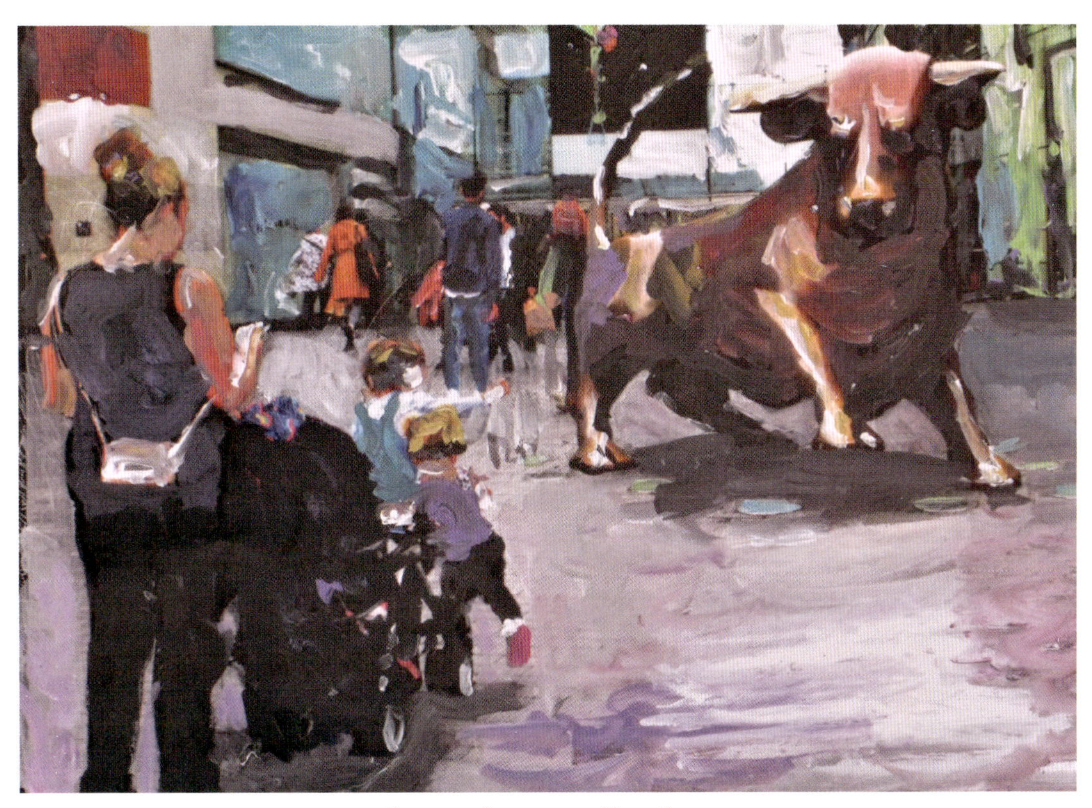

DANIEL STEDMAN, THE BULL

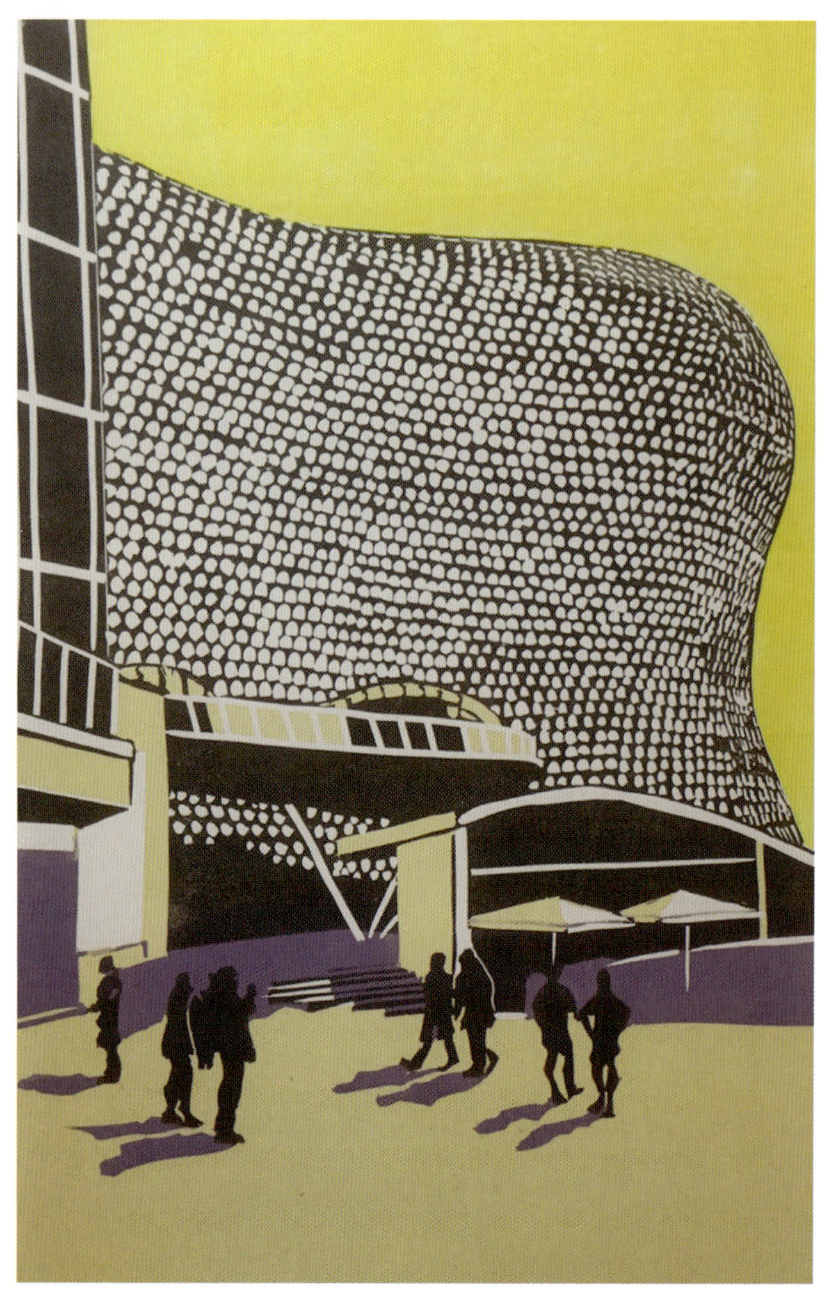

ANDY TROMANS, BULLRING

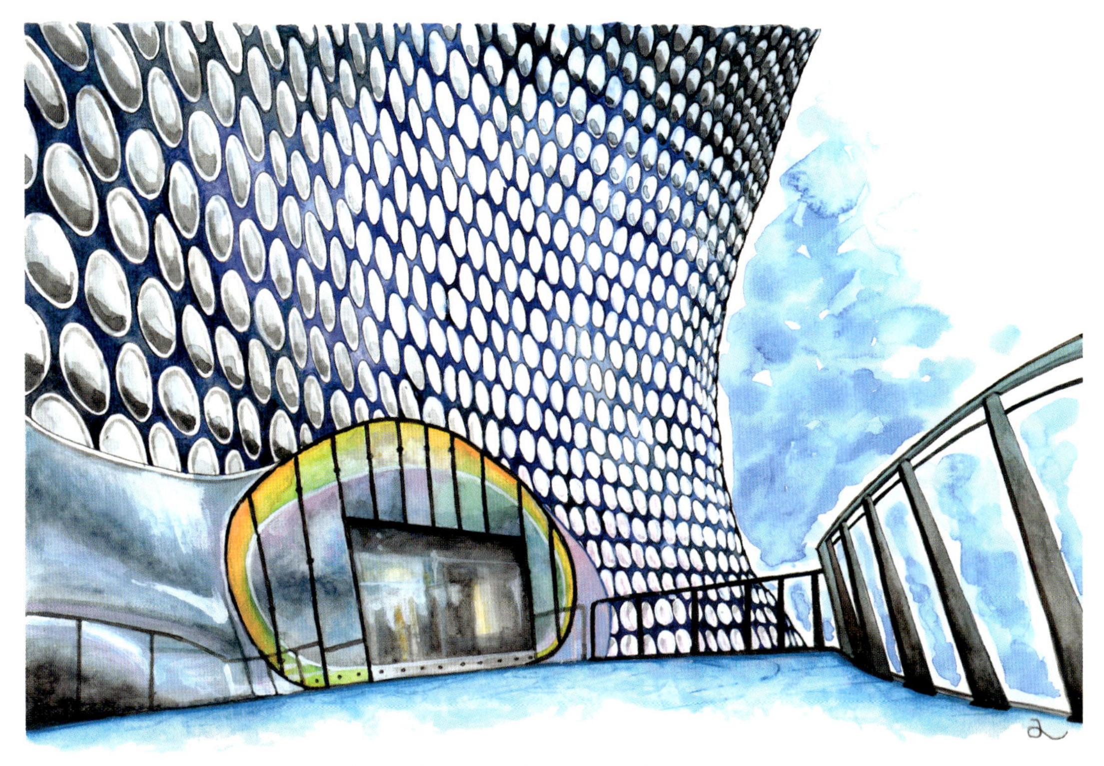

JILLY OXLADE-ARNOTT, SELFRIDGES

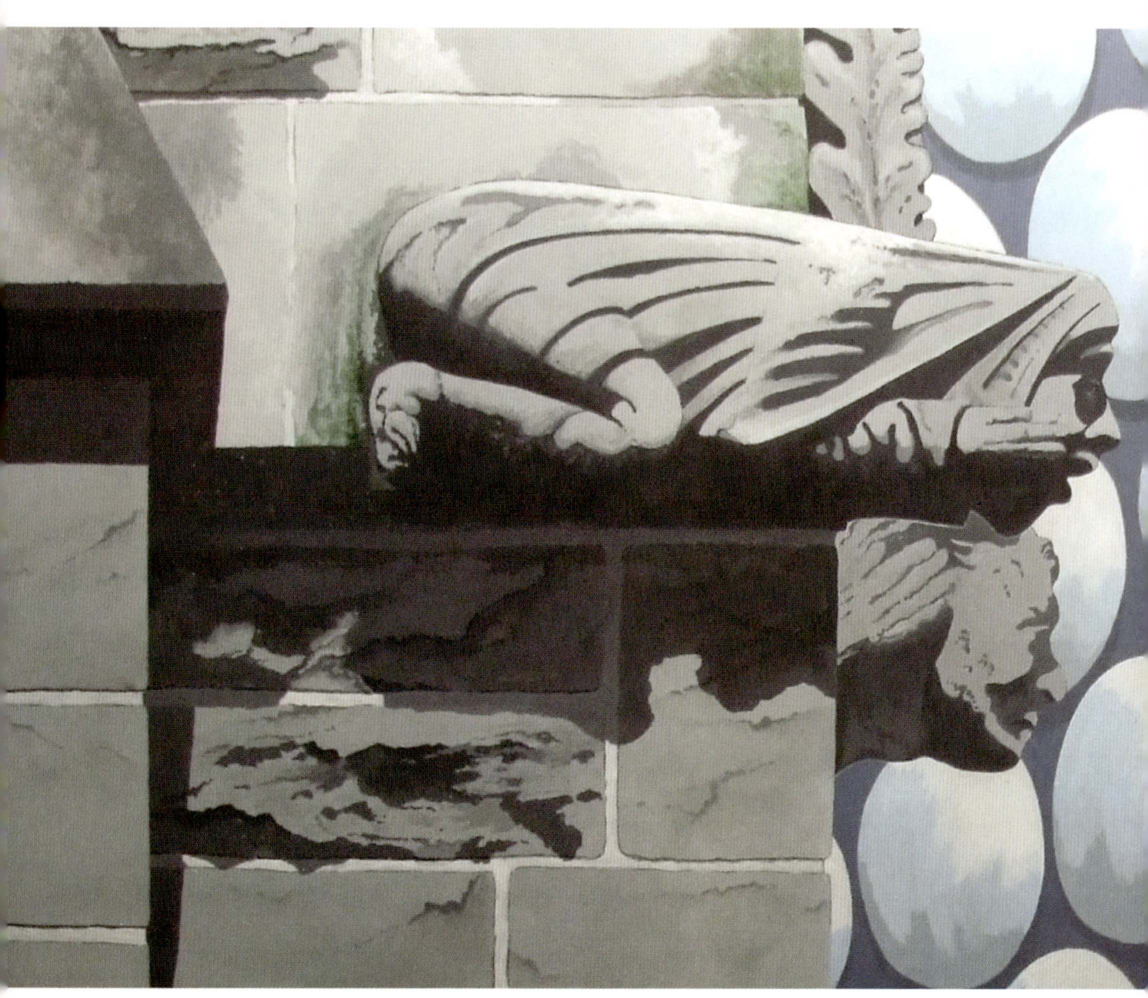

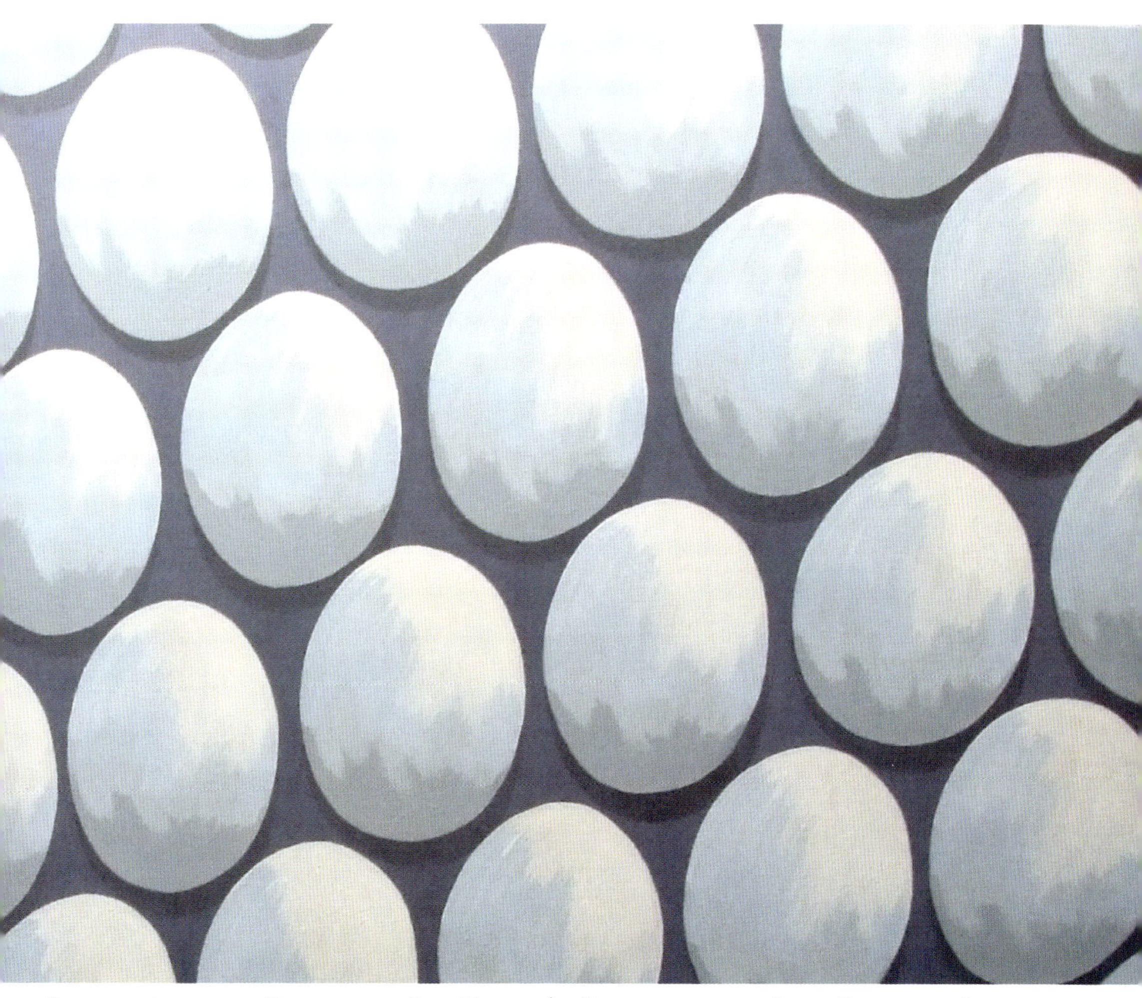

GRAHAM LEONARD KING RBSA, ST. MARTIN'S CHURCH IN THE BULL RING AND SELFRIDGES

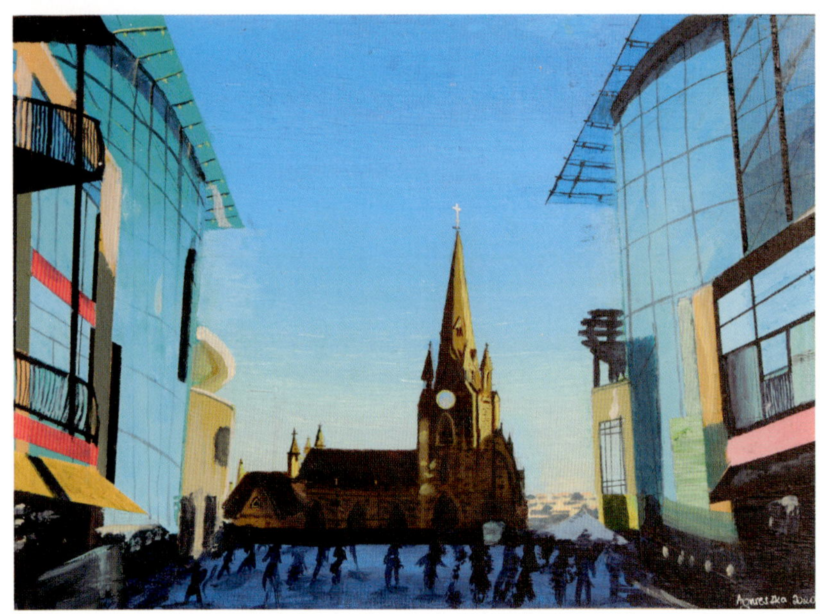

AGNIESZKA KLIMASZEWSKA, ST. MARTIN'S CHURCH IN THE BULL RING

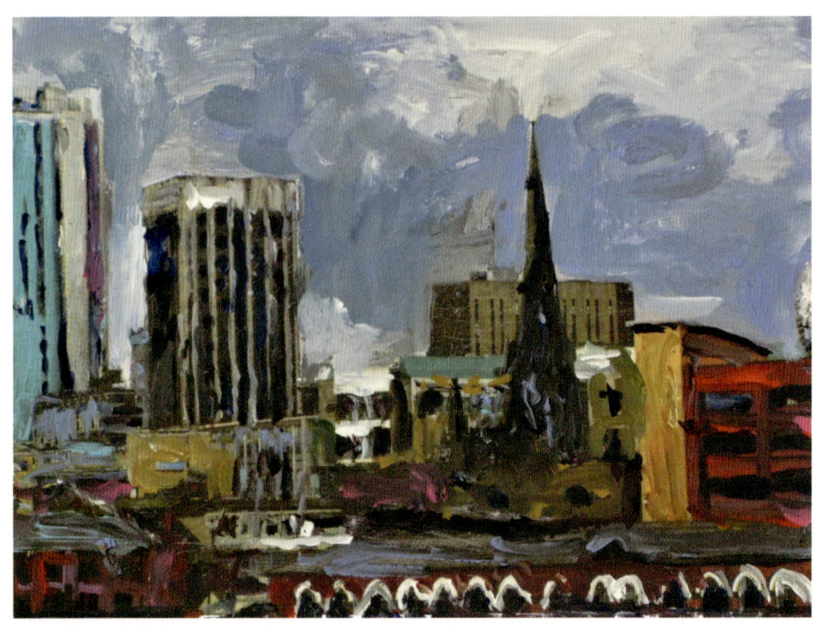

DANIEL STEDMAN, BIRMINGHAM FROM DIGBETH

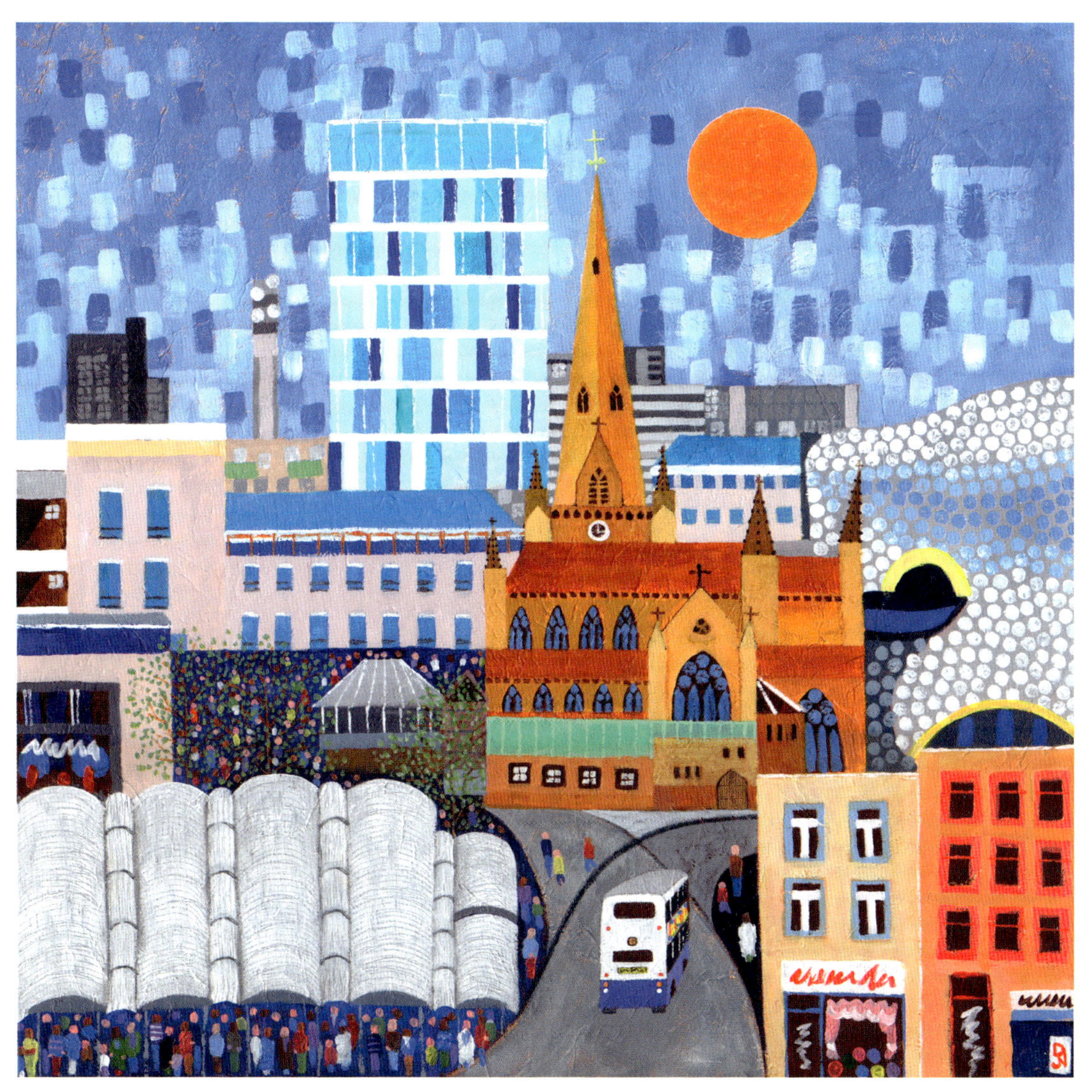

David Newton, St. Martin's Church in the Bull Ring

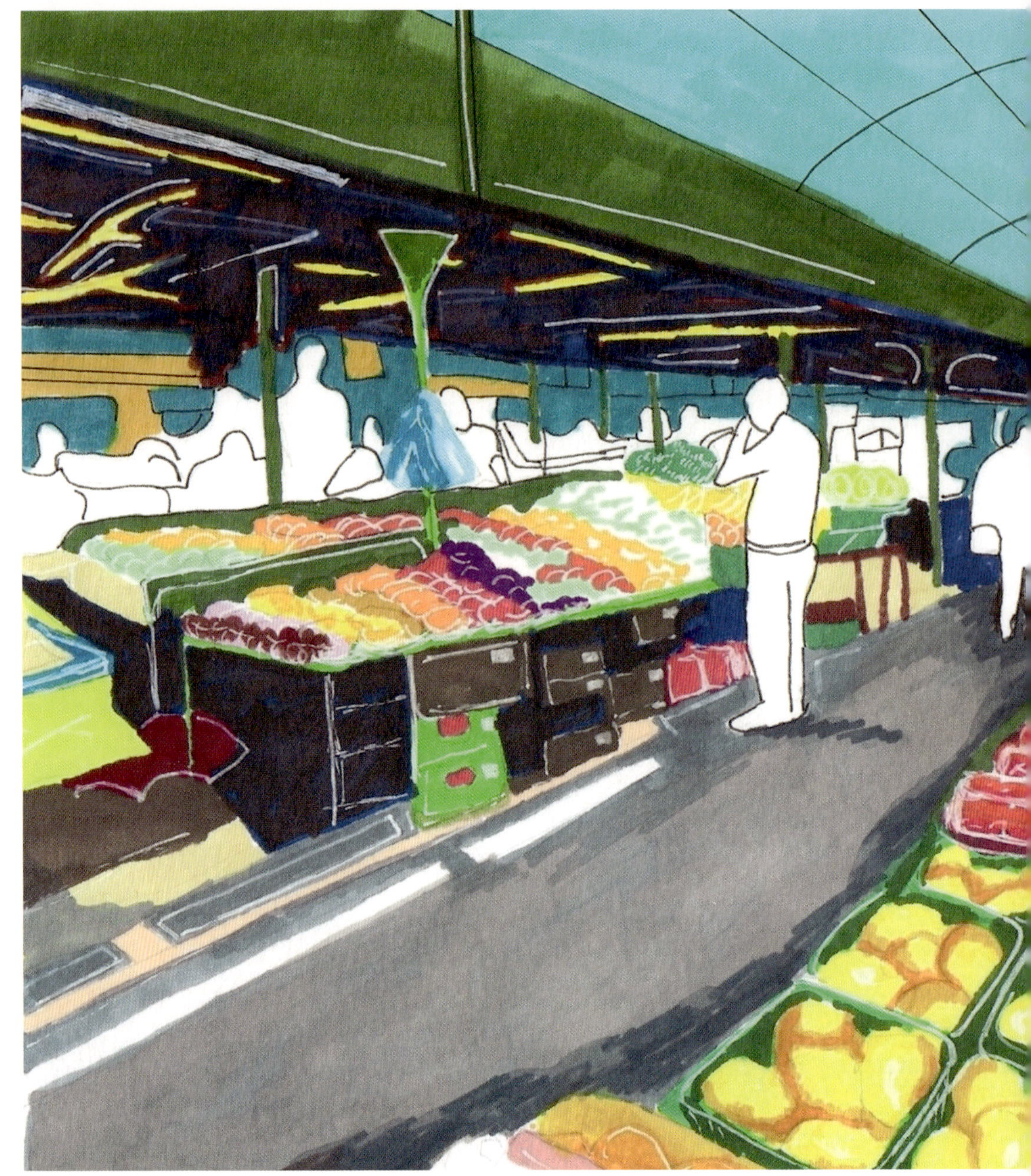

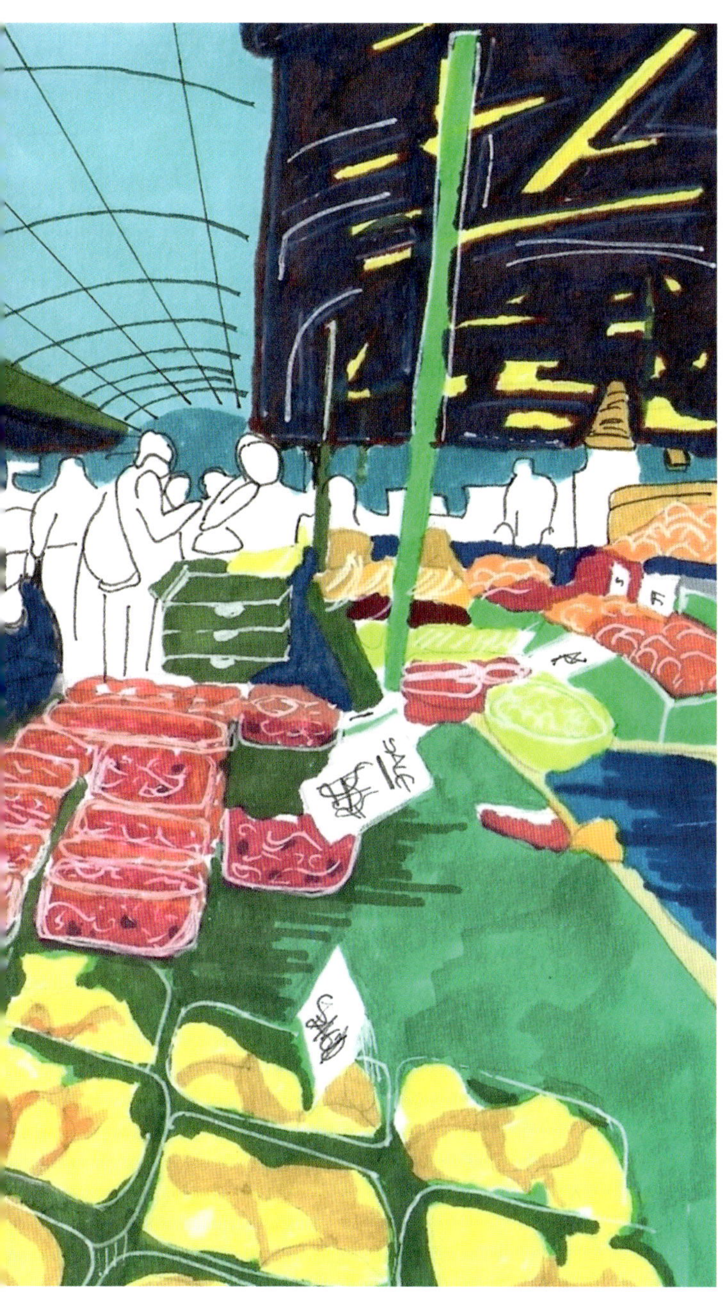

SANA ALI,
THE BULL RING MARKET

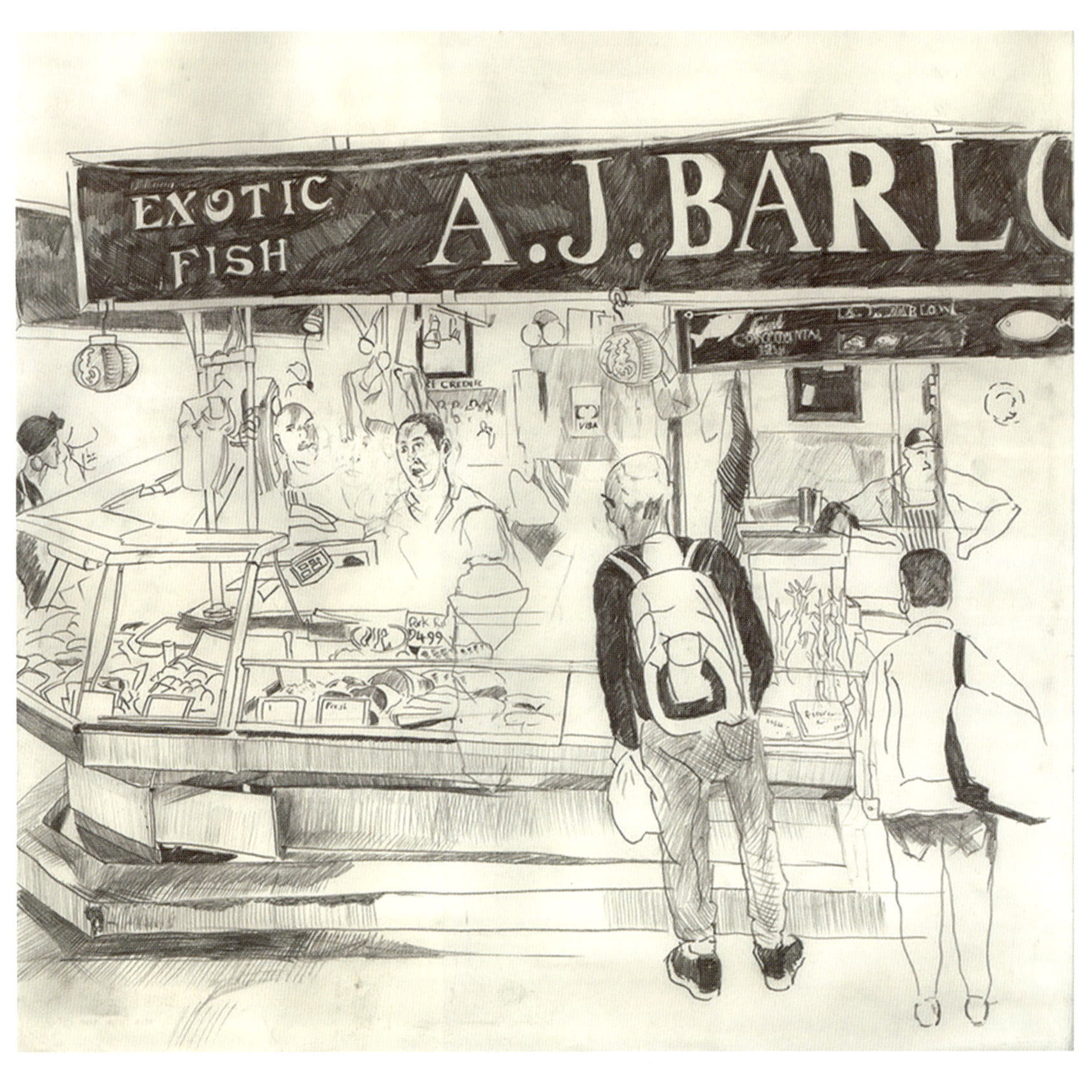

NICHOLAS SIMS, EXOTIC FISH IN THE BULL RING OPEN MARKET

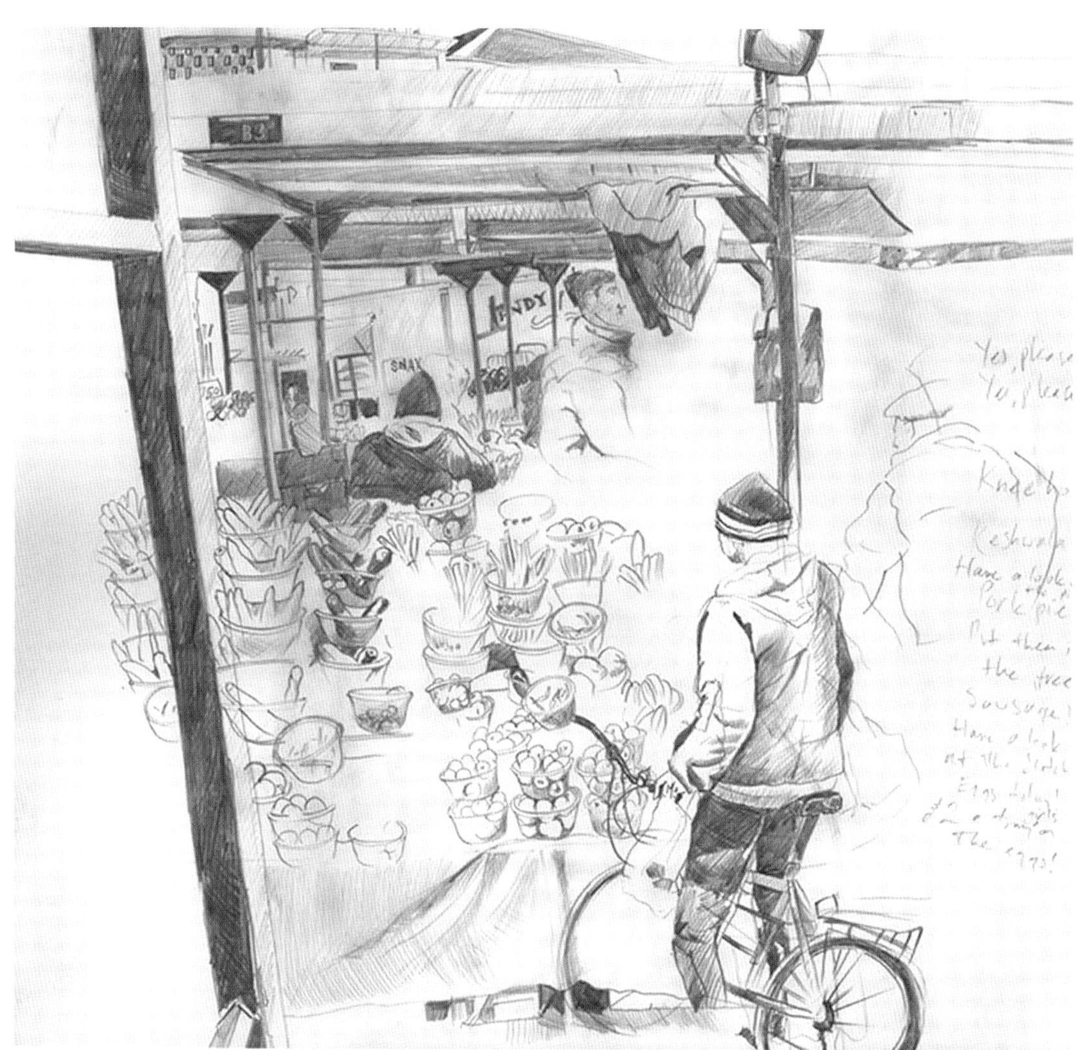

NICHOLAS SIMS, FRUIT 'N' VEG IN THE BULL RING OPEN MARKET

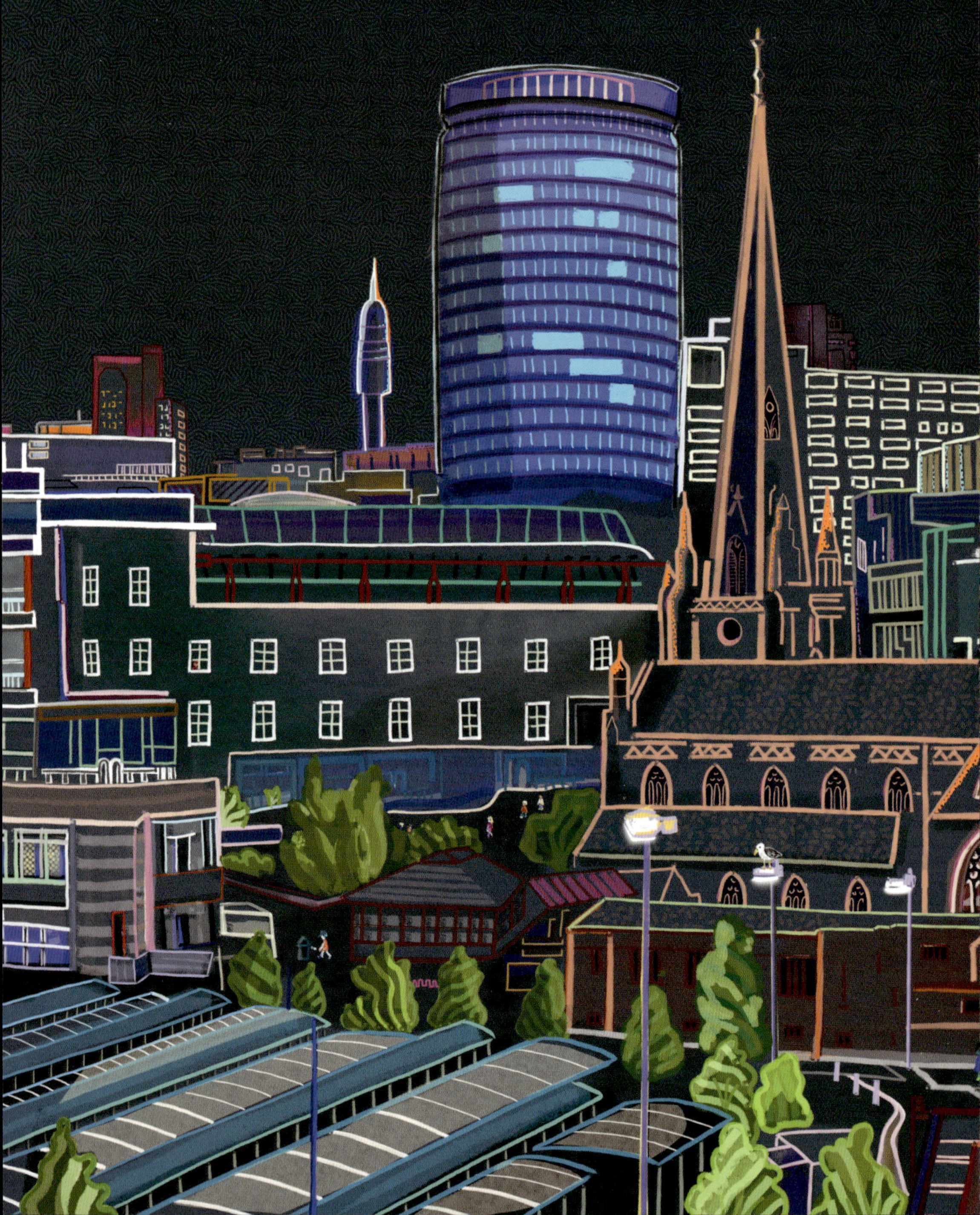

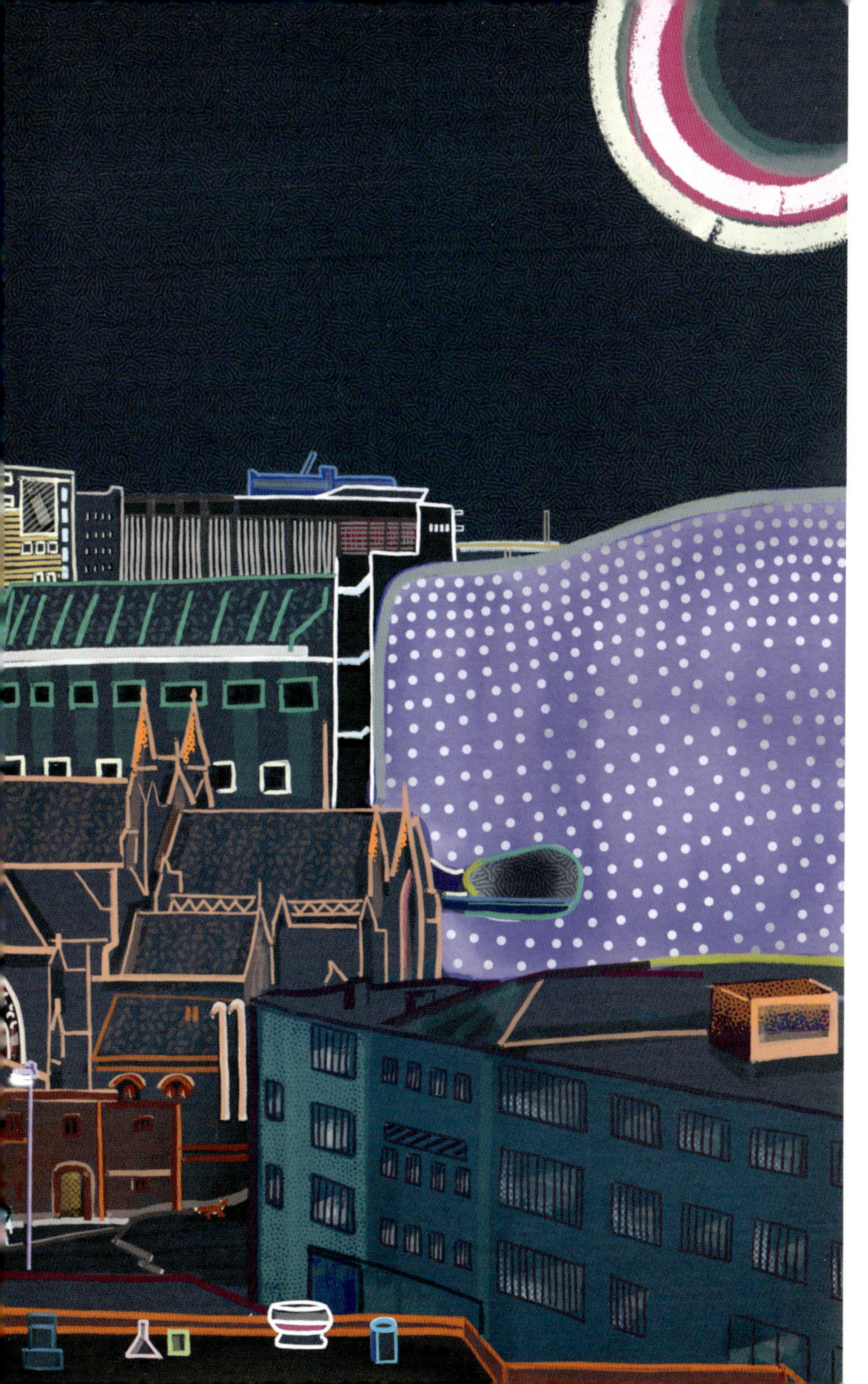

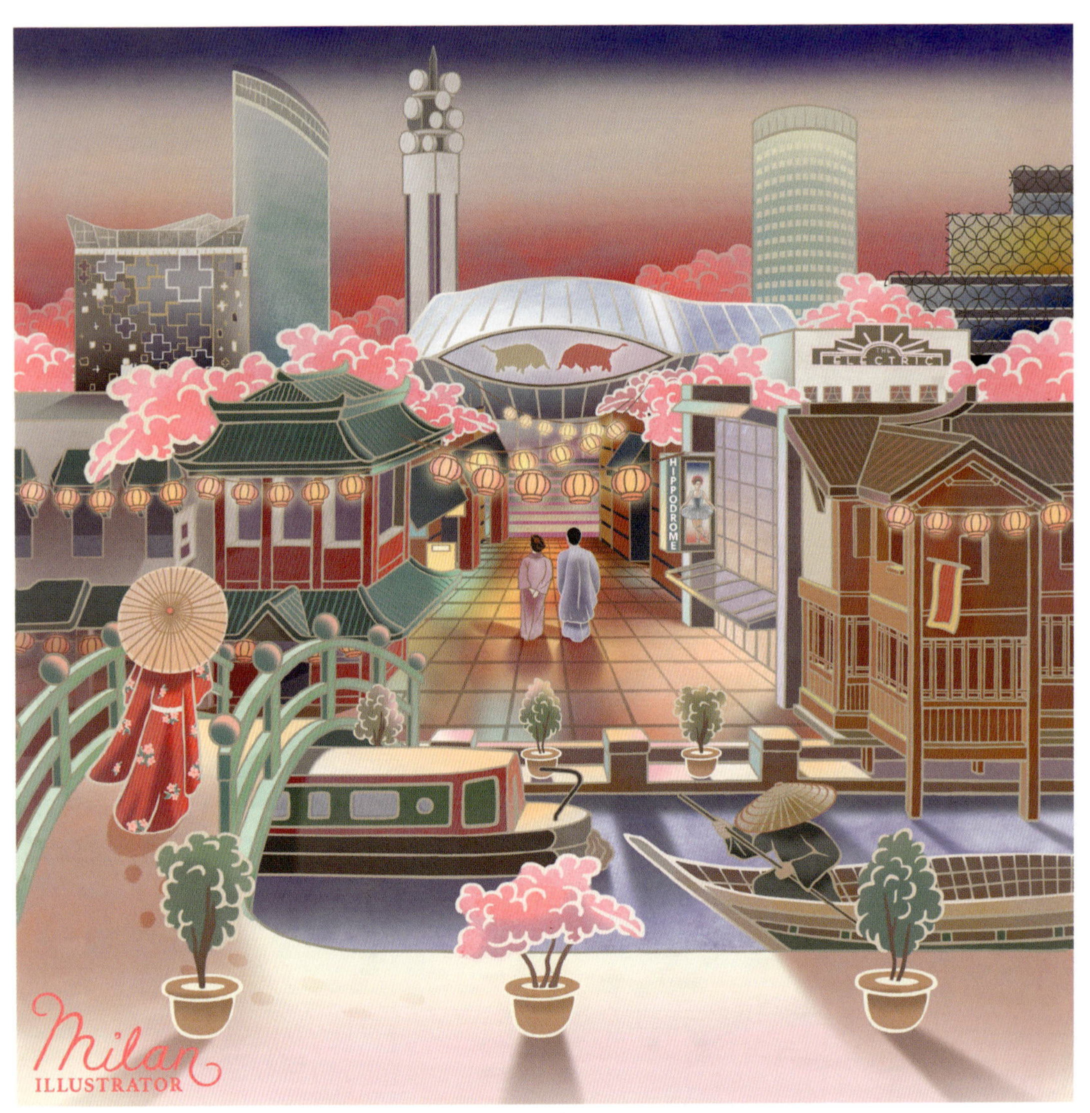

Milan Topalović, Chinatown

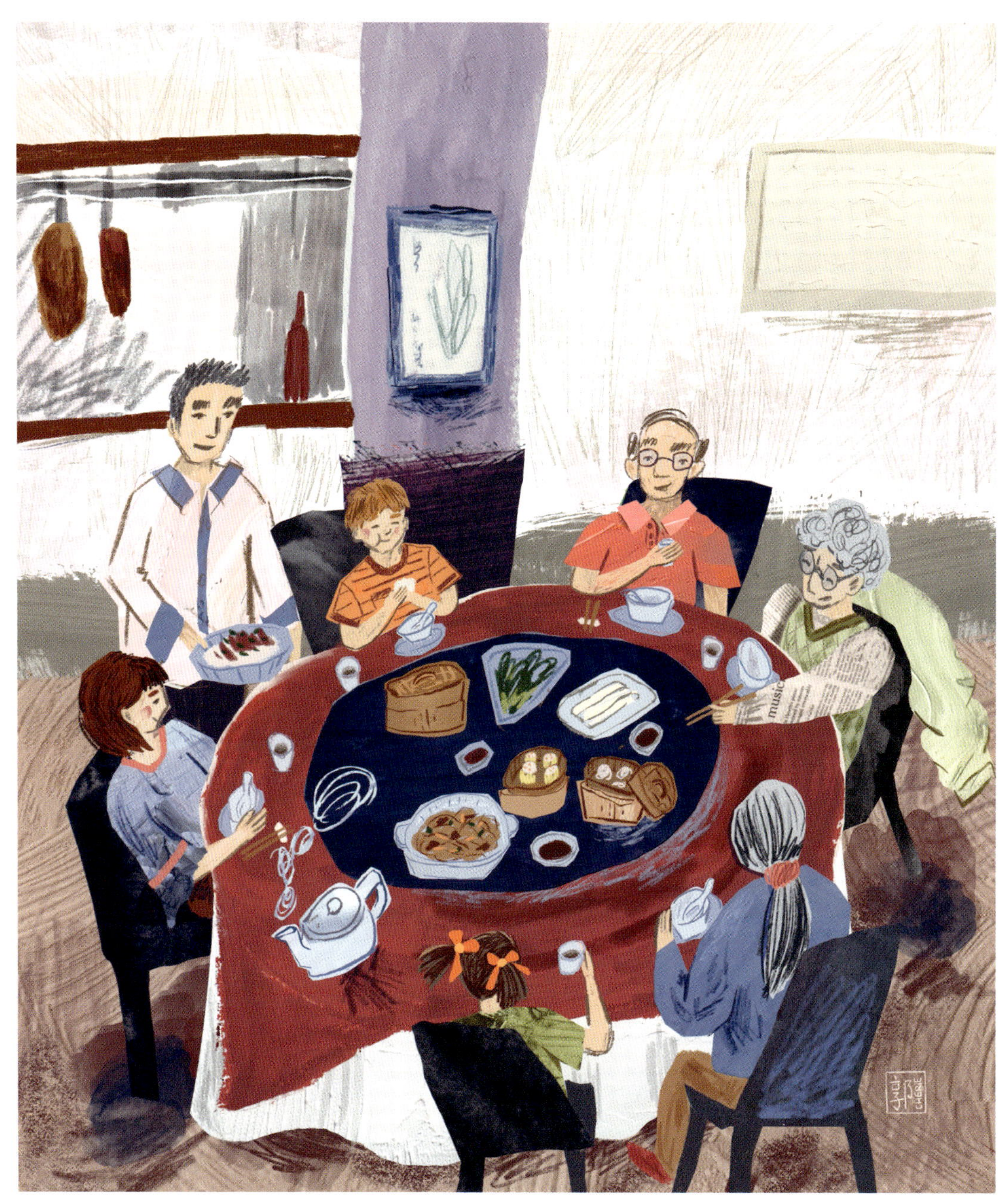

CHERIE KWOK, KEN HO RESTAURANT

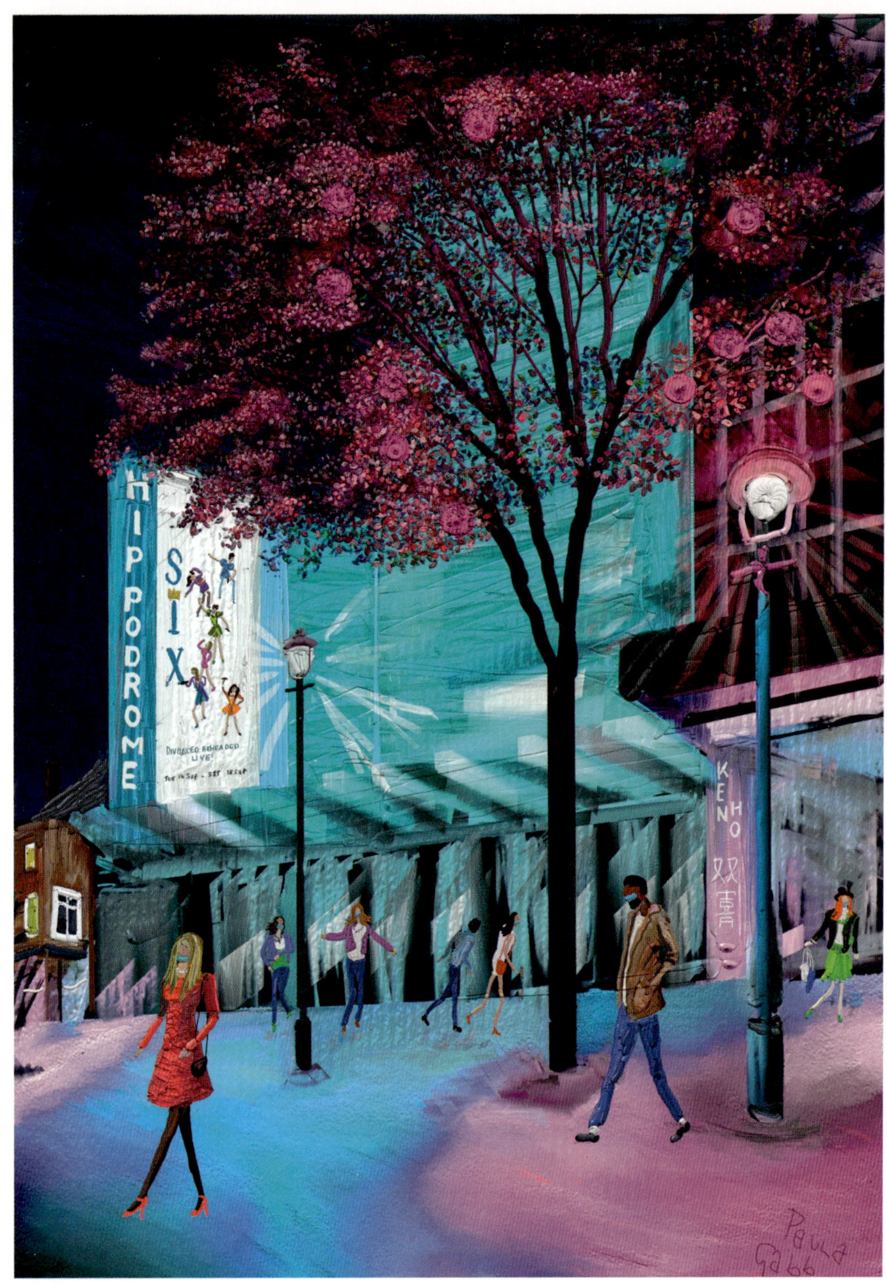

PAULA GABB, BIRMINGHAM HIPPODROME

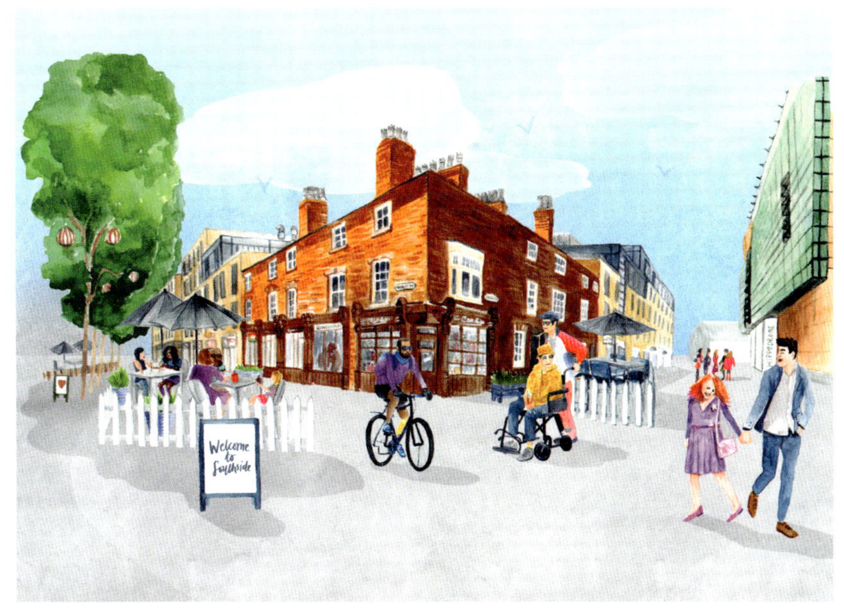

KATHERINE TROMANS, BIRMINGHAM BACK TO BACKS

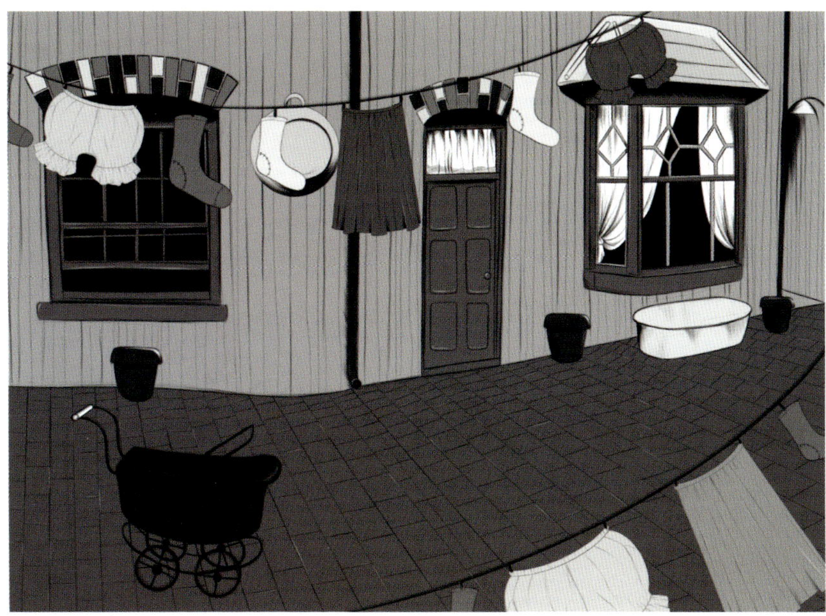

CASEY JOAN HARWOOD, BIRMINGHAM BACK TO BACKS

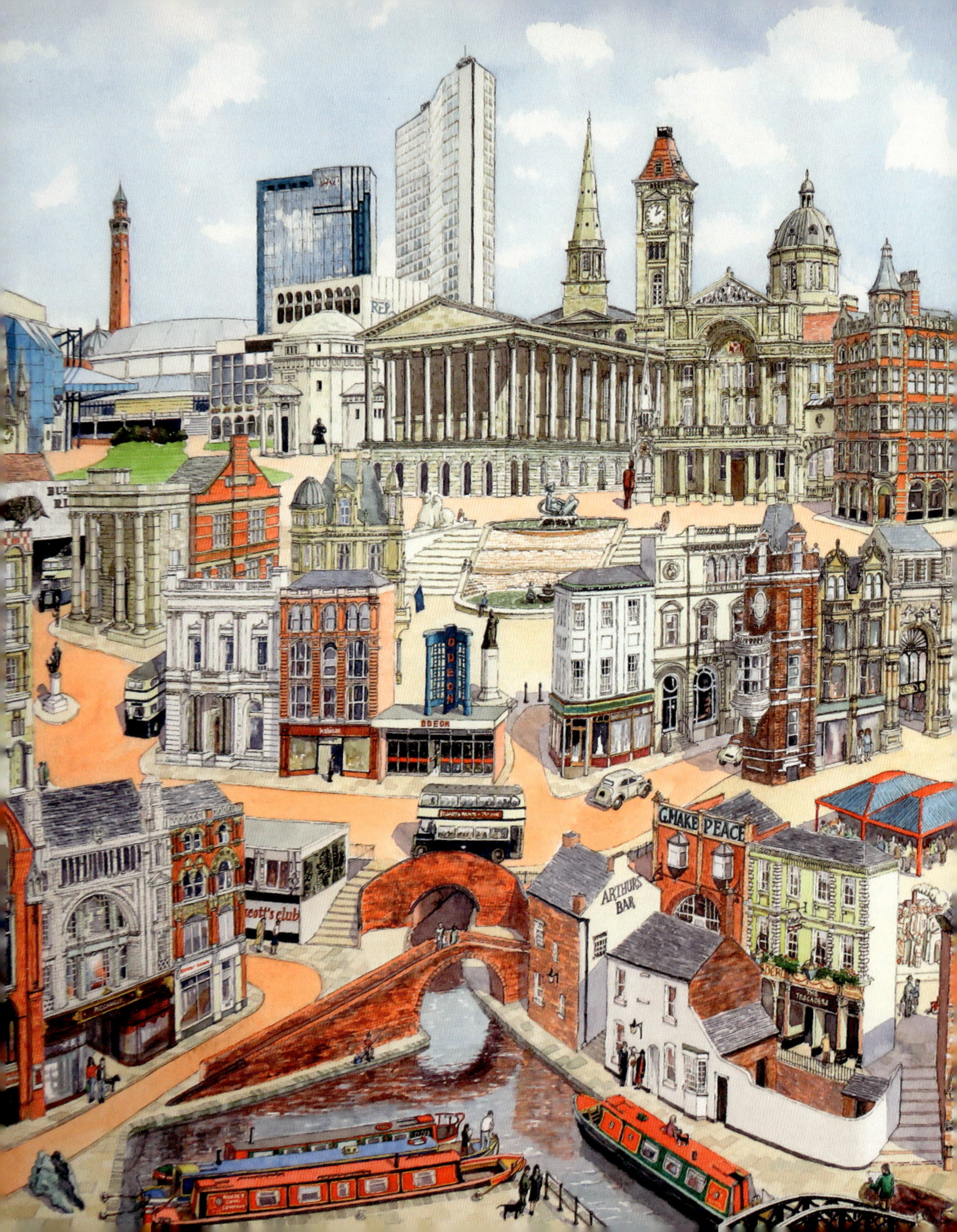
Scott's Club
ODEON
ODEON
ARTHURS BAR
G.MAKE PEACE

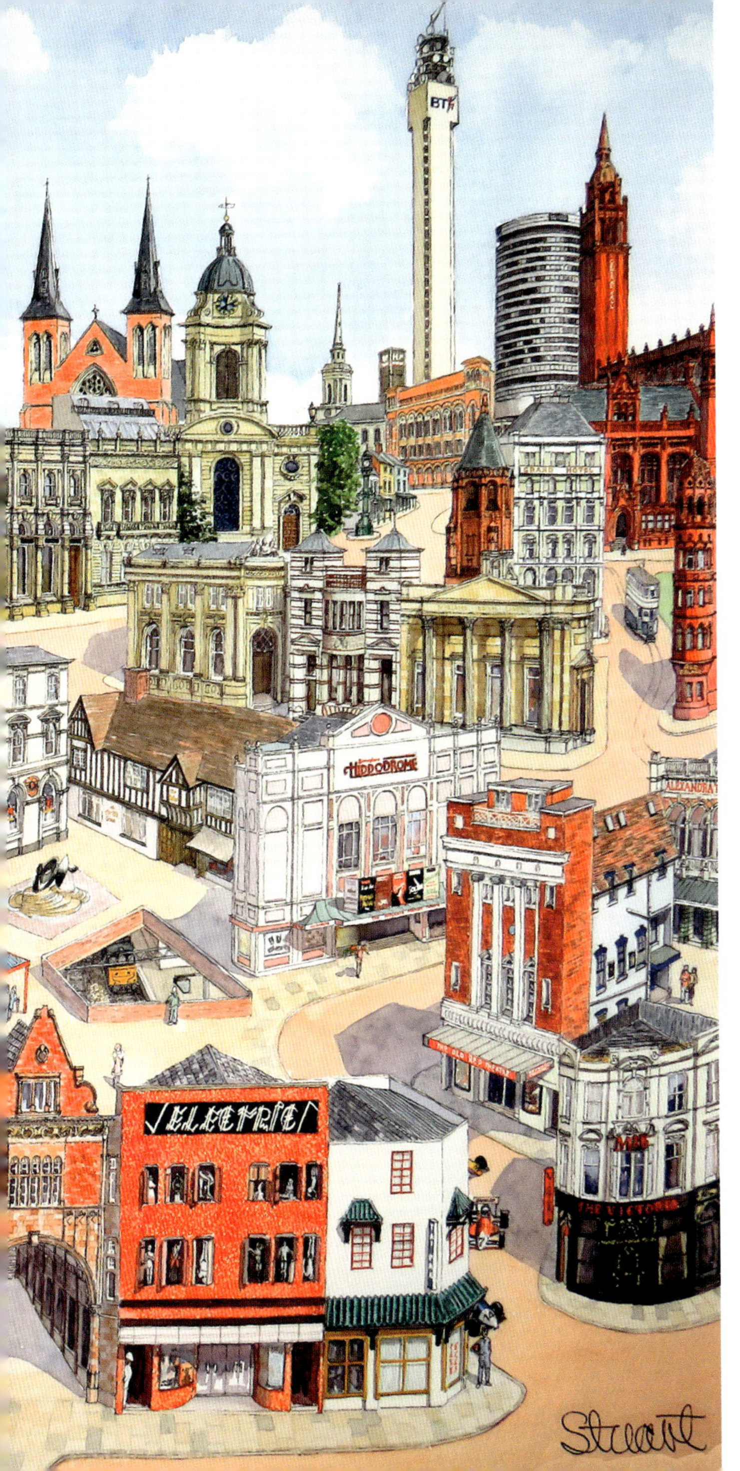

MARTIN STUART MOORE,
MEMORIES OF BIRMINGHAM

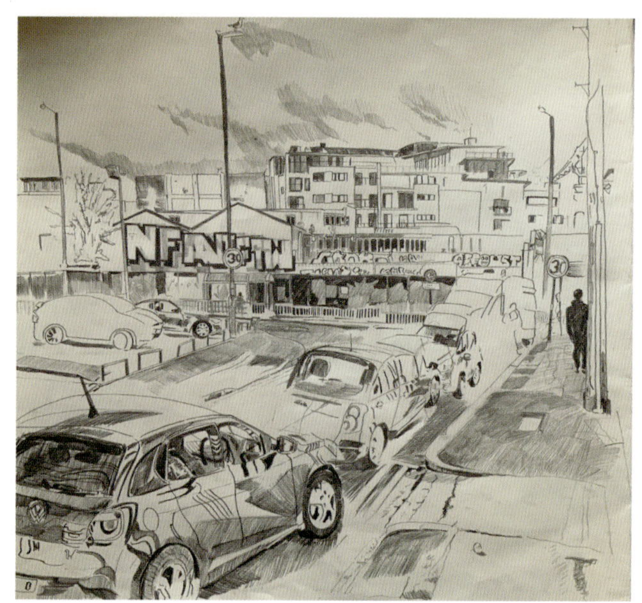

Nicholas Sims, Digbeth

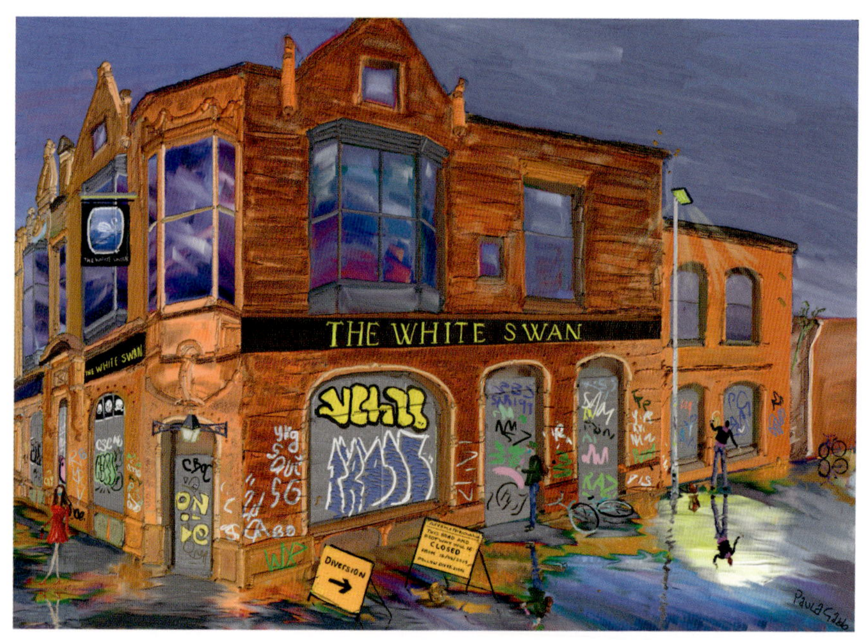

Paula Gabb, The White Swan

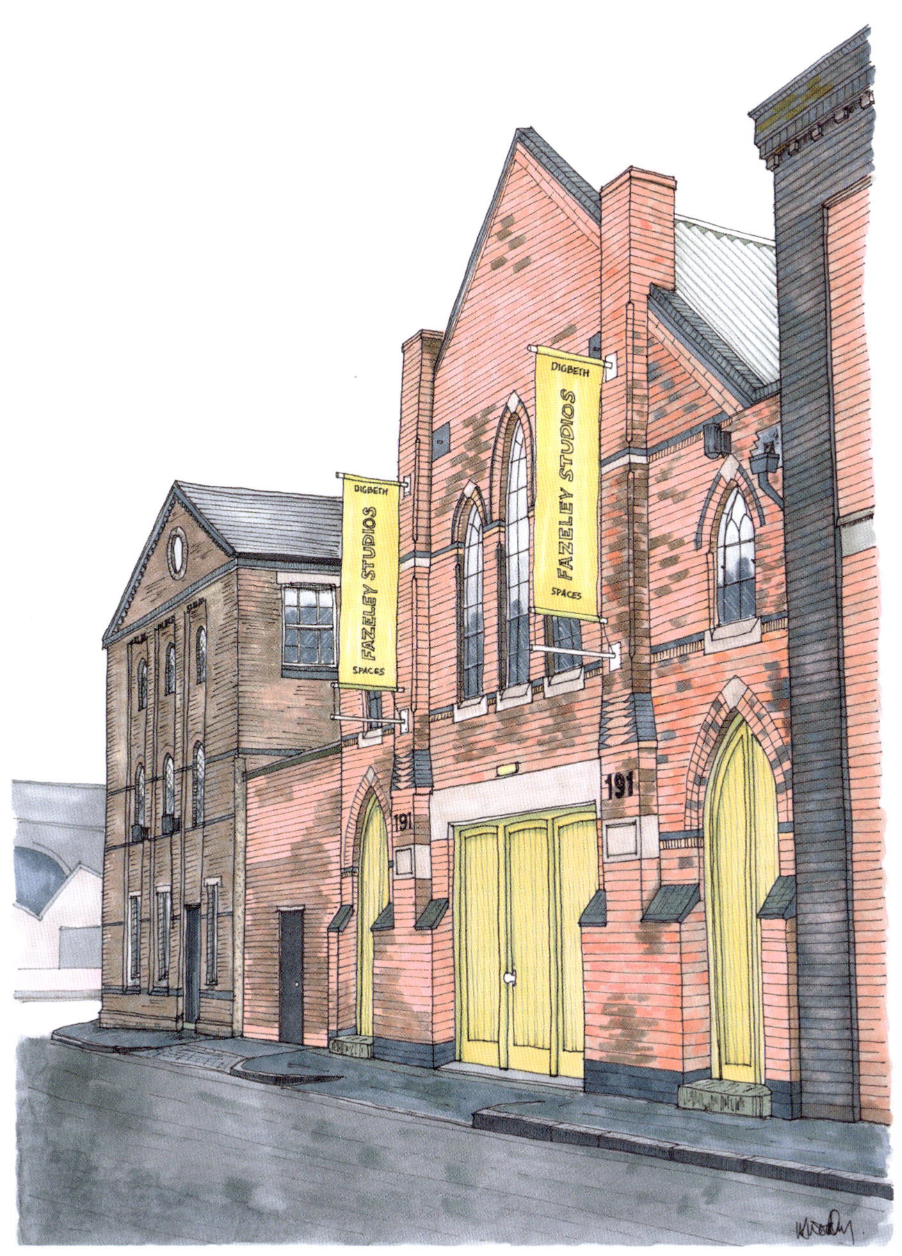

IAN WOODLEY, FAZELEY STUDIOS

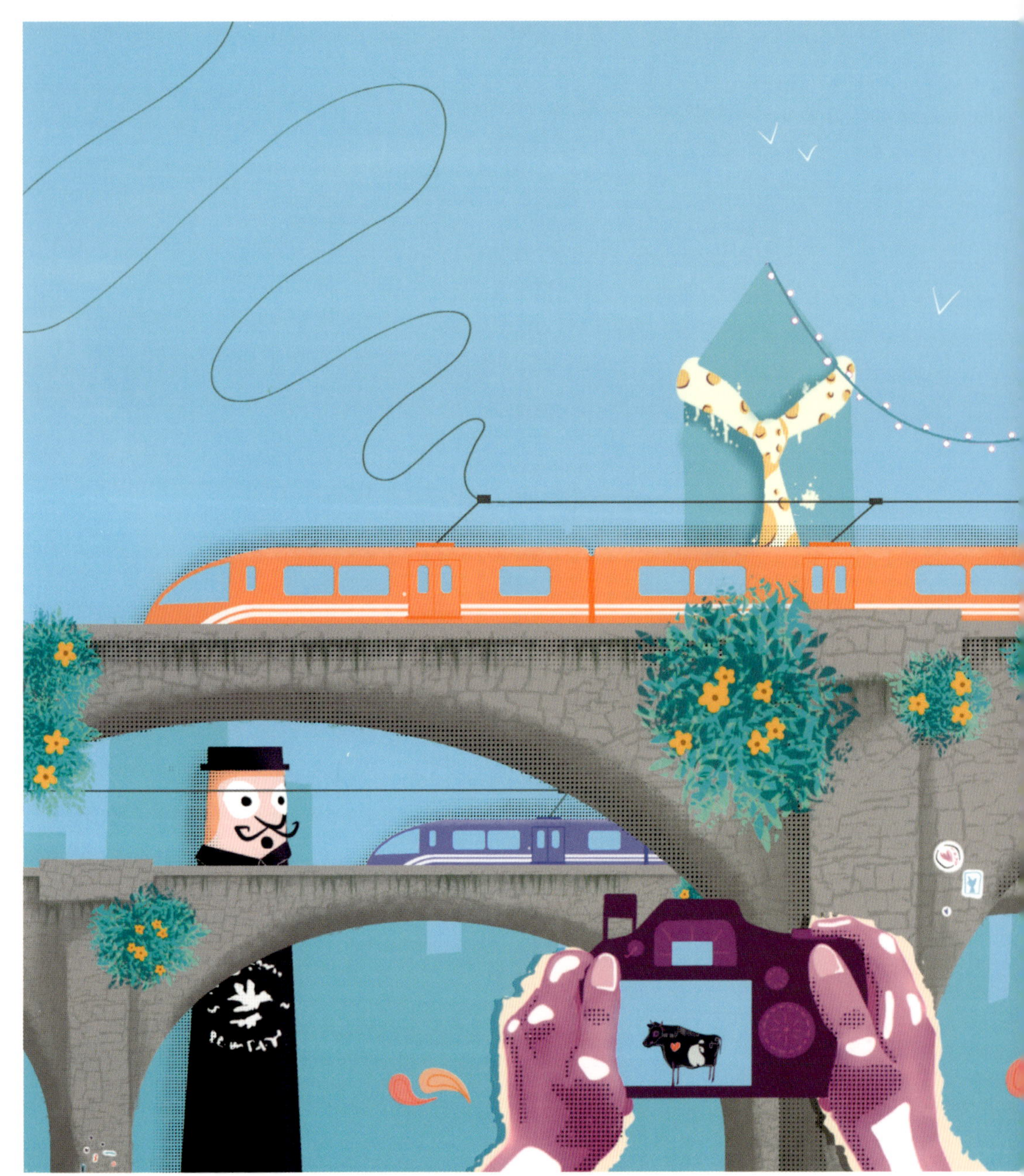

PEUGEOT

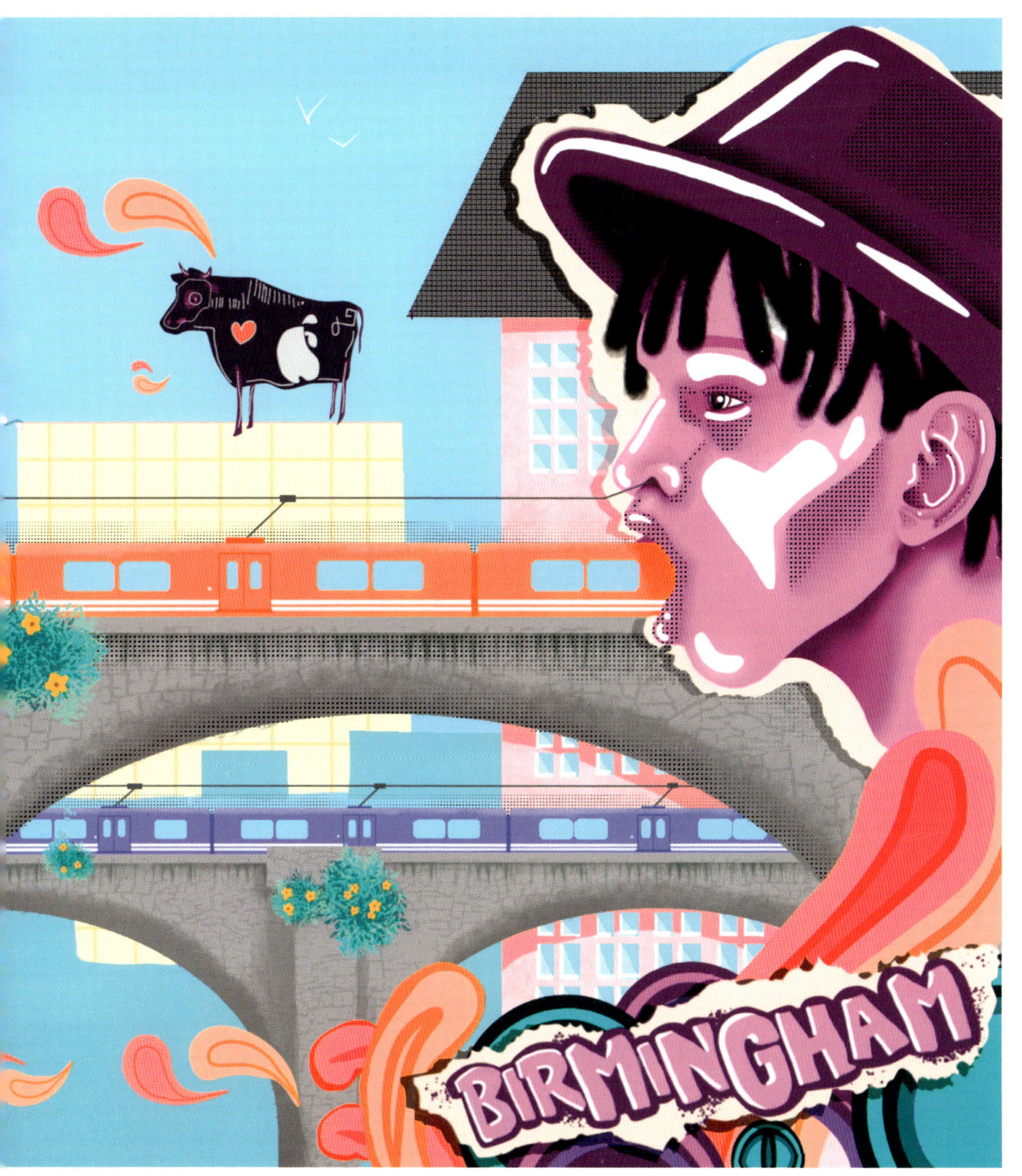

ELEANOR GARRETT, DIGBETH STREETS

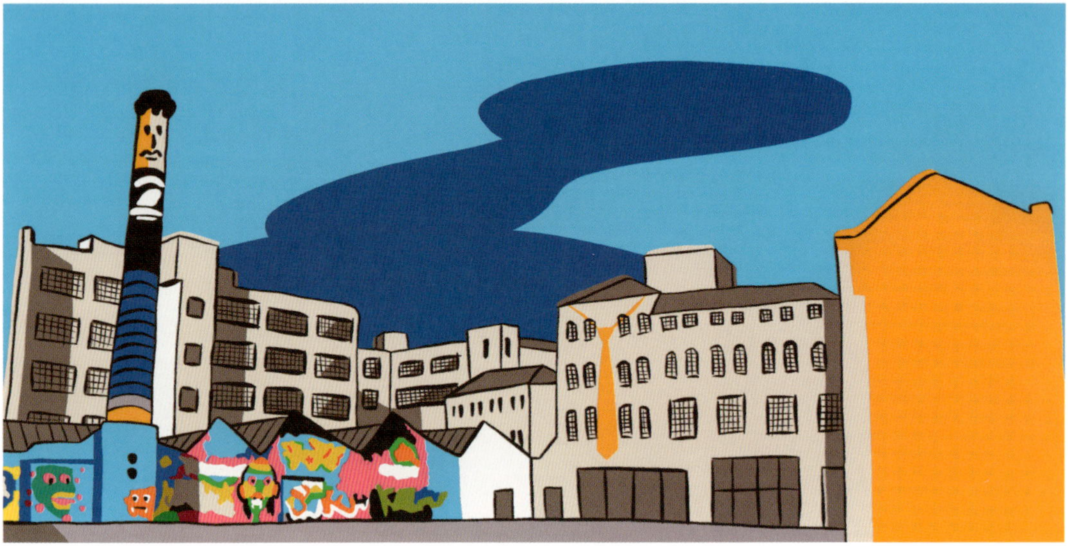

ANNA REUBEN, CUSTARD FACTORY

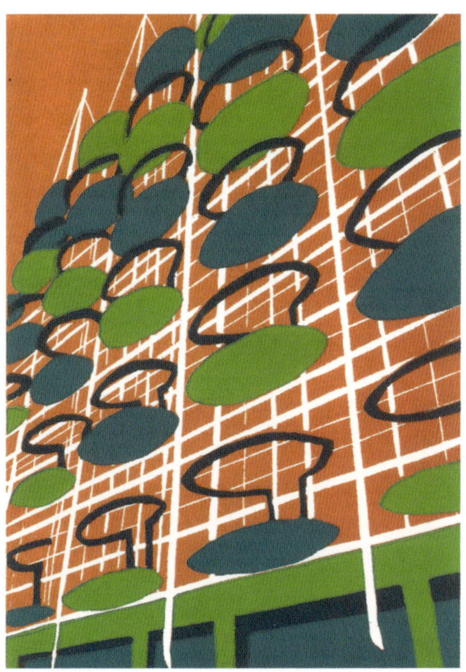

JENNIE ING, CUSTARD FACTORY

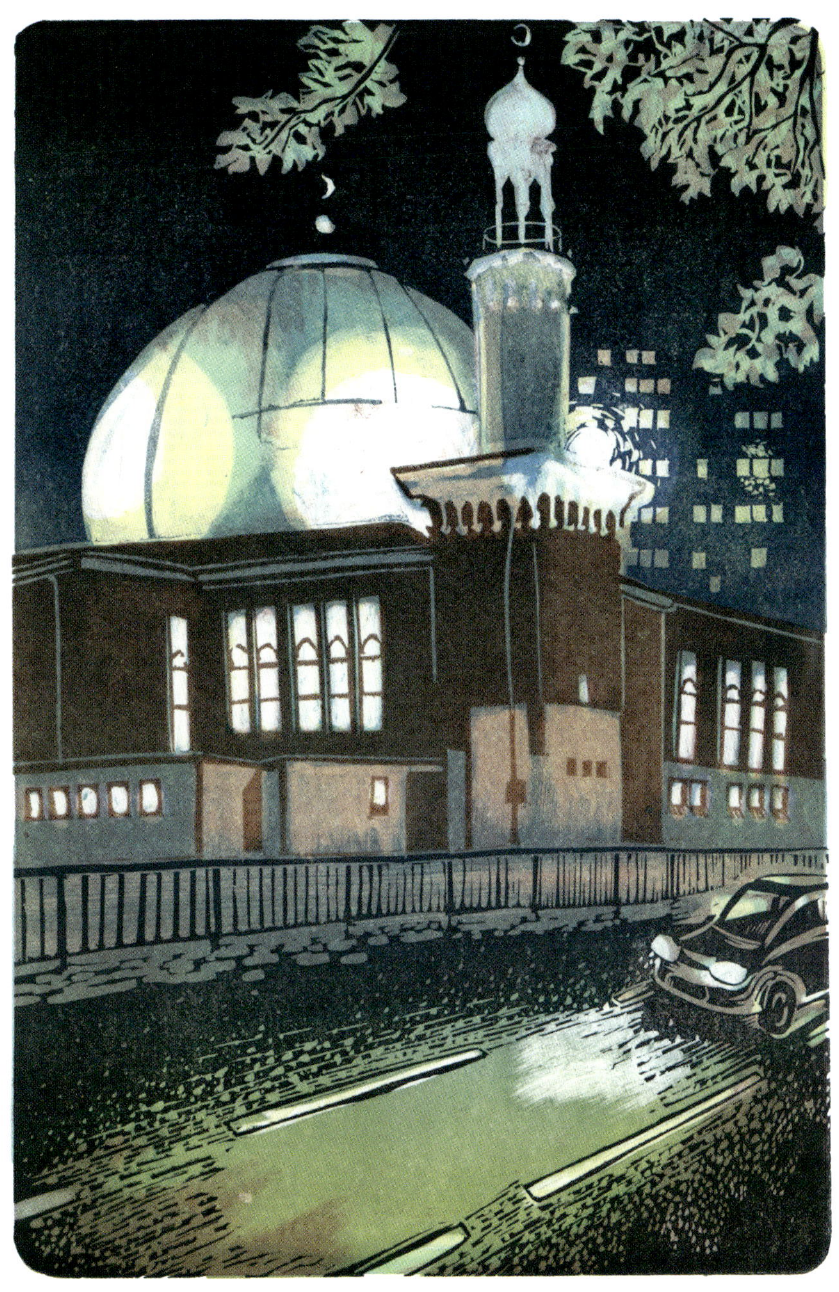

MIKE ALLISON, BIRMINGHAM CENTRAL MOSQUE

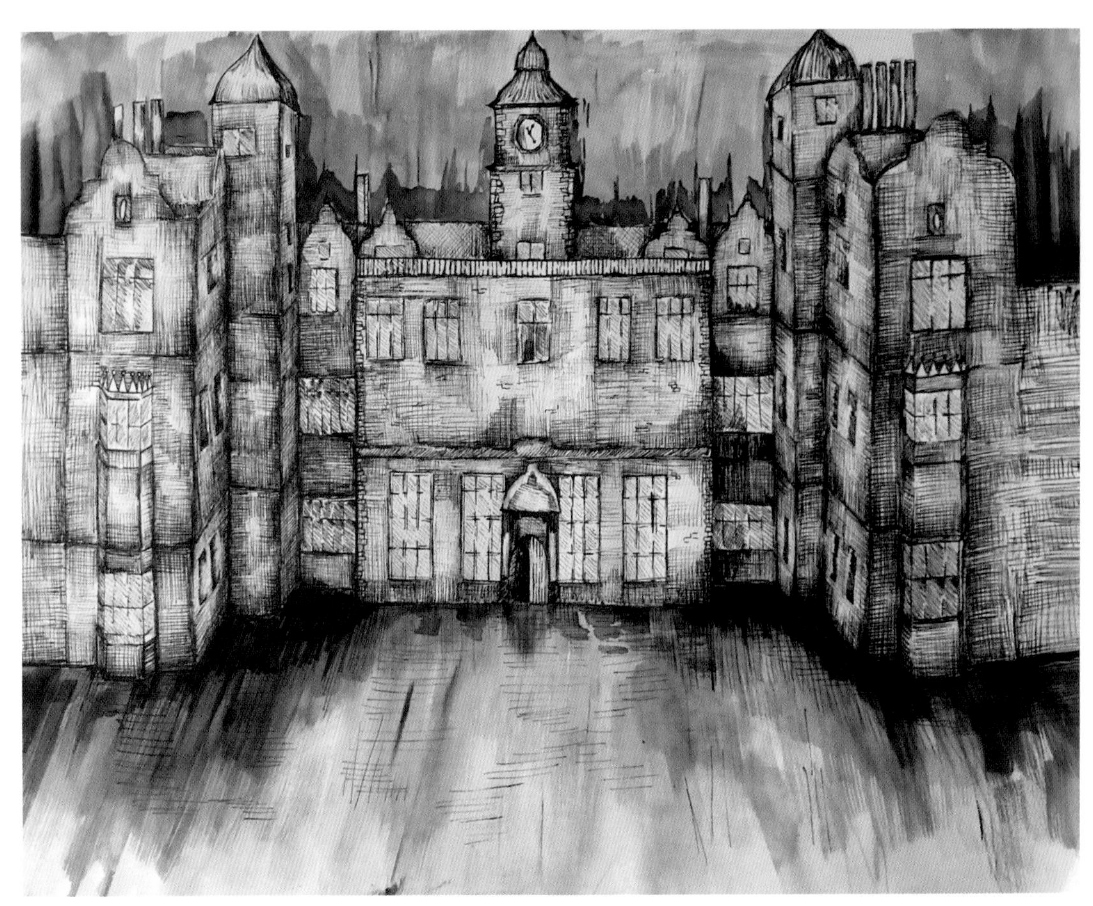

Lucy Murray, Aston Hall

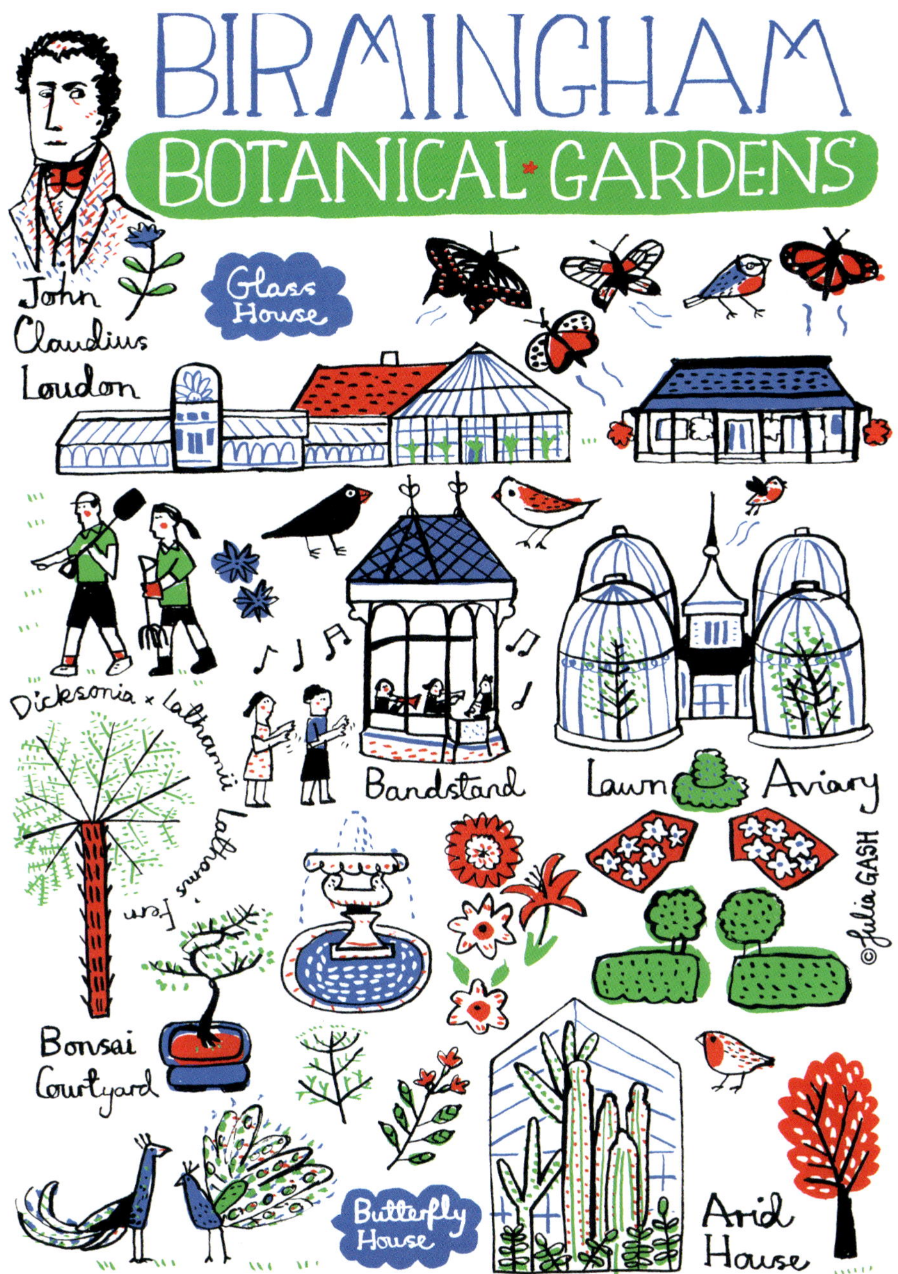

Julia Gash, The Birmingham Botanical Gardens

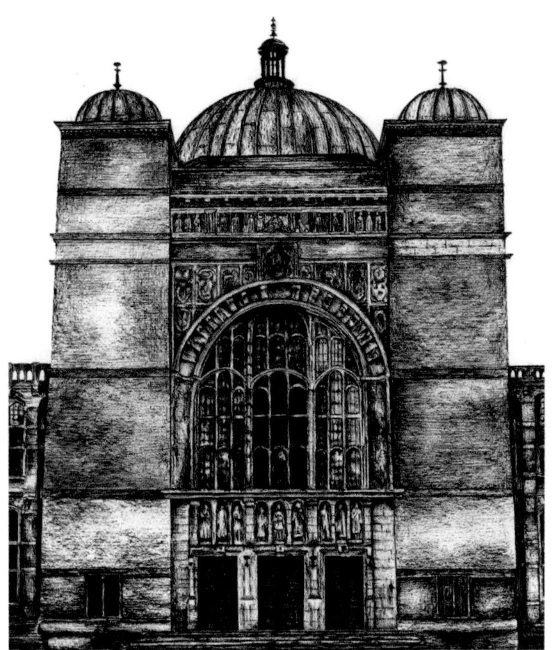

H ELENA C HECKLEY , A STON W EBB B UILDING

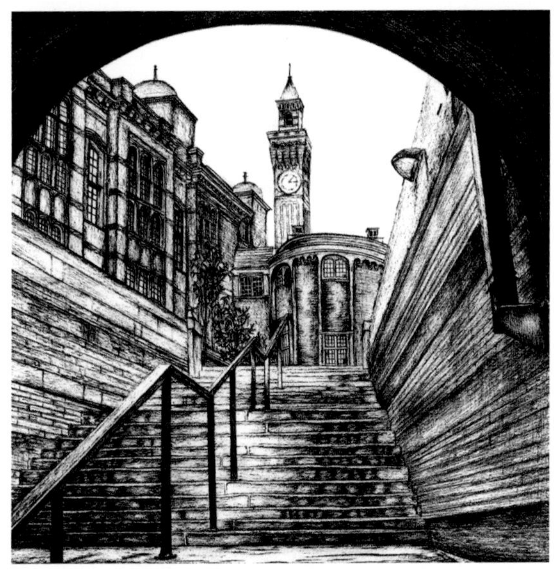

H ELENA C HECKLEY , U NIVERSITY OF B IRMINGHAM

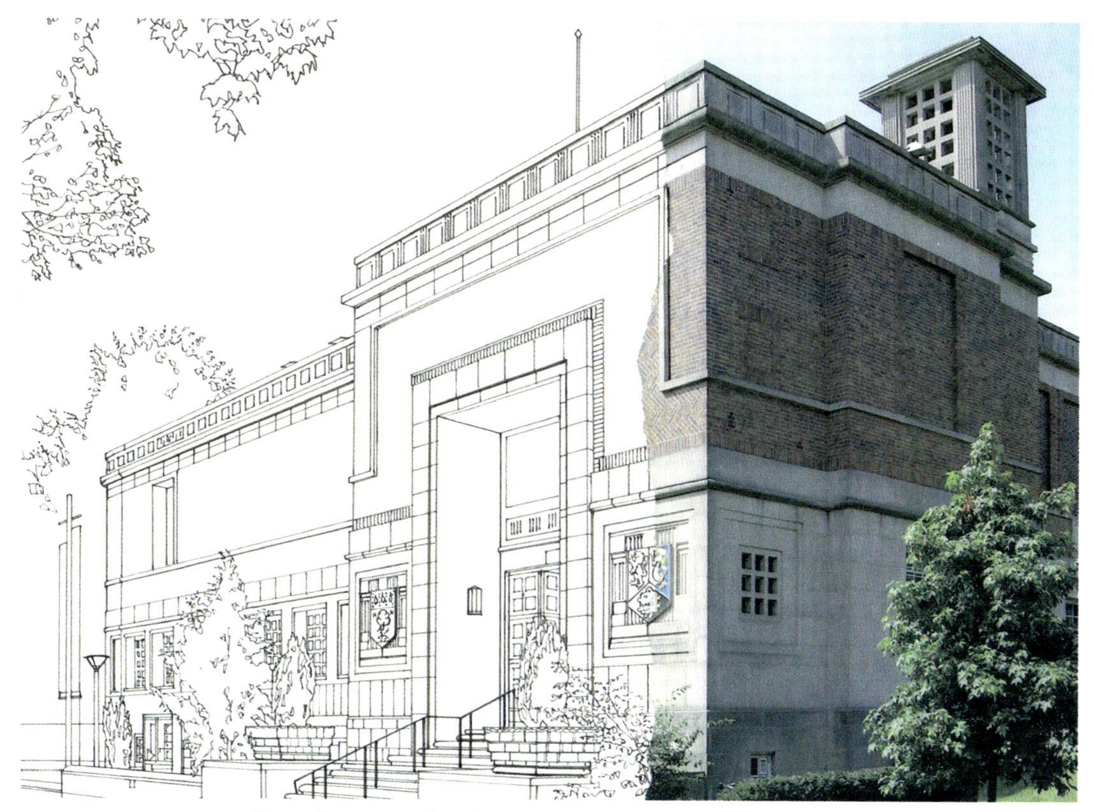

GARY IZZARD, THE BARBER INSTITUTE OF FINE ARTS

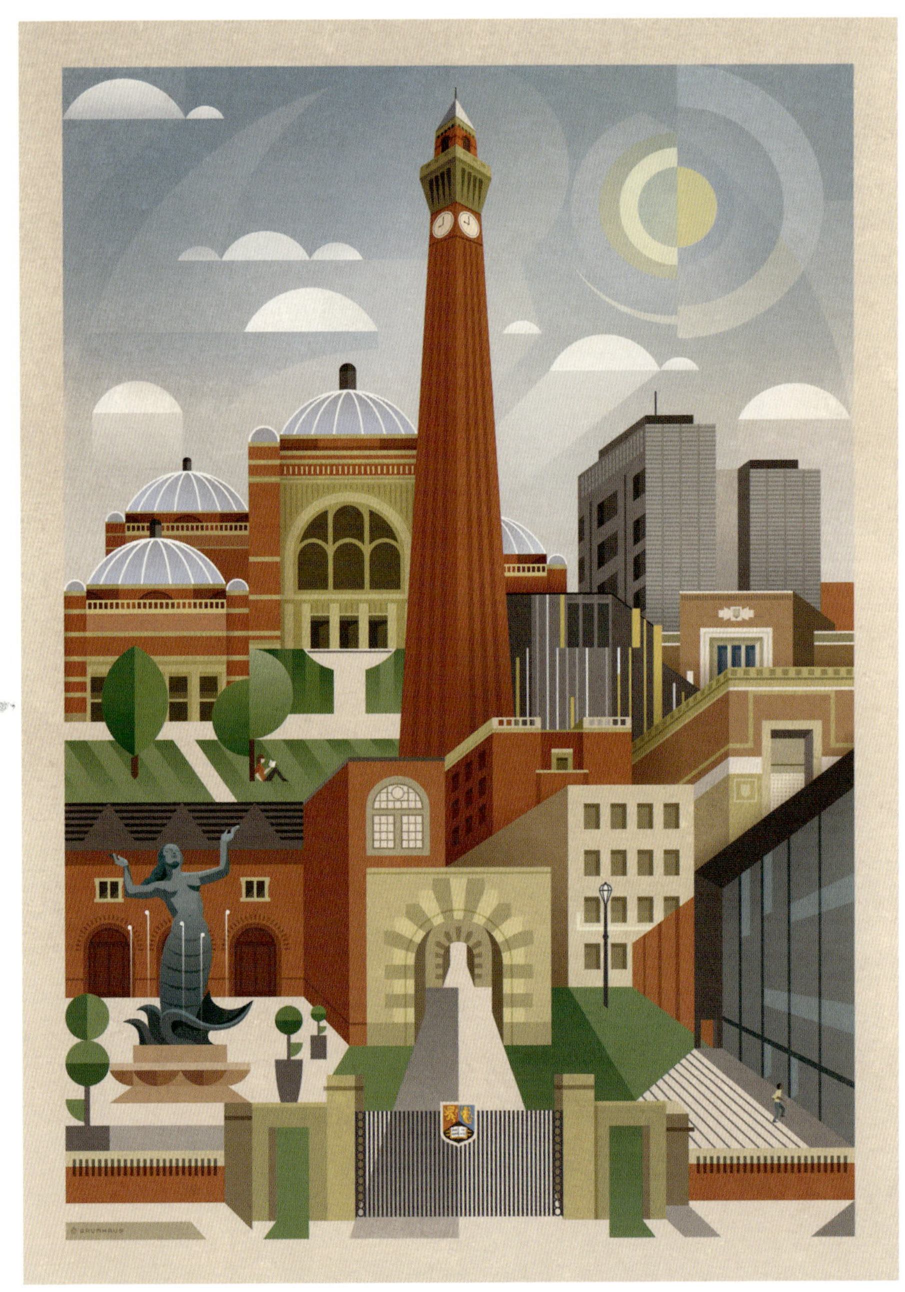

Alexander Edwards (Brumhaus), University of Birmingham

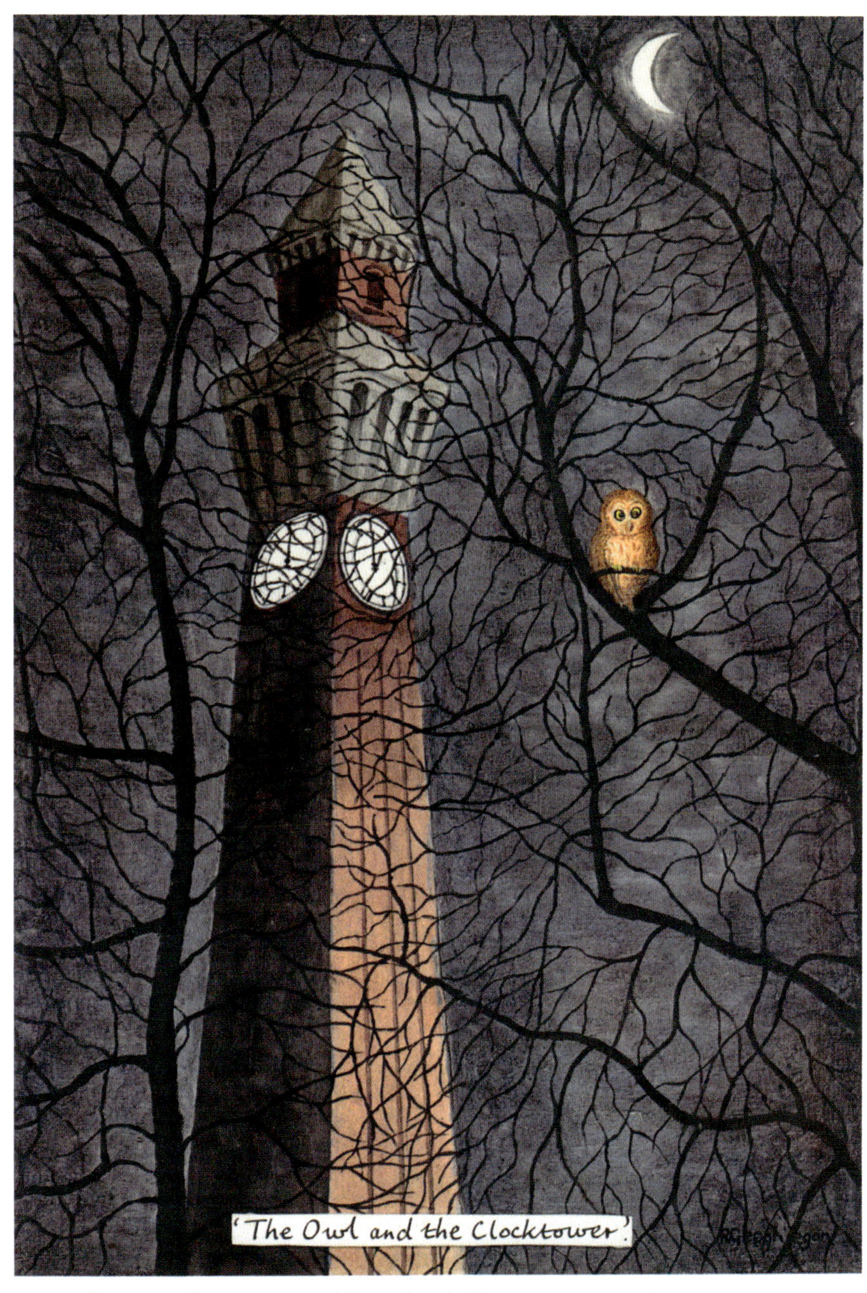

ROBERT GEOGHEGAN 'OLD JOE' UNIVERSITY OF BIRMINGHAM

119

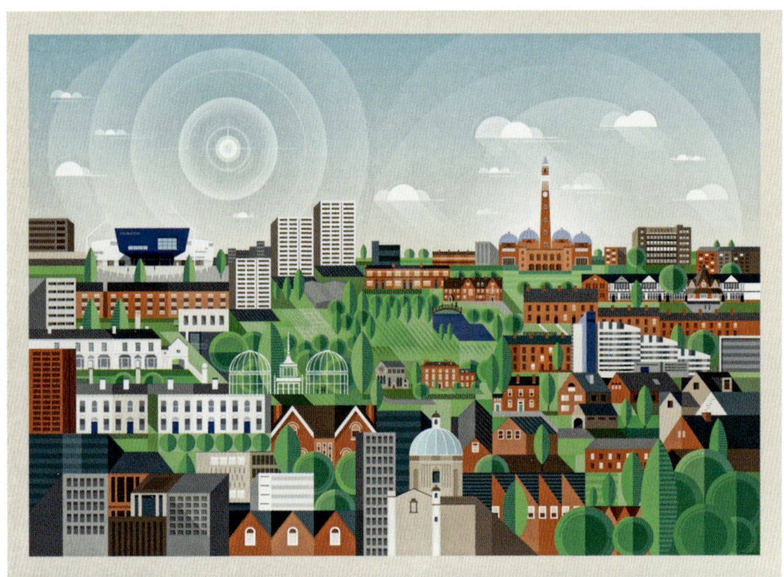

A L E X A N D E R   E D W A R D S   (B R U M H A U S) ,   E D G B A S T O N

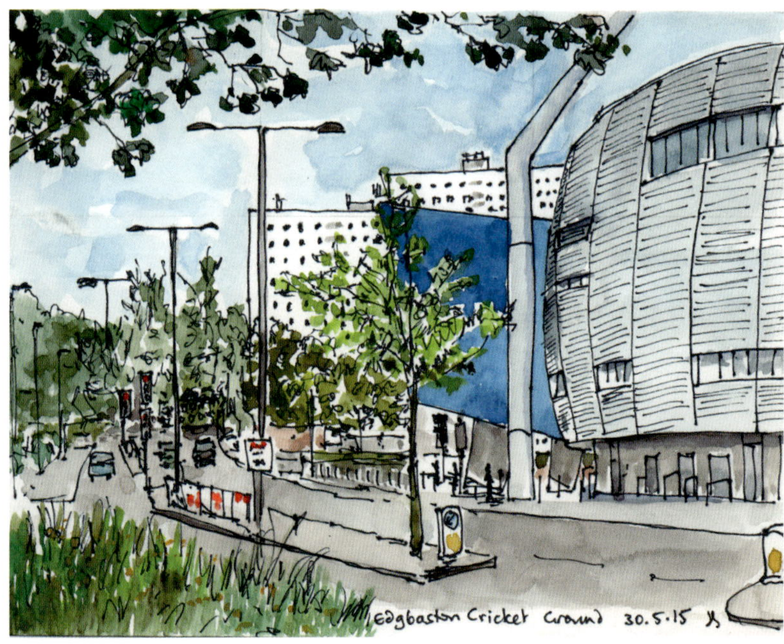

J A N E T   S C O T T ,   E D G B A S T O N   C R I C K E T   G R O U N D

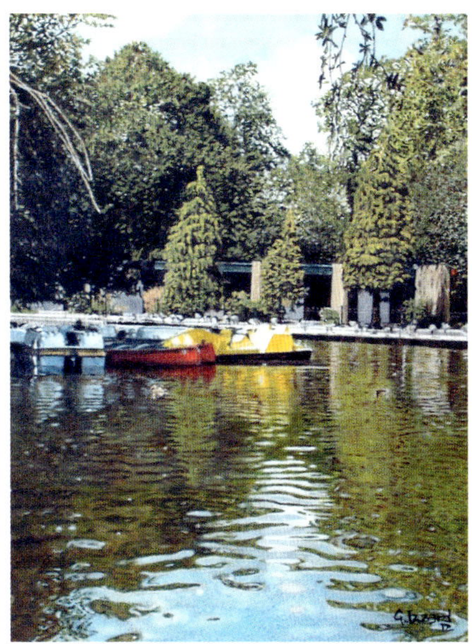

GARY IZZARD, CANNON HILL PARK

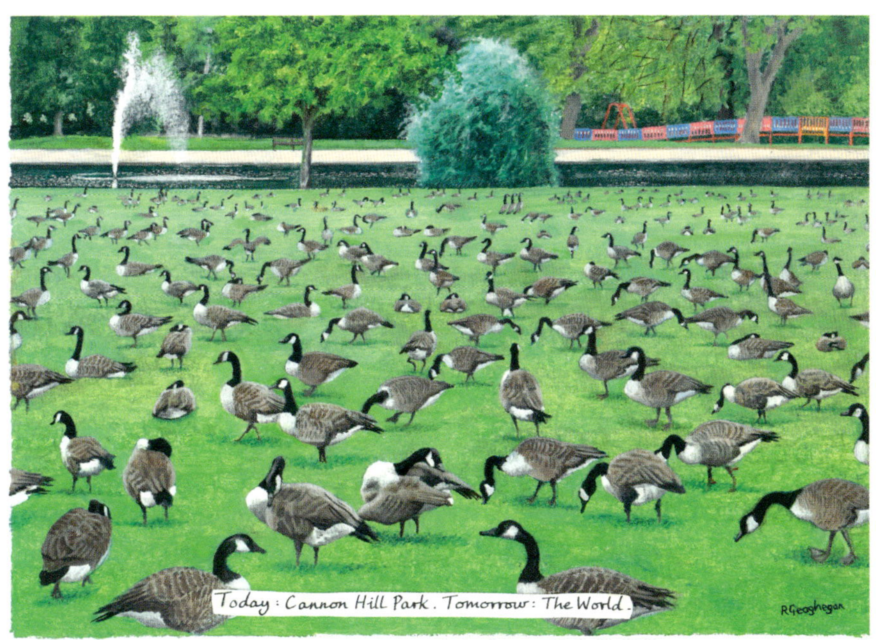

ROBERT GEOGHEGAN, CANNON HILL PARK

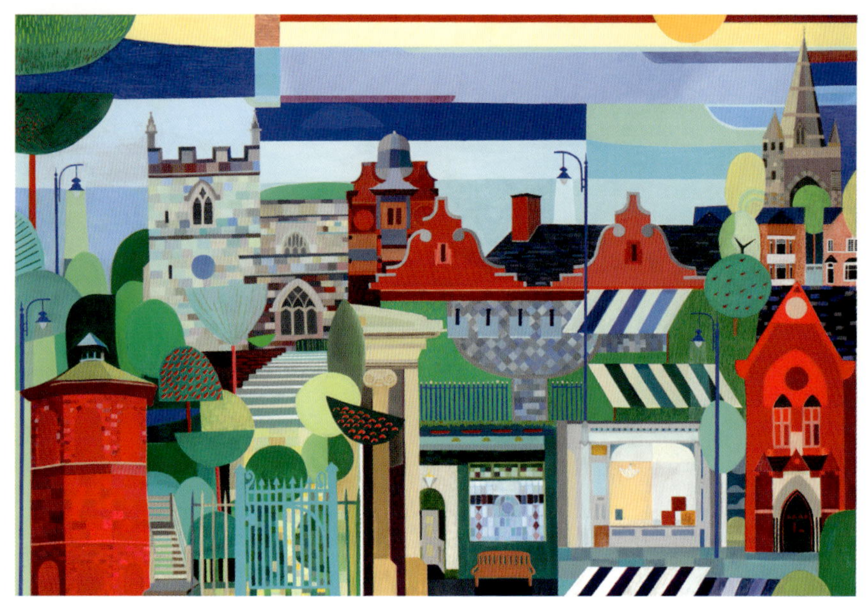

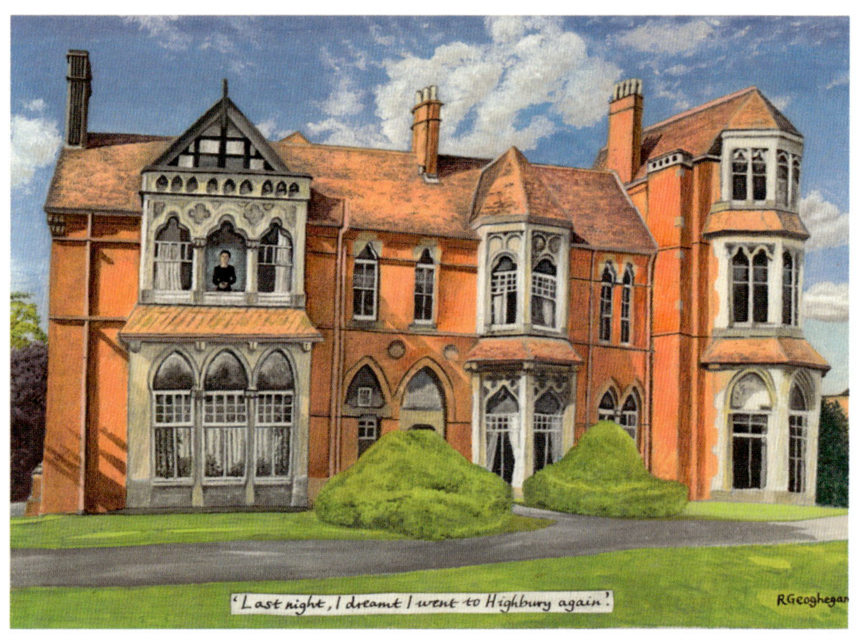

ROBERT GEOGHEGAN, HIGHBURY HALL

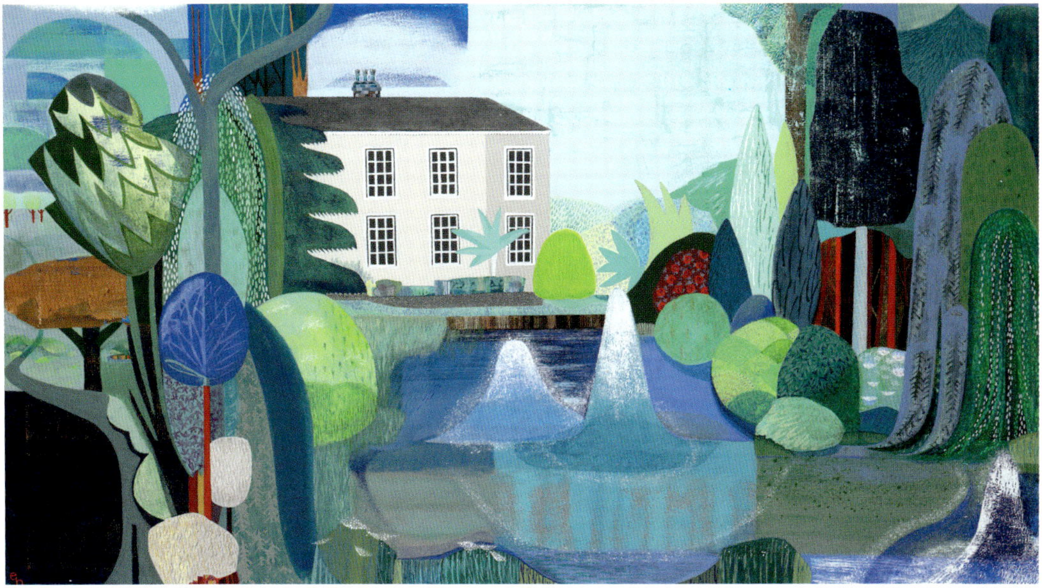

EMMA HARDICKER, KINGS HEATH PARK

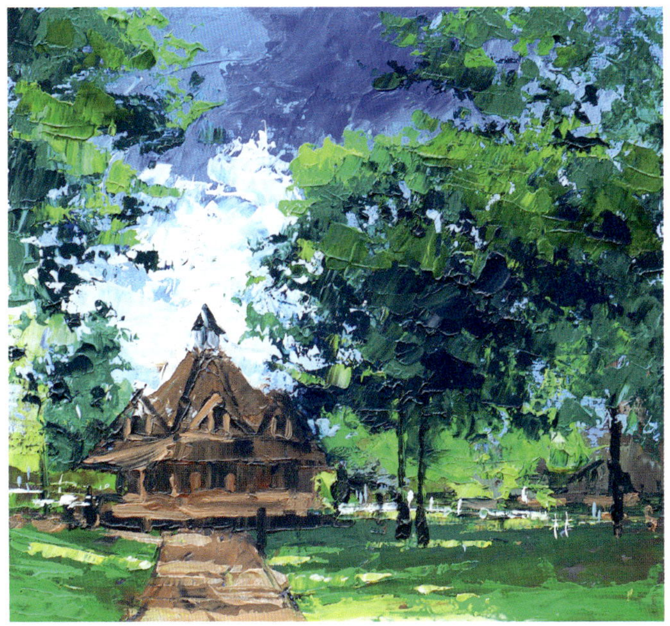

COLIN CARRUTHERS, BOURNVILLE GREEN

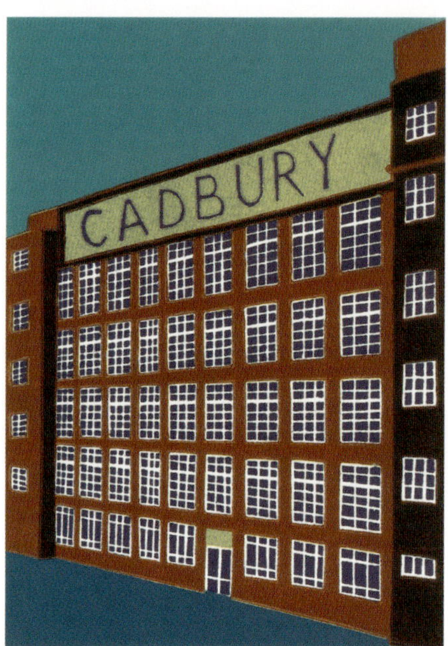

J E N N I E I N G , C A D B U R Y

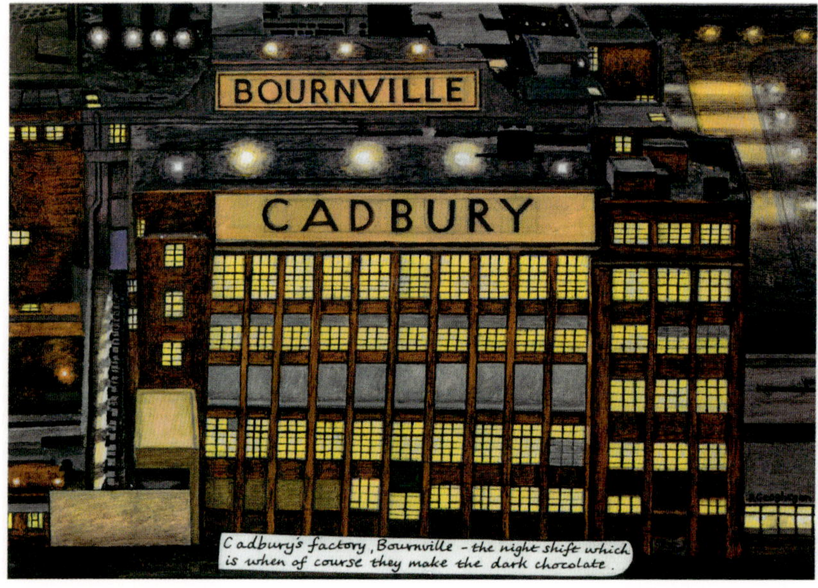

R O B E R T G E O G H E G A N , C A D B U R Y N I G H T S H I F T

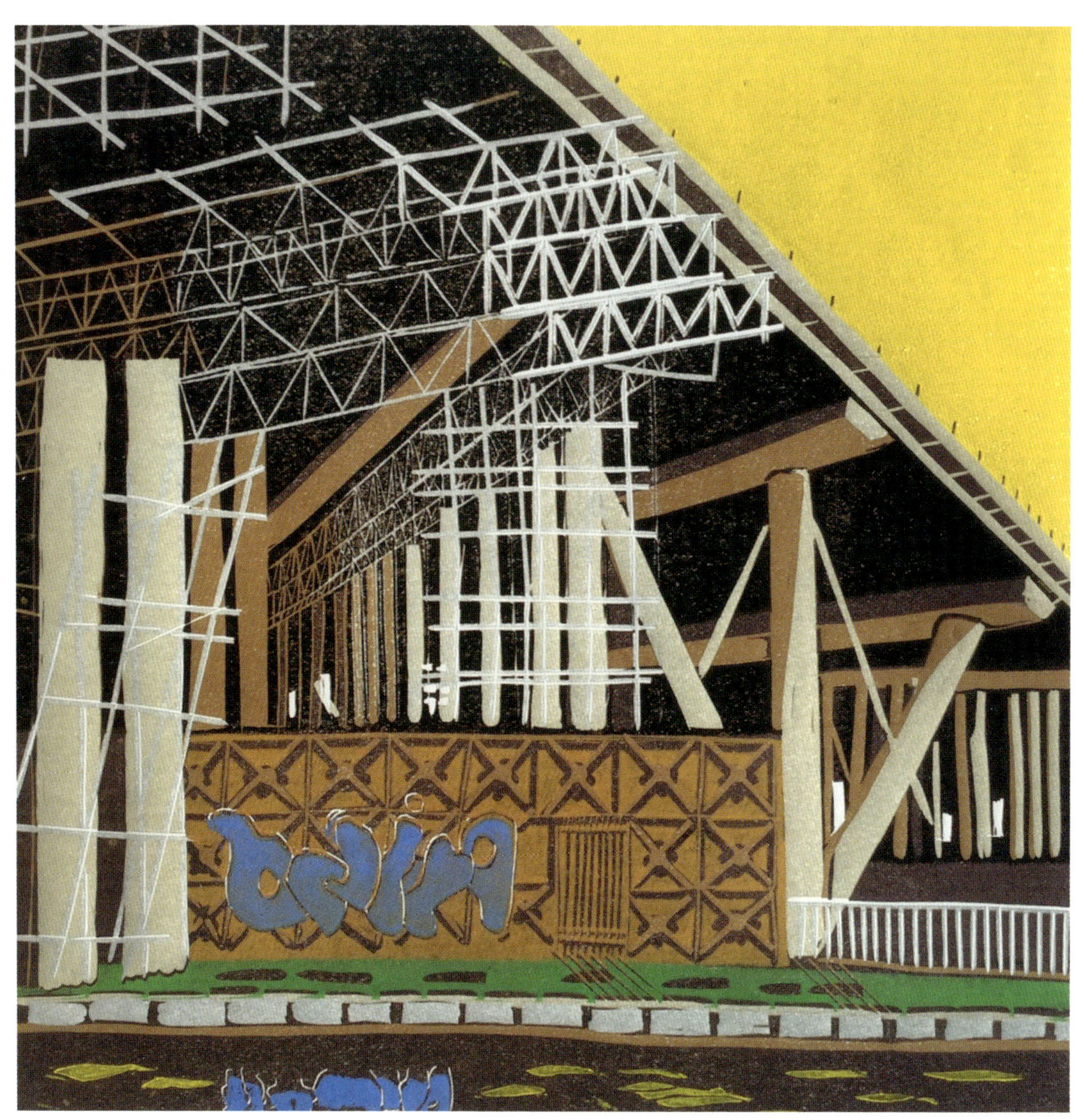

ANDY TROMANS, M6 MOTORWAY

ARTIST CREDITS

Artists' work can be found on the pages listed in parentheses.

Agnieszka Klimaszewska (40, 94)
artbyagnes.co.uk
Animal, landscape and cityscape paintings on canvas, board and wood

Alexander Edwards (Brumhaus) (23, 33, 59, 66, 88, 118, 120)
www.brumhaus.uk
Prints which explore architecture and modernism, using a hard-edged, graphic style

Amanda Godden (22)
amandagodden67@gmail.com
Pen and watercolour composition with collage detail

Andy Tromans (90, 125)
www.andytromans.co.uk
Painter and printmaker, urban and rural subjects

Anna Reuben (11, 112)
instagram.com/annaintheworks
Fun and quirky artwork created using digital tools

Barbara Gibson (67)
www.barbaragibson.pl
Analogue and digital collage artist producing content for editorial and advertising

Becca Moody (31)
etsy.com/uk/shop/BeccaMoodyArt
Acrylic and oil painting with a focus on colour and natural forms

Bethany Dartnell (14, 35)
bethanydartnell@msn.com
An architecture enthusiast whose work features the Brutalist buildings from Birmingham's skyline

Casey Joan Harwood (105)
caseyjoanart.com
Digital illustrator

Caroline Johnson (16, 17)
artistsmock@hotmail.co.uk
Fine artist and printmaker. Graphic depictions of urban and other subject matter

Carrick Siddell (11, 57)
www.carricksiddell.com
Contemporary cityscape oil paintings inspired by travel and light

Cherie Kwok (103)
cheriekwok.co.uk
Work focusing on cultural identity, mental health and social issues

Chris Eckersley (25, 83)
chriseckersley.co.uk
An artist and designer with a passion for architectural space

Colin Carruthers (123)
www.colincarruthers.com
Acrylic painting on canvas

Daniel Stedman (13, 37, 75, 81, 89, 94)
daniestedman@yahoo.co.uk
Acrylic painting, pen, ink pencil and printmaking

David Newton (8, 95)
davidnewton4art@gmail.com
Naive cityscapes and contemporary Art Nouveau in acrylics and mixed media

Ed Isaacs RBSA (68)
Twitter: @IsaacsEd
Drawing in a range of media and styles

Eleanor Garrett (111)
eleanorbgarrett@gmail.com
Exploring mixed media with digital and traditional approaches

Emma Bennett (cover)
www.emmabennettcollage.co.uk
Vibrant hand-cut collage, book cover illustration and children's book illustrations

Emma Hardicker (122, 123)
emmahardicker.com
Painter and printmaker with a contemporary style filled with pattern and colour

Eric Gaskell (54, 62, 63, 80)
egdesign.co.uk
Multi-block, reduction and single
colour linocuts of coast, town and
canal

Gary Izzard (117, 121)
garyizzard@blueyonder.co.uk
Many years experience in graphic
design, fine art and illustration

Georgia Chapman (21)
georgiachapmanblog.wordpress.
com/
Illustration student and practising
portrait artist based in Birmingham

Grace Warren (21)
instagram.com/ecargoart/
Illustrations created in a wide range
of mediums

**Graham Leonard King RBSA
(93)**
www.grahamleonardking.co.uk
Landscapes and portraits in acrylics

Helena Checkley (116)
helenacheckleyart@gmail.com
High detail studies using pen,
watercolour and acrylic

Ian Woodley (30, 109)
ghouseart.co.uk
Architectural surveyor and
Illustrator specialising in hand-
drawn pen and ink drawings

Ilona Drew (19, 30)
idrewthis.co.uk
Colourful unique mixed media
artwork inspired by beautiful
architecture

Janet Scott (60, 73, 120)
janet9scott@gmail.com
Sketcher en plein air using fineliner
pen and watercolour

Jenny Seddon (map)
www.jennyseddon.com
Illustration and screen prints

Jennie Ing (12, 15, 42, 112, 124)
www.jennieingart.co.uk
Linocut prints inspired by city
architecture and views

Jilly Oxlade-Arnott (78, 84, 91)
archiimp.com
Bold watercolour and fine line ink
artist specialising in architecture

John Maule-ffinch (64, 65, 69)
johndmff28@gmail.com
Urban scenes in watercolour and
mixed media

Julia Gash (115)
juliagash.co.uk
A playful and honest vision of the
world in which we live

Karen Cross (26, 27, 45, 85)
www.kciphotography.co.uk
Digital graphic art pieces of
Birmingham city centre in bright
multicolour

Kate Rafiq (101)
etsy.com/shop/KateRafiqStudio
Children's picture book author,
illustrator, publisher and digital
artist

Katherine Tromans (105)
katherinetromans.com
A freelance illustrator and designer,
with a specialism in watercolour

Kevin Parrish (41)
kevinparrish.co.uk
Traditional fine art oil painter of
railway scenes and various other
genre

Kevin Line RBSA (71)
kevinline-portraits.co.uk
Realist grisaille portraits painted
with charcoal, dust and the fingers

Linda Nevill RBSA (56)
lindanevill.com
Printmaking and painting,
cityscapes and landscapes

Lois Cheshire (36)
@ lois.chesh (Instagram)
Illustrations using a range of
mediums, including pen, paint and
pencil

Lucy Murray (114)
Lucymu0@gmail.com
Drawing from pen and watercolour

**Lynn Jeffery RBSA
(46, 48, 50, 74)**
lynn.jeffery@live.com
Stencil and photo silk-screen print

**Margaret Fairhead RBSA
(60, 74)**
margaretfairhead@talktalk.net
Urban/rural landscapes and other
topics, freely machine stitched over
painted surface

Marta Kochanek (69, 70)
www.martakochanek.com
Advertising photographer
producing intricate 1/24 scale
models for sets and as hobby

Martin Stuart Moore (107)
stuartsoriginals.com
Cityscape prints in capriccio
style

Mike Allison (10, 18, 20, 32, 49, 55, 79, 113)
100views.net
Various original printmaking
methods forming a series of
100 views

Milan Topalović (19, 102)
milanillustrator.com
A Birmingham illustrator
inspired by Art Deco and
1950s film and travel posters

Nicholas Sims (47, 98, 99, 108)
nicholassims.info
An artist who enjoys working
on-the-spot with pencil

Paula Gabb (9, 34, 44, 104, 108)
instagram.com/paula_gabb
City-life artist using oils,
acrylics or digital paintings
using a palette knife

Paul Hipkiss RBSA (52, 53)
lynn.jeffery@live.com
Stenciled colours, overprinted
with a linocut print

Peter Shread (39, 61)
Petershread@gmail.com
Oil painter and printmaker
producing images in both
wood and linocut

Rob Leckey (45)
robleckeyart.com
Mixed media painting with
collage

Robert Geoghegan (29, 119, 121, 122, 124)
robspaintings.com
Paintings about different
aspects of Birmingham with a
comic twist

Sam Bailey (28, 40, 76, 77)
sambaileyfineart.co.uk
Oil painter of landscapes,
cityscapes, street scenes and
portraits

Samantha Brown (14)
samanthaa_bbrown@yahoo.com
Showing love to brutalist
buildings in a range of
mediums and styles

Sana Ali (97)
Asana0127x@gmail.com
Pen markers, colour or dark
and a variety of adapting skills

Steve Evans (43, 51)
SteveEvans49@aol.com
Drawings on various materials
such as paper, Perspex and
board

Steve Millward (58, 86)
stevemillward@hotmail.co.uk
Artist and printmaker

Tom Tebby (87)
www.tomtebby.com
Digital collage/screen print
using vintage photography of
Birmingham, circa 1972

Xinying Tang (72)
tangxinying.aria@gmail.com
Paintings made using acrylic
markers

Every effort has been made to correctly credit contributors. In the case of any omissions or
errors we would be pleased to make appropriate corrections in future editions.

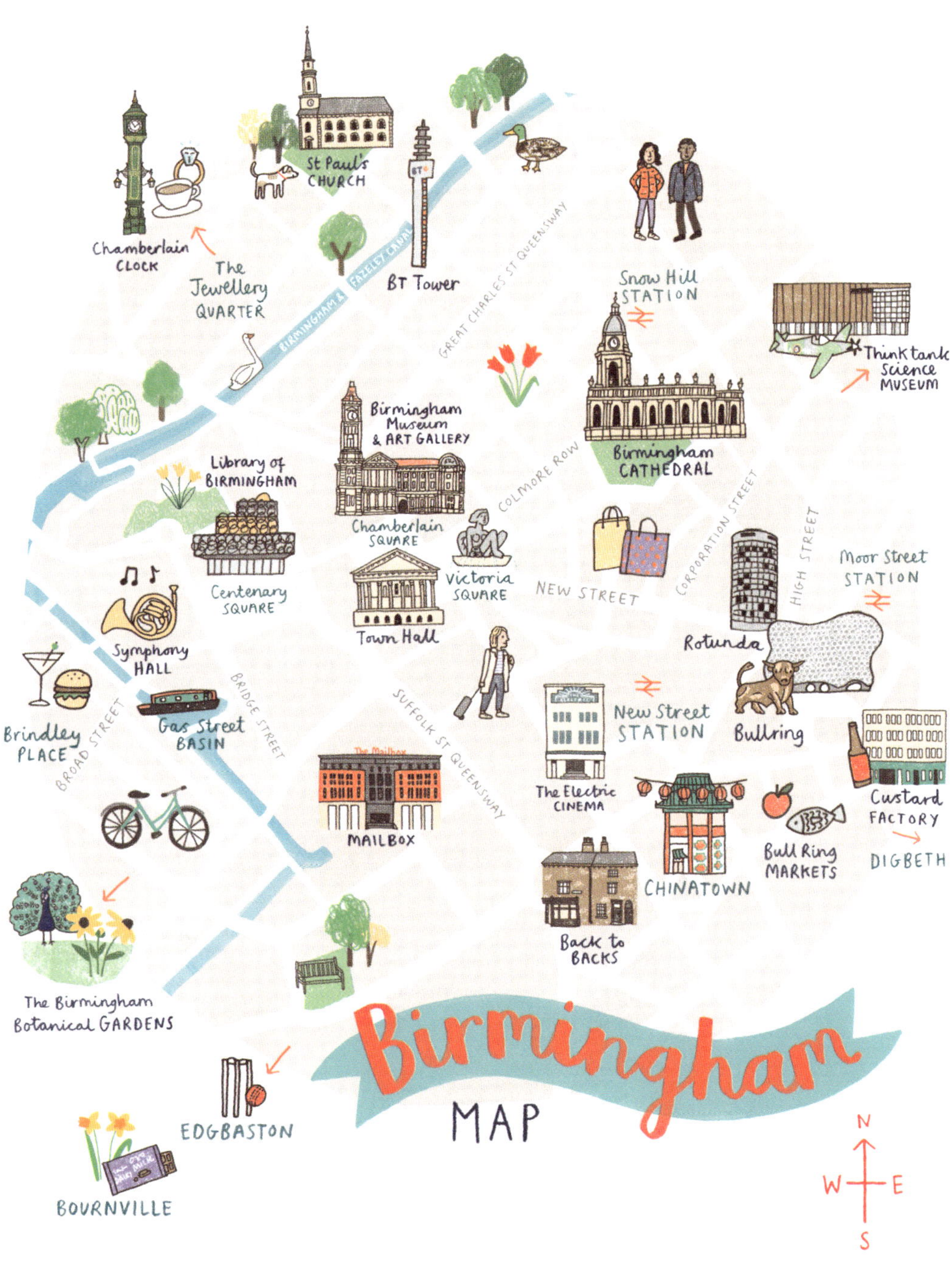

Chamberlain CLOCK
St Paul's CHURCH
The Jewellery QUARTER
BT Tower
Snow Hill STATION
Think tank Science MUSEUM
BIRMINGHAM & FAZELEY CANAL
GREAT CHARLES ST QUEENSWAY
Birmingham Museum & ART GALLERY
Library of BIRMINGHAM
Birmingham CATHEDRAL
COLMORE ROW
Chamberlain SQUARE
Centenary SQUARE
Victoria SQUARE
NEW STREET
CORPORATION STREET
HIGH STREET
Moor Street STATION
Symphony HALL
Town Hall
Rotunda
Brindley PLACE
Gas Street BASIN
BRIDGE STREET
BROAD STREET
SUFFOLK ST QUEENSWAY
New Street STATION
Bullring
Custard FACTORY
The Mailbox
MAILBOX
The Electric CINEMA
CHINATOWN
Bull Ring MARKETS
DIGBETH
Back to BACKS
The Birmingham Botanical GARDENS
EDGBASTON
BOURNVILLE
DAIRY MILK
Birmingham MAP
N
W E
S

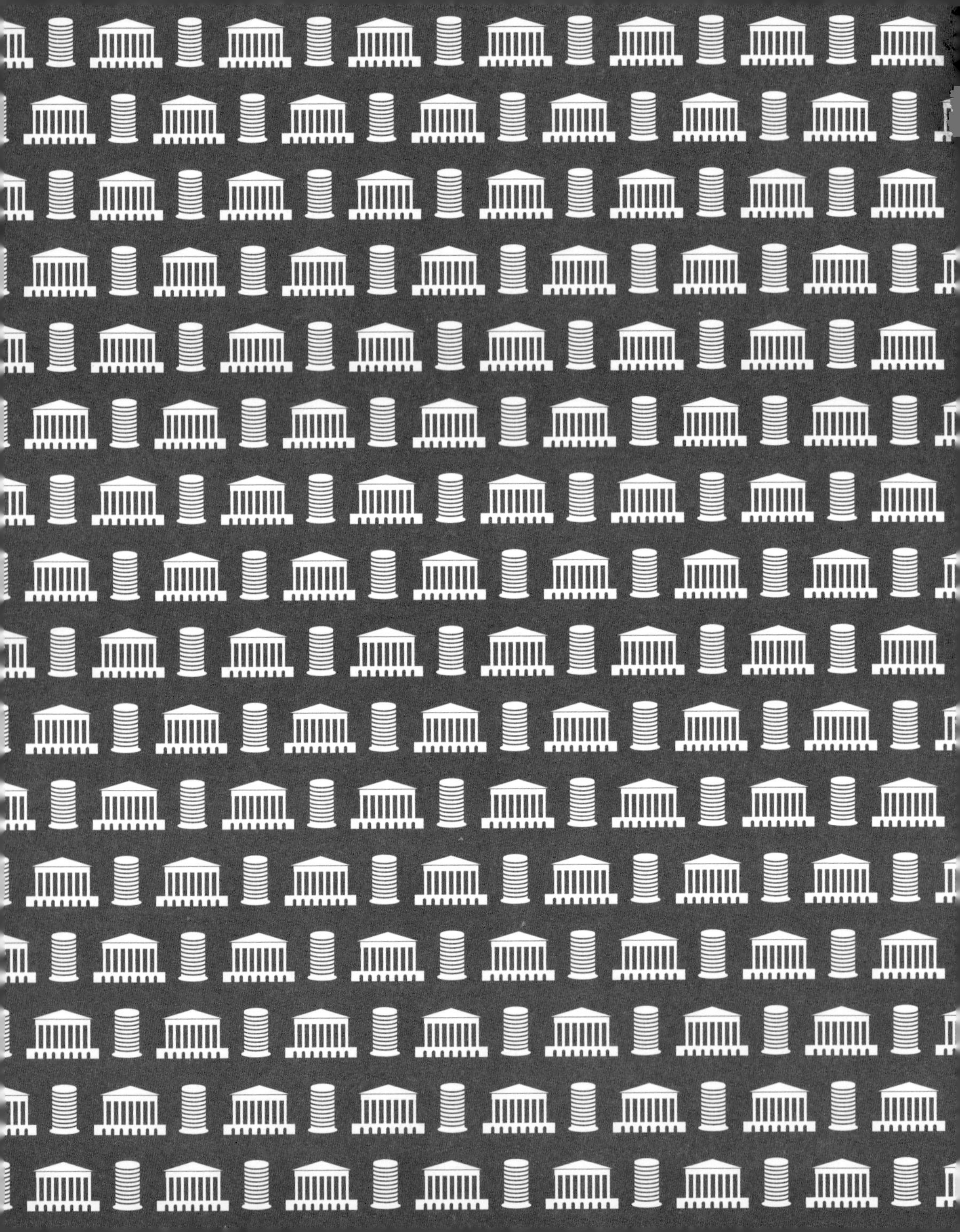